OUIDA

Ouida

Helena Esser

EER
Edward Everett Root, Publishers, Brighton, 2024.

EER
Edward Everett Root, Publishers, Co. Ltd.,
Atlas Chambers, 33 West Street, Brighton, Sussex, BN1 2RE, England.
Full details of our stock-holding overseas agents in America, Australia, China, Europe and Japan, and how to order our books, are given on our website.
www.eerpublishing.com

edwardeverettroot@yahoo.co.uk

We stand with Ukraine!
EER books are **NOT** available for sale in Russia or Belarus.

© Helena Esser, *Ouida*

ISBN: 9781915115140 Hardback
ISBN: 9781915115157 Paperback
ISBN: 9781915115164 eBook

This edition © Edward Everett Root Publishers Co. Ltd., 2024.

Key Popular Women Writers series, no.7.

Helena Esser has asserted her right to be identified as the owner of the copyright of this Work in accordance with the copyright, Designs and Patents Act 1988 as the owner of this work.

All rights reserved. No part of this publication may be reproduced, stored in a retrieval system or transmitted in any form or by any means, electronic, mechanical, photocopying, recording or otherwise, without the prior permission of the copyright owner.

Design and production by Pageset Ltd., High Wycombe, Buckinghamshire.

KEY POPULAR WOMEN WRITERS

Series editors:
Janine Hatter and Helena Ifill.

This innovative new series delivers original and transformative, peer reviewed, feminist research into the work of leading women writers who were widely read in their time, but who have been under-represented in the canon.

The series offers critical, historical and aesthetic contributions to current literary and theoretical work. Each volume concentrates on one writer.

The first seven titles are available:
- *Geraldine Jewsbury* by Abigail Burnham Bloom.
- *Florence Marryat* by Catherine Pope.
- *Margaret Oliphant* by Valerie Sanders.
- *Mrs. Henry Wood* by Mariaconcetta Costantini.
- *Frances Trollope* by Carolyn Lambert.
- *Rhoda Broughton* by Tamar Heller.
- *Ouida* by Helena Esser.

These will be followed by contracted volumes on:
- *Eliza Lynn Linton*
- *Marie Corelli*
- *Mary Elizabeth Braddon*
- *Mary Shelley*
- *Charlotte Riddell*

We are also now seeking authors for volumes on:
- *Daphne Du Maurier*
- *Edith Wharton*

The series volumes interrogate the ways in which women writers, their creative processes and published material can be considered feminist, and explore how recent developments in feminist theory can enrich our understanding of popular women's lives and literature.

The authors rethink established popular writers and their works, and rediscover and re-evaluate authors who have been largely neglected – often since their initial burst of success in their own historical period. This neglect is often due to the exclusivity and insular nature of the canon which has its roots in the Victorian critical drive to perpetuate a division between high and low culture.

In response, our definition of the "popular" is broadly interpreted to encompass women writers who were read by large sections of the public, and who wrote for the mass publishing market. The series therefore challenges this arbitrary divide, creating a new and dynamic dialogue regarding the canon's expansion by introducing readers to previously under-researched women writers who were nevertheless prolific, known and influential.

Studying the work of these authors can tell us much about women's writing, creativity and publishing practice, and about how popular fiction intervened in pressing political, social and cultural issues surrounding gender, history and women's role in society.

This is an important and timely series that is inspired by, interrogates, and speaks to a new wave of feminism, new definitions of sex and gender, and new considerations of intersectionality. It also reflects growing interest in popular fiction, as well as a feminist desire to broaden and diversify the literary canon.

Ultimately the series sheds light on women writers whose work deserves greater recognition, facilitates and inspires further research, and paves the way for introducing these key women writers into the canon and modern-day studies.

The series editors

DR. JANINE HATTER is an academic based at the University of Hull. She is the President of the Victorian Popular Fiction Association and Associate Editor of *Victorian Popular Fictions*, the journal of the VPFA. With Nickianne Moody she has edited the volume *Fashion and Material Culture in Victorian Fiction and Periodicals*, already published by *EER*. Her research interests centre on nineteenth-century literature, art and culture, with particular emphasis on popular fiction. She has published on Mary Braddon, Bram Stoker, the theatre and identity, and Victorian women's life writing, as well as on her wider research interests of nineteenth to twenty-first century Science Fiction and the Gothic.

DR. HELENA IFILL is a Senior Lecturer at the University of Aberdeen where she is Director of the Centre for the Novel. She is the Secretary of the Victorian Popular Fiction Association and editor of *Victorian Popular Fictions,* the journal of the VPFA. Her monograph, *Creating Character* was published in 2018 and she has written articles on a range of topics including sensation fiction, the Gothic, and the interactions between Victorian popular fiction and the medical sciences.

About the author

Helena Esser completed her PhD on "Urban Imaginaries of Victorian London in Steampunk Fiction" at Birkbeck College in 2020, and pursued her interest in Ouida alongside. She has published on steampunk in the *London Literary Journal* (11:2, 2014), *Cahiers victoriens et éduardiens* (87, 2018), *Otherness: Essays & Studies* (7:1, 2019), and *Humanities* (11:1, 2022), and on neo-Victorianism in *Neo-Victorian Studies* (11:1, 2018) and the *Victorian Popular Fictions Journal* (2:1, 2020). She is currently co-organising the Victorian Popular Fiction Association's reading group on 'The Third Sex'. Her research on Ouida, which she has presented at the VPFA Annual Conferences, has been awarded the Greta Depedge PGR Prize 2019 and received honorary mention in the 2020 Margaret Elize Harkness Prize.

Contents

Acknowledgements xi

Introduction. Florid, and Fervent, and Fanciful. 1

Chapter 1. Beau Sabreurs: Homosocial Masculinity 23

Chapter 2. Soldiers and Spies: Women in Masculine Space . . . 53

Chapter 3. French Novels and Femmes Galantes: Agency, Cosmopolitanism, Spectacle 79

Chapter 4. Aces and Aesthetes: Sex, Violence, Marriage 109

Chapter 5. The Artist as Critic: Italy, Decadence, and the Politics of Beauty. 145

Conclusion. High Priestess of the Impossible 179

Bibliography 193

Index. 209

Acknowledgements

This book has been a joy to write. My heartfelt thanks to Janine Hatter and Helena Ifill for providing me with the opportunity to explore the ever-fascinating Ouida and learn all that I have learned. Thank you for your support, feedback, and expert editorship.

My deepest gratitude goes out to the wonderful, warm, and welcoming community of excellent scholars gathered under the banner of the Victorian Popular Fiction Association, where I have been fortunate to experience so much collegiality, inspiration, enthusiasm, and encouragement. Among them, I would like especially to thank Andrew King, whose verve, endless generosity, and readiness to share his expertise have been invaluable, and Jesse Erickson, whose boundless creativity, passion, and ready assistance in all matters Ouida are a source of constant inspiration. My thanks also to the lovely Lorraine Dubuisson, for her kindness and generosity, for many enthused discussions, and for her indispensable feedback. I am particularly grateful to the members of the Third Sex Reading Group who joined our two Ouida-themed sessions for their open-minded and engaging discussion of my in-progress ideas, to Jane Jordan for her kind and thought-provoking feedback on Ouida scholarship, and to Will Sutton, for his generous feedback and continued support.

My sincere appreciation to the VPFA for awarding my research the Greta Depledge Prize in 2019, and to Ana Parejo Vadillo for awarding me honourable mention for the Margaret Elize Harkness

Prize in 2020, both of which encouraged me enormously.

Finally, all my thanks to Frankie Dytor for organising an incredible Study Day with me, and to everyone who joined us, both as speakers and listeners, to explore our high-priestess of the impossible.

This book is for you.

INTRODUCTION

Florid, and Fervent, and Fanciful

Few conclusions may be drawn about Ouida's life and work with certainty. She was an individualist and avid libertarian who neither conformed to dominant literary, cultural, or gendered conventions of the nineteenth century, nor neatly affirms our present-day expectations of Victorian literature. This, however, is precisely why she deserves much more scholarly attention: she does not sit comfortably within established genealogies and canons of 'the Victorian'. Instead, she challenges, confounds, and complicates dominant meta-narratives of Victorian paradigms about gender, genre, culture, and identity, and compels us to re-evaluate them.

After all, Ouida was a self-supporting female writer who never married, was wholly uninterested in the middle class, the domestic sphere, or realism, and she inspired the New Woman – yet, her criticism of early feminist politics put her at odds with the parameters of 1980s feminist scholarship, which summarily disqualified her from its canon. Subsequent scholarship has troubled such simplistic dismissals. Reclaiming Ouida as a remarkable woman and writer, and a much-discussed celebrity in her time, remains a crucially and undeservedly neglected undertaking.

Ouida's Literary World
Ouida's place within the field of 'Victorian literature' is, like everything about her, complex and not seldom contradictory, but importantly reveals the tensions between the gender politics

of literary production and reception in the nineteenth century. Her vast, vivid, even hyper-real literary world earned her a large, devoted readership that included John Ruskin, Alfred, Lord Tennyson, Oscar Wilde, Max Beerbohm, and the Italian royal family. Over a forty-five-year-long career, she wrote twenty-nine best-selling novels, five novellas, fourteen short story collections, two volumes of essays, and countless non-fiction articles. She was published in Britain and the US, translated into German, French, Italian, Spanish, Dutch, Polish, Czech, Hungarian, Finnish, Russian, and Japanese, and pirated, parodied, and put on stage or film innumerable times. In 1920, W. H. Mallock summarised the appeal of her "foreign princes, mysterious dukes – masters of untold millions – and of fabulous English guardsmen whose bedrooms in Knightsbridge Barracks were inlaid with silver and tortoise-shell" (124).

First thought a male writer of "muscular" adventures in the style of Alfred Lawrence, Ouida soon became a household name of Victorian popular culture alongside – and rivalling – sensation novelists Mary Elizabeth Braddon, Rhoda Broughton, and Wilkie Collins. The latter she welcomed to her salon at the newly-built Langham hotel (see Steel, 1990: 22–4), together with Robert Browning, John Everett Millais, Algernon Swinburne – one reviewer attributed to her work the characteristics of "[r]ed-hot passion and ultra-Swinburnian fleshiness" ("Novels", 1880: 841) – as well as dashing military men, and explorer Richard Burton, with whom she maintained a life-long correspondence. Among her guests was also Oscar Wilde, whose aestheticist style she influenced, with whom she collaborated on his magazine, *The Woman's World* (Schaffer, 2002: 213–4; see also Elfenbein, 1995: 235; Fitzsimons, 2015), and who praised her "florid, and fervent, and fanciful" style and called her "the last of the romantics" (Wilde, 1889: 3). More than once, she was identified as having "the honor of having, to some extent, anticipated Zola" (Preston, 1886: 50) or as making Émile Zola appear "clean-tasted by comparison" ("New Novels", 1878: 2). Indeed, Ouida came to be known as a writer of French novels (see Jordan, 2014b) who did for fashionable drawing rooms what Zola did to cellars (see Fiske, 1880). Her Italian novels in turn won the praise of John Ruskin and Henry James. *Fin-de-siècle* decadents like Max Beerbohm admired her "irresistible élan" and "sustained vitality" (Beerbohm, 1899, original emphasis); G. S. Street reviewed her in *The Yellow Book* and expressed his continued enjoyment of her work. Likewise, her novels influenced a generation of New Woman writers (Gilbert, 1999: 173; Schaffer, 2001: 47), inspired Jack London (1917 [1994]: 512) and Dorothy Richardson, and drew the admiration of Marie Corelli and Vernon Lee. As such, Ouida's name and work were an integral part of the Victorian literary culture and popular consciousness, although more often than not as a controversial figure.

Her novels and the transgressive morals they espoused polarised opinion; they sparked enjoyment, inspiration, and even admiration in some, derision and outrage in others. Harriet Waters Preston, for example, writing for *The Atlantic Monthly*, identified Ouida as a "flagrant romanticist", whose dazzling literary world consisted of "ardent love and furious war; of vast riches and dazzling pomp; of heroic virtues and brutal crimes", and of "tremendous adventures, enormous windfalls, crushing catastrophes, and miraculous escapes" (1886: 47). While she questioned Ouida's espousal of aristocratic pomp and adultery, she also called her unparalleled among living female writers, an author whose books revealed "a truly remarkable wealth of invention and no mean constructive power", and whose "endless variety of striking figures and picturesque situations, combined with an independence of conventionalities, whether moral or literary, [...] moves one to something like awe" (50). One anonymous reviewer called her "the Chopin of dramatic narration" and "of surpassing brilliance" ("'Whitehall' Portraits", 1878: 484), another attested her genius, but also cautioned that "those eloquent rhapsodies of lurid description" might lead astray foolish and uneducated readers ("Contemporary Literature", 1879: 334). Marie Corelli likewise called Ouida "a woman of *genius*" (1890: 362, original emphasis; see Moody, 2013), and attested that there was "no living author who has the same rush, fire and beauty of language", but also felt compelled to state: "[l]et it not be imagined that I, or any of us, for that matter, seek to defend 'Ouida's' system of morals as set forth in her books" (1890: 365). A. K. Fiske, on the other hand, charged her work with offenses against propriety, found it insulting and distressing, particularly from a woman unappreciative of the healthy and pure domestic sphere, and declared her un-English (see Fiske, 1880). Vincent E. H. Murray declared "the fact that a silly and ignorant woman should write novels which are at once vulgar, nasty, and immoral in tendency, could not, in itself, be a matter of interest for readers of the CONTEMPORARY REVIEW", but also warned that her work would "breed a pestilence so foul as to poison the very life-blood of our nation" (1873: 935). Accusations of moral corruption, as is well documented in scholarship, were regularly levelled at sensation fiction, with its bigamy plots, villainous women, and murder. Ouida, who was then, and still is, often classed, albeit awkwardly, with sensation fiction, nevertheless flouted even those daring genre conventions by granting happy endings to adulteresses and divorcées, or discussing marital rape. "Why this was tolerated in Ouida's novels", Pamela Gilbert admits, "is unclear" (2005: 143). One reason, as both Gilbert and Jane Jordan have suggested, and as I will discuss, might be that Ouida's novels were perceived to be French novels written in English (see Jordan, 2009b; 2014b). However, here this conundrum illustrates Ouida's uncertain place within the Victorian literary marketplace.

Indeed, while many agreed on her stylistic and narrative prowess, her merit as an artist remained, paradoxically, under discussion. Reviewer Ella, for example, lauds Ouida's work as "marked by beauty and vigour of language, delicacy of thought, and richness of imagination", but also points out her tendency towards exuberance and the extreme, proclaiming her "essentially a careless writer" (1877: 369), and concludes that "the general influence of her novels is unhealthy" (372). Beerbohm, who dedicated his essay collection *More* (1899) to Ouida "with his love", praised her "force and energy so exuberant and indefatigable" (1899: 109), a "description which is the result of true vision" (112): "[h]er every page is a riot of unpolished epigrams and unpolished poetry of vision, with a hundred discursions and redundancies. She cannot say a thing once; she must repeat it again and again, and, with every repetition, so it seems to me, she says it with greater force and charm. Her style is a veritable cascade" (109–10). Willa Cather calls Ouida "one of the brightest minds of the last generation" and admits "it would be hard to find a better plot" than that of *Under Two Flags* (1867) (1895: 7). However, while the novel contains "the rudiments of a great style", Cather also finds it "the most drivelling nonsense and mawkish sentimentality and contemptible feminine weakness to be found anywhere" (7). Indeed, Cather declares that Ouida's novels "fill me with the same sense of disgust that Oscar Wilde's books do" (7). Nonetheless, what amounted, to Cather, to "one rank morass of misguided genius and wasted power" (7), others recognised as artistry: both Ouida and, later, Wilde, after all, became known for their aesthetic, highly visual, and witty style, and larger-than-life characters – yet only one of them has become a staple of the Victorian canon.

"The picturesqueness of modern life", said Beerbohm, "transfigured by imagination, embellished by fancy, that is her *forte*" (1899: 111, original emphasis). At the same time, Fiske identified Zola-esque realism, or what he calls "coarseness and foulness" (1880: 80) in Ouida's depiction of high society (83), prompted by a remark by Ouida herself in her novel *Moths* (1880 [2005]: 431). Identified with masculine adventure, sensationalist taboo-breaking, French realism, and British aesthetes, a prolific narrator and storyteller who "grips [...] with her every plot" (110), Ouida's novels were nonetheless reviewed by critics, as

G. S. Street diagnosed, "with simple merriment or a frankly contemptuous patronage" and placed "below writers without a tenth of her ability" (1895: 167, 176). Beerbohm, paradoxically, declared: "Ouida is not, and never was, an artist" (1899: 106). Why did profuse adulations for her narrative skill not translate into respect for her work? Corelli, in accusing male authors of being "ungallantly jealous of a woman's brain that proves in any respect sharper, quicker, and more subtle than [their] own" (365) no doubt has a point – though one suspects she is espousing her own cause here as much as Ouida's. Critics, for example, were swift and elaborate in pointing out inconsistencies and inaccuracies in Ouida's novels, which were littered with allusions to Classical and contemporary literature or popular culture, and while such errors should not be explained away, we should remember that Ouida was not university-educated, but self-taught. Instead of scrutinising her work thus, we should, as Janine Hatter and Helena Ifill suggest, understand that popular women writers like Ouida were "writing for audiences that they considered to be capable and engaged readers" (2021: 6–7), and examine how they mobilised popular culture to create shared frames of reference.

Another reason for Ouida's troubled place in the literary field, as Celia Phillips, Jane Jordan, and Andrew King have shown, was Ouida's complicated, vulnerable, and often disadvantageous relationship with publishers and the literary market. For example, whereas Ouida considered herself an artist with a cultured, cosmopolitan readership, in 1876, Chatto & Windus purchased the rights to her new novels and back catalogue behind her back from Chapman & Hall, and began to market her work towards the popular market in increasingly cheap editions (see Jordan, 2011a; King, 2013c). As Celia Phillips remarks: as "a middle-class woman with no financial resources, [Ouida] was painfully vulnerable in the business world of that 'gentleman's' trade, and neither Frederick Chapman nor Andrew Chatto resisted the temptation to exploit her" (1978: 215). Conceiving of her work "in wholly commercial terms for a seemingly undiscerning readership" (Jordan, 2011a: 42), they published yellow-back editions with safely sentimental cover illustrations (King, 2013c: 21) that falsely advertised her increasingly serious work and undermined the artistic praise she had received, for example, for *Ariadnê* (1877) and *A Village Commune* (1881) (see Jordan, 2011a: 42): "[h]er novels were marketed, priced and packaged like popular fiction for a popular reader, and the literary establishment judged her accordingly" (54). While such democratisation made her work widely available, as King shows, Ouida profited less and less from the sales of her books, and was driven into financial ruin at the end of her life (King, 2013c).

As a female writer of commercially and sometimes critically successful novels, essays, and short stories, who nevertheless suffered under the gendered biases of the literary market, Ouida not only powerfully encapsulates the strengths and weaknesses of popular fiction, and reflects the "tastes and preoccupations" of her readership (Hatter and Ifill, 2021: 6), but throws into relief a multitude of Victorian cultural currents. As a nexus of various fields of tension, she illuminates conventions, practises and expectations related to literary production, genre, and gender, troubles high and low brow binaries, highlights relationships between publishing and readerships, and provides a case study for nineteenth-century literary celebrity. For, whereas Ouida's work resisted assimilation into any one tradition, "the 'Ouida' morals", "'Ouida' exaggerations" and "'Ouida eloquence" (Corelli, 1890: 365) became its very own "familiar institution" (Street, 1895: 168), and came to imply dashing guardsmen, flamboyant, "swift and strong" and daring writing (see Beerbohm, 1899: 115), "undisguised sensuality" (Acland, 1874: 827), exotic and cosmopolitan settings, and, often, female agency. Indeed, Dorothy Richardson, in *Pilgrimage* (1915–38), catalyses her protagonist's cathartic awakening through the experience of reading Ouida: "Ouida, Ouida, she would muse with the book at last in her hands. I want bad things – strong bad things ... It doesn't matter, Italy, the sky, bright hot landscapes, things happening. I don't care what people think or say. I am older than anyone here in this house. I am myself" (1917: 286).

This, then, was Ouida to her readers: entertainment, exuberance, scandal, vicarious exploration of and participation in the cosmopolitan world. For herself, she knew to cultivate a more mysterious identity (see Jordan, 2011b: 221) and so became synonymous with her work, less "a member of Society" rather than "a representative of the republic of letters" ("'Whitehall' Portraits", 1878: 484). Nonetheless, at this point, the question arises: who was Ouida?

Biography

Ouida was born Marie Louise Ramé on 1 January, 1839 in Bury St. Edmunds in Suffolk, but would later style herself "de la Ramée". Her mother, Susan Sutton, came from a family of local wine importers. Her father, Louis Ramé, worked as a French teacher, but his frequent absences gave rise to rumours about him being a French spy for the exiled Louis Napoleon, and one Bury resident later claimed Ramé was "commonly supposed to have a gambling 'hell or hells' [...] in Paris" (Gedge, 1920: 387). He left his family in 1850, and the persistent and appropriately romantic myth tells of his demise in the Franco-Prussian war (1870–71). Despite his absence in her life, which left Ouida in charge of supporting her mother and grandmother throughout their lives, Ouida identified strongly with her French heritage. Whereas growing up without the guardianship and financial support of a male figure will have lastingly influenced Ouida, for example by inspiring her life-long exploration of female characters struggling to exert agency within patriarchal society, to diagnose either her or her fiction with "fetishistic attempts to substitute the loss of her father", as some studies do (Schroeder and Holt, 2008: 15; Sutherland, 1995), seems somewhat outdated.

In 1857, Ouida and her family relocated to West London, where she met surgeon William Francis Ainsworth. Through his connections to his cousin Harris' *Bentley's Miscellany*, Ouida began to publish her first stories between 1859 and 1861 under the pseudonym "Ouida", derived from a childhood mispronunciation of her name, Louisa. She was twenty years old. In 1861, *Granville de Vigne*, her first novel, was serialised in another of Harris' magazines and published in 1863 as a triple-decker by Chapman and Hall. A tale of *beau sabreurs*, adventuresses, bigamy, and war, it was modelled on the fiction of George Alfred Lawrence and the then-emergent sensation genre. It was followed by *Strathmore* (1865), *Chandos* (1866), *Idalia* and *Under Two Flags*, both serialised in 1867, the latter in the military magazine *Army and Navy Review*. Ouida began publishing in the US through Lippincott and in Germany through Baron Tauchnitz, based in Leipzig, with whom she entertained a life-long correspondence and friendship (Esser, forthcoming [2024]). For the first years of her career, Ouida was thought to be a male writer and "gentleman rake" writing about his own set (King, 2015: 1227), so well did she mimic and portray male spaces like racecourses, clubs, and battlefields. When her feminine gender was discovered, praise turned to scepticism: she was trespassing (see Jordan, 2011b: 224).

In 1866, her grandmother died. Ouida moved into the newly established Langham Hotel, where she held a salon to which she invited prominent artists and writers, and surrounded herself with military men, whose open talk she would encourage. Whereas it was long supposed those conversations inspired *Under Two Flags*' authentic prose, Jane Jordan convincingly argues that the novel, already serialised when Ouida moved, had a literary inspiration, namely Colonel Poulett Cameron's *Romance of Military Life* (1853) (Jordan, 2013: 65) – indeed, Ouida dedicated the novel to him.

In 1871, after a tour of the continent, Ouida and her mother moved to Florence, where they took the eleventh-century Villa Farinola, and where Ouida would live with her many dogs and mingle with European high society. By now, she had published various short stories as well as *Tricotrin* (1869), *Puck* (1870), and *Folle-Farine* (1871), which would be followed by *A Dog of Flanders* (1872) of enduring international fame. In Italy, Ouida turned towards Italian politics, debates of art, and satirical portraits of high society with *Pascarèl* (1874), *Two Little Wooden Shoes* (1874), *Signa* (1875), *Ariadnê* (1877) and *Friendship* (1878). The latter is an imminently readable *roman à clef* about her ultimately frustrated relationship with the Marchese della Stufa and her rivalry with his mistress, Janet Ross, which caused no little awkwardness in Florentine circles. How big a celebrity Ouida was at the time may be illustrated by the fact Edmund Yates profiled her for the series "Celebrities at Home" for his magazine, *World* (September 1876, published 1877), where she was featured alongside aristocratic men, artists, and scientists as only one of four women featured (the others were Empress Eugénie, Sarah Bernhardt, and fellow writer, Mary E. Braddon [Jordan, 2011a: 39–40]). Still, at the same time, as detailed above, Chatto & Windus purchased Ouida's copyright from Chapman & Hall without her approval.

In *Moths* (1880), published at the same time as Zola's *Nana*, Ouida satirised high society and the marriage market with biting wit and esprit, discussed the taboo topic of marital rape, and scandalised audiences by depicting, possibly for the first time, a divorced woman living happily. *A Village Commune* (1881), no less political, portrayed political corruption and the Italian countryside. With her short story collection *Bimbi* (1882), dedicated to the teenage prince Vittorio Emmanuele, she outlined her moral vision for Italy's future. After *In Maremma* (1882), Ouida turned from Italy back to social satire, increasingly biting in its proto-Wildean witticisms (see Schaffer, 2002; Fitzsimons, 2015) and critique. *Wanda* (1883), *Princess Napraxine* (1884), *Othmar* (1885), *Guilderoy* (1889), and *Syrlin* (1890) also stand out through their aestheticist qualities (see Schaffer, 2000).

In the winter of 1886, Ouida returned to London and the

Langham, where she was received as a celebrity, and also met Wilde, beginning a collaboration for his *Women's World* (1888–89). However, through her difficulties with her publishers, who paid her less while profiting from reprints of her earlier work (King, 2013c: 25), she was writing more short stories, essays, and opinion pieces, and could not well afford the trip to London. Her later, shorter novels *Toxin* (1895) and *The Waters of Edera* (1900) centred on political statements around vivisection and environmentalism, respectively. Her 1897 novel, *The Massarenes*, once more turned to her forte, social satire, spectacle, and commodity culture. By now, Ouida lived in increasingly unstable circumstances. Her mother had died in 1893, she moved often and was evicted from her rented villa in 1903, losing her possessions, including the manuscript for her last novel, to her landlady. She won the ensuing court case but had to rewrite the novel from memory. *Helianthus* (1908) remains unfinished but is a clever and perceptive fantasy about mounting political tension in Europe, and its indictment of militarism and warmongering, written six years before the First World War, seems especially perceptive. The year before her death by pneumonia at the age of sixty-nine, well-wishing publications by Marie Corelli and Vernon Lee, courting for charity for her, had exposed Ouida's poverty to the British public, much to her outrage, and she had been awarded a Civil List Pension. Ouida died on January 25th, 1908, in Viareggio, and was buried in Bagni di Lucca. In Britain, the *Daily Mirror* raised a public subscription to erect a monument in her birthplace, Bury St. Edmunds.

Ouida remained a staple of popular consciousness for a long time. Her private but eccentric life and work inspired four biographies: Elizabeth Lee's *Ouida: A Memoir* (1914), Yvonne Ffrench's *Ouida: A Study in Ostentation* (1938), Monica Stirling's *The Fine and Wicked* (1950), and Eileen Bigland's *Ouida: The Passionate Victorian* (1951). After that, interest waned and Ouida, expelled from canons of Victorian literature by virtue of her "popular" status and gender, lapsed into obscurity. Her novels went out of print, with the exceptions of the 1995 Oxford World's Classic edition of *Under Two Flags,* edited by John Sutherland, Natalie Schroeder's editions of *Moths* (2005) and *In Maremma* (2006), as well as Andrew King's edition of *The Massarenes* for Carolyn Oulton's *New Woman Fiction* series (2011). The memory of Ouida has been shaped from the beginning by her author persona, but also by her biographies, which all reflect the dominant gender politics of their time and attempt to portray her patronisingly and unsympathetically in turns as a deluded eccentric or a tragically jilted, naive woman (for corrective accounts, see Jordan 1995; Jordan 2009a; King, 2015). As such, they have lastingly damaged her literary reputation. However, both Ouida's reputation and her status in the cultural consciousness underwent another significant, if equally detrimental, evaluation through second-wave feminist scholarship.

The Struggle with Feminism

In 1894, Ouida responded to Sarah Grand's essay in the *North American Review*, "The New Aspect of the Woman Question", with mocking critique – and in so doing, coined the term "New Woman". Superficial readings of what is, no doubt, a polemic essay, by second-wave feminists (1960s-80s) resulted in branding Ouida an "anti-feminist" and have rendered "Ouida invisible within today's canon" (Gilbert, 1999: 170). Whereas subsequent readings of the essay have troubled and questioned Ouida's opposition to the New Woman (Gilbert, 1999; Schaffer, 2002; Hager, 2014; King, 2011b; Pykett, 2016), that initial judgment, essentially disqualifying Ouida from canon-revisionist feminist scholarship, has lastingly shaped her legacy. Considering that here, once again, Ouida becomes a catalyst that spotlights the attitudes, biases, and politics with which we approach her, and which underlie ever-developing feminist criticism at various points in history, it is worth discussing Ouida's relationship with feminism, not least as a foundational framework of this study.

The 1890s New Woman, as Sally Ledger and Thalia Schaffer observe, was an idealised collective symbol, a semi-fictional, "discursive phenomenon" emerging out of a multitude of literary and non-fiction texts, cartoons, as well as real working women, novelists, campaigners, and bicyclists, and as such mutable to its creator's intentions (Ledger, 1997: 3; Schaffer, 2001: 39, 45). As a pioneering figure, she embodied women seeking autonomy in a male-dominated society, mainly through problematising marriage as an institution of violence and oppression and by demanding education, careers, sexual freedom, dress reforms, and the right to vote. Second-wave feminism, itself championing New Woman ideals such as participation in public life, rejection of marriage as an institution, or dress reform, thus canonised her as the essential feminist foremother within an imagined teleological genealogy of steady emancipation, and struggled to assimilate diverging views or alternative visions. Whereas Elaine Showalter's seminal study *A Literature of Their Own* identified Ouida as part of a proto-feminist generation expressing "female anger, frustration, and sexual energy more directly than had been done before" (1977: 160), she was disqualified as a New Woman writer due to her scepticism.

However, in her essay, Ouida is far from siding with conservative anti-suffragists like Eliza Lynn Linton, and as far as ever from espousing Ruskinian ideals of women as domestic angels. Ironically, it is Sarah Grand who emerges as a "difference feminist" championing ideals of feminine purity and rooting her argument for greater public responsibility in "women's natural housewifely and maternal instincts" (Schaffer, 2001: 41). No wonder Ouida mocked Grand's vision of the New Woman as superior to other women, patronisingly "prescrib[ing] the remedy" (Ouida, 1894 [1895]b: 206). Indeed, Ouida is well aware of women's troubled status in Victorian society (Hager, 2014: 97), but rather accuses women like Grand of demanding abstract privileges instead of becoming politically active from their current position, for example in the realm of animal rights: "[w]oman, whether new or old, leaves immense fields of culture untilled, immense areas of influence wholly neglected. She does almost nothing with the resources she possesses because, her whole energy is concentrated on desiring and demanding those she has not" (Ouida, 1894 [1895] b: 211). As Schaffer perceptively argues, Ouida also constructs the New Woman as a grotesque Other in order to present her own activism and her views as "moderate and reasonable" in comparison (Schaffer, 2001: 42, 45).

This study does not aim to re-claim Ouida as a forgotten feminist foremother – not least because that, in itself, is a fraught endeavour – but instead to highlight that, regardless of the frameworks she adopted or rejected, Ouida was nonetheless acutely aware of, and invested in, the ways gender shapes agency and participation within a capitalist patriarchal society, and as such has much to offer. Concurrently, I argue we must pay attention to the ways in which scholarship is shaped by external frameworks. Pamela Gilbert recounts how canon-revisionist scholarship itself was shaped, well into the 1990s, by academic imperatives of the time:

> We were fighting three battles, the first two of which had to be fought just to get the author an audience: first, to justify attention to a woman author as a feminist foremother; second, to justify the relation of that author to a 'great tradition' in which aesthetic innovation and filiation are important measures of evaluation. But women's writing and popular writing often cannot be read within these categories of filiation. [...] Thus our third battle was to find a mode of reading that fully respected the complexities of our subject. And this battle we are still fighting. (Gilbert, 2013: 39)

In the interest of fully representing the complexities of our subject, we must revisit and re-contextualise Ouida's role in and relationship with Victorian femininity and proto-feminism, as Gilbert, Schaffer, Pykett, and Hager have done. After all, whereas what is now known as first-wave feminism of the 1890s to 1910s ultimately catalysed itself around the demand for suffrage, it was far from a monolithic movement towards a clearly mapped-out, teleological notion of progress. Entangled in "often a problematic and contradictory relation" to "*fin-de-siècle* utopianism, socialism, imperialism, Aestheticism and Decadence, urbanism, mass culture, sex science, psychoanalysis, economics, eugenics, the discourses of evolution (and degeneration), and definitions of masculinity" (Pykett, 2002: xii), New Woman writers "coexisted with conservative thinking as they upheld racial and social hierarchies" (Richardson, 2002: lxi). Against this backdrop, Ouida's exile from feminist history seems increasingly arbitrary, not least because, as several scholars have noted, New Woman subjects like "the horrors of the marriage market" and the notion of "socially sanctioned loveless marriages as a form of prostitution" (Pykett, 2016: 38), are central to her work. Moreover, not only does Ouida's own life as an unmarried, self-supporting woman who frequently challenged social norms qualify her as a New Woman role model (Schaffer, 2001: 47), but so does her fiction "anticipate the active, assertive, sexually liberated, or alternatively the highly sensitive, pure, and morally elevated New Woman heroine who resists the constraints of conventional nineteenth-century gender roles" (Pykett, 2016: 38). Gilbert has argued this for *Under Two Flags* (in 1999), Hager for *Princess Napraxine* (in 2014), and Pykett for *Moths* and *The Massarenes* (in 2016), but Ouida's rebellion against constricting social conventions and her exploration of emancipatory models of (female) agency and independence are, as this study explores, fundamental to her work at large. She herself stated: "[n]o one can accuse me of any political prejudices. My writings have alternatively been accused of a reactionary conservatism and a dangerous socialism, so that I may without presumption claim to be impartial: I love conservatism when it means the preservation of beautiful things, I love revolution when it means the destruction of vile ones" (Ouida, 1881: 214–5). As such, Ouida was an individualist and libertarian (see King, 2011b), who rejected Grand's New Woman as too homogeneous and thus too restrictive (King, 2011a: viii). Her politics were equally individualist and often contradictory: she valorised aristocratic glamour, cosmopolitan travel, dashing guardsmen, and feminine youth and beauty, yet also espoused a fiercely democratic spirit, hated capitalism, and championed animal rights and environmentalism. She deployed misogynist language and was so critical of women that she was said to "hate her own sex" (Corelli, 1890: 363), yet her female characters are complex, angry, act with agency, and escape Victorian narrative moralistic conventions that govern popular fiction to this day (see Primorac, 2018). In the end, her views may best be summarised by G. S. Street, who attests her a "genuine and passionate love of beauty, as she conceives it, and a genuine and passionate hatred of injustice and oppression" (1895: 175).

About This Book

Then as now, Ouida's life and work provide a powerful prism through which to draw out the biases, gendered ideologies, and politics that underpin Victorian publishing practise, readerships, and contemporary scholarship, thus shaping genre, canon formation, and feminist reception. But she also deserves attention in her own right, as a masterful storyteller and a woman with strong convictions. Her prose is eloquent, exuberant, and evocative, her powerful imagination conjures exciting settings for vicarious consumption, and her narrative style is, for lack of a less anachronistic descriptor, cinematic. Her plots and characters are elaborately created and potently condensed to types of swashbuckling or romantic allure, demanding, as Gilbert notes, an affective response and evaluation that takes place "in the world outside the text, the world of readers" (2013: 47), just as much popular fiction does today. Ouida expertly engineers those responses from her standpoint of critique (47), but also as a narrator, crafting settings and situations always for the greatest dramatic effect. It is no wonder her fiction was so often adapted for the stage or later, early film. This is to say, while a closer inspection of her dramatic skill lies outside the scope of this study, Ouida's status as a writer of popular fiction should not obscure her considerable literary or narrative talents, which after all won her a large and loyal readership.

Scholarship on Ouida has long reflected her uneasy relationship with canons, genres, and categorisations. While there is a variety of analyses from dedicated Ouida scholars such as Natalie Schroeder, Lyn Pykett, Pamela Gilbert, Talia Schaffer, Jane Jordan, and Andrew King, these chapters and articles often appear under a variety of frameworks within Victorian studies, with only two full-length studies and one special journal issue (*Anglistica Pisana*, 6.1/2, 2009) dedicated to her, one dedicated to a close reading of her work (Schroeder and Holt, 2008), and one examining her relationship with popular culture (Jordan and King, 2013). Traditionally, Ouida has been treated, albeit uneasily, as a sensation writer (Showalter, 1977; Schroeder, 1988; Poster, 1996; Gilbert, 2005; Jordan, 1995; Marucci, 2009; Jordan 2011b; Schroeder and Schroeder, 2011; Hager, 2014), but second-wave scholarship has focused on the genre as one written by women for women, and so relegated Ouida, who also wrote for men, to the margins (Jordan, 2011b: 222). Discussions of her depiction of homosocial friendships abound (Gilbert, 2005; Jordan, 2011b; Jordan, 2013; Oulton, 2007; Schroeder and Holt, 2008), but it might be interesting to explore the *beau sabreur* type, for which she became famous, from other angles, such as genre: Jordan has commented on Ouida's connection to George Lawrence (2011b, 2013), but there is more to be said. Although gender in *Under Two Flags* has been discussed broadly (Peck, 1998; Gilbert, 1999; Schroeder and Holt, 2008; Addcox, 2009; Jordan, 2011b; Schroeder and

Schroeder, 2011; Vrachnas, 2017; Clarke, 2022), little has been made of the novel's qualities as desert adventure (Sutherland, 1995; Embry, 2010). Likewise, whereas Jordan has explored Ouida's French identity (Jordan, 2009b; 2014a; 2014b), there is more to discover about her transcultural influences. Her Italian novels and relationships have been discussed in *Anglistica Pisana* (6, 2009), by Jordan (2009c) and King (2009) and, as outlined above, she is increasingly discussed in relation to the New Woman (Gilbert, 1999; Schaffer, 2002; Hager, 2014; Pykett, 2016), or in terms of her connections to *fin-de-siècle* culture (Schaffer 2000; Schaffer 2002; Fitzsimons, 2015; Bristow, 2015; Hallum, 2015; Denisoff, 2022). Other avenues of inquiry have been publishing and author identity (Phillips, 1978; Molloy, 2008; Jordan, 2009a; 2011a; forthcoming [2024]; Dubuisson, 2013; Vrachnas, 2013; Law, 2013; King, 2013c), identity and celebrity (Jordan, 1995; Moore, 2011; Dubuisson, 2021), environmentalism (Carroll, 2019; Denisoff, 2022), animal rights (Sanders Pollock, 2005; Pireddu, 2014), mobility (Parkins, 2009: 49–61), artistry (King, 2009; 2013a), politics (Maltz, 2009; King, 2011b; Pykett, 2013: Ambrosini, 2013), and legacies (Geraghty, 2019; Erickson, 2020, Rainwater, 2021). While it is thus difficult to assemble an overview of the field of "Ouida studies", these approaches reflect the many aspects under which Ouida may be discussed, as well as her uneasiness within canons and genealogies.

Indeed, rather than try to shoehorn her work into any one tradition, this study aims to examine her work as much on its own terms as possible; that is, as a woman writing successfully both within and against historical currents, exploring independence and rebellious gender politics, and engaging in manifold and complex ways with the socio-political and cultural landscape around her.

My approach in doing so is influenced by the social-media-based, grass-roots-activist, and popular culture feminism of the fourth wave that has been gaining momentum since the 2010s (see Baumgardner, 2011; Munro, 2013; Jenkins et. al. 2016;

Zimmerman, 2017). The 1990s and 2000s' post-feminism responded to the second wave's perceived earnestness with a youthful, 'Girl Power', free market feminism that entangled women in the market economy as self-curating consumers on the one hand, and expanded into queer and post-colonial feminism on the other (see Whelehan, 1995; Genz; 2009; McRobbie, 2009). The fourth wave is heralded by a new generation of digital natives who engage with feminist ideas in the non-academic spaces of social media and participatory culture, and endorsed by public figures and celebrities who recognise that championing social justice and widespread recognition of minority voices has become socially acceptable, even desirable, as well as carried over into activism such as the Black Lives Matter, #MeToo, and the Women's March movements (Rivers, 2017; Pilcher and Whelehan, 2017; Clark-Parsons, 2022). Fourth-wave feminism continues to challenge conservative and white-centric feminisms, and, is "transaffirmative and intersectional, attentive to how classism, racism, ableism, geographical location, and other forms of discrimination and privilege differentially shape women's lives" (Cooke, 2020: 4). It explores gender on a broader scale, taking into account queer sexualities and (toxic) masculinities, and, in response to emerging and vocal right-wing populism, threats to women's reproductive rights, enduring pay gaps, and endemic sexual harassment, both in everyday and workplace situations. It especially scrutinises systemic inequalities (social, cultural, economic, political) in institutionalised patriarchal power structures such as the workplace, public spaces, and the media; "it is sobering", comments Jennifer Cooke, "to recognise that women's hard-won legal rights and positions in society are more fragile than we might have supposed" (2020: 4). Turning our "attention to both media portrayals of women, and the impact of popular culture on women's lives" (Rivers, 2017: 16), that is both how 'woman' is constructed and re-negotiated in popular discourse, and how concepts such as sexuality, agency, and empowerment remain entangled in a capitalist marketplace, indeed provides a fruitful framework for (re-)evaluating popular women writers. My interest accordingly lies in how Ouida treats gender binaries, femininity, (toxic) masculinity, consent, female agency, and commodity culture. I aim to make visible how Ouida so often challenges, transgresses, and subverts binary Victorian notions of gender without categorising character attributes as either 'masculine' or 'feminine', that is, without re-inscribing that binary.

In that endeavour, this study moves through Ouida's oeuvre in a broadly chronological way, charting her evolving exploration of gender, identity, politics, and economies of spectacle through pertinent examples from her fiction and non-fiction, highlighting connections, echoes, and through-lines. Each chapter also situates her work in the context of larger, trans-cultural social and literary movements and so illustrates how integral popular fiction is not only to the literary marketplace, but the circulation of ideas and narratives across genres and readerships.

Chapter 1 examines Ouida's early novels, focussing on her relationship with masculinity and male homosocial relationships. It considers how she, inspired by George Lawrence's work, re-imagines the *beau sabreur* against contemporary military and muscular ideals emerging in and through the Crimean War, how her clubland dandies relate to evolving ideals of heroic masculinity, and how her dandy soldier hero Bertie Cecil both anticipates and defies later versions of the chivalric adventurer as imagined by New Imperialist authors like H. Rider Haggard or George Alfred Henty. By contextualising Cecil within a French colonial project, Ouida disentangles her hero to some degree from national identity and is free to voice colonial critique and explore a core staple of her work, the subject of individual liberty.

Chapter 2 revisits her two 1867 novels, *Idalia* and *Under Two Flags*, with a focus on her transgressive female heroines, whom Ouida imagines as active agents within international political frameworks. Both navigate male-defined, military and political settings and manage to find independence and even heroism in these heterotopic, liminal spaces. By disentangling her heroines from gender norms, Ouida mobilises the adventure genre not only to craft vicarious fantasies of agency but also to examine and expose ideas about 'femininity' as socially constructed. At the same time, Ouida navigates the limits of female rebellion and agency when her heroines fall in love and become entangled in sexual politics in new ways.

Chapter 3 concerns itself with Ouida's provocative, even scandalous female adventuresses, present throughout her work and usually escaping the Victorian narrative justice that punishes the Fallen Woman. It examines how Ouida negotiates female self-direction within and against the patriarchal order through the failures and successes of her so-called Femme Galantes, but also contextualises the type against what I suggest are her real-world inspirations: celebrity courtesans of the French Second Empire. By comparing Ouida's satirical and critical portraits against real women like Marie Duplessis or Cora Pearl, as well as male-authored narratives by Alexandre Dumas *fils*, Émile Zola, and Octave Feuillet, we gain a deeper understanding of Ouida's exploration of female independence.

Chapter 4 discusses another core theme of Ouida's work: her criticism of the institution of marriage. By deploying Gothic parody or mobilising a uniquely female aestheticism, Ouida not only tackles taboo topics such as marital rape and happy divorcées but also makes visible how women are objectified and commodified through the marriage market. Anticipating key concerns of New Woman fiction, Ouida investigates how sex and marriage compromise women's social, economic, and physical integrity, and explores queer, female asexuality as a site of possible resistance and even empowerment.

Chapter 5 examines Ouida's identity as an artist and critic. It considers how she portrays women artists in her fiction, developing the concept of the independent, exceptional artist-genius whose unique insights and capacity for sympathy oblige them to voice critique as a social responsibility. It also looks at how she channelled the anti-capitalist, anti-imperial, anti-modern politics she voiced across multiple non-fiction essays into her later fiction. As such, it investigates how Ouida mobilised narrative and popular fiction as an important site of social diagnosis and critique.

CHAPTER 1

Beau Sabreurs: Homosocial Masculinity

Introduction: Guardsman Heroes

In the contemporary Victorian imagination, Ouida was firmly identified with "her guardsmen", hedonistic adventurers who, with "their fair, silken mustachios and their glen-garries and their velvet jackets" are "pegs for luxury and romance" (Beerbohm, 1899: 112). They are seen "gambling on credit for fabulous stakes, and rise 'fresh as paint' to go on duty in the morning", and are identified both with "aristocratic superciliousness" and "muscles of steel" ("Contemporary Literature", 1879: 334). As *Blackwood's Edinburgh Magazine* quips, they "could be reckoned upon at a moment's notice for a manly decision in the most momentous question, or for a heroic deed of superb self-sacrifice. For they had a code of honour and virtue of their own, though it was a code that clashed with the old-fashioned decalogue; and if they swindled a friend or seduced his wife, they would always back his bills to any amount" (334). Whereas the latter part is persiflage, here outlined is the *beau sabreur* hero, great in sport and love and war, which George Alfred Lawrence's 1857 novel *Guy Livingstone* had pioneered. Intrinsically, the Ouidean hero is, however, also "inimitable alike in his grace of person and in the perfection of his taste": while he may refuse "the bedchamber assigned to him, on the plea that he could not sleep under a false Fragonard", this essentially romantic figure is familiar with "Cairene Bazaars" as with "the incomparable grace and brilliance of the Court of Hapsburg" (Beerbohm, 1899: 113).

Jane Jordan has discussed the influence of Lawrence's *Guy Livingstone* on Ouida's early fiction (Jordan, 2011a), especially with regard to the constellation of male friendships threatened by a femme fatale. This motif is also central to Mary Braddon's *Lady Audley's Secret*, which was serialised concurrently with Ouida's first novel, *Granville de Vigne* (serialised 1861–63, later published as *Held in Bondage* in 1863), and which was published by the Tinsley Brothers, who also published Ouida and Lawrence. Indeed, as contemporaries noted, Ouida synthesised Lawrence's popular heroes with newly emerging sensation fiction: "[t]he words are those of Guy Livingstone, but the plot is that of Miss Braddon" (*Westminster Review*, qtd. in Jordan, 2011b: 224).

However, whereas Ouida's relationship with the sensation genre is well established, her adoption of Lawrence's brand of muscular masculinity merits a closer look, both against the historical context of a newly emerging heroic ideal, and because she, as a young female writer, successfully adopted and re-imagined a male genre for male audiences. Her heroes may be inheritors of the silver-fork dandy of Disraeli and Bulwer Lytton (Schroeder and Holt, 2008: 20; Jordan, 2013: 53), but they are also rooted firmly in the new, heroic masculine ideal which emerged out of the Crimean War, which was potently configured in Thomas Hughes' *Tom Brown's School Days* (1857) and central to Lawrence's fiction, and which became the masculine ideal of chivalry and courage, and which dominated the nineteenth century until the First World War (Bristow, 1991; Hall, 1994; Girouard, 1981).

This chapter examines Ouida's male heroes. It establishes the historical context out of which her dandy adventurers arise by comparing *Held in Bondage* against Lawrence's novels, especially *Guy Livingstone* and *Sword and Gown* (1859), and examines both in the context of emerging masculine ideals. It then provides a close reading of Bertie Cecil, the hero of *Under Two Flags*, as the essential Ouida hero of that era and, while keeping in mind also the protagonists of *Strathmore* (1865) and *Chandos* (1866), discusses how Cecil embodies an aristocratic ideal as a Clubland dandy embroiled in close, male, homosocial friendships. Against the context of real-life inspirations, such as Ouida's Langham salon, and well-known guardsman Frederick Burnaby, the chapter then turns towards Cecil's escapades in the French Algerian desert. By contrasting how Ouida configures this colonial context, the Bedouin, and the French military, I examine how her soldier hero both anticipates and undermines the muscular hero of 1880s New Imperialism espoused by H. Rider Haggard, G. A. Henty, and Arthur Conan Doyle, especially in the wake of General Gordon's death at Khartoum in 1885. By way of conclusion, I discuss Ouida's relationship with and intervention in a male-aligned genre and market.

The Six Hundred

Held in Bondage begins in the masculine realm of boys' schools like Eton and Rugby, with a distinct note of nostalgia: "[w]hat a royal time it was!" (Ouida, 1863 [1891]: 3). The boyish idyll of cricket, smoking, fishing, boating, swimming, riding, and flirtations with shop girls soon matures to "dear old Trinity", where sunshine, roaring fires, picnics and rowing reflect a joyful indolence imbued with generations-deep tradition, embodied by the river Cam:

> Where grave philosophers have watched the setting sun die out of the sky, as the glories of their own youth have died away unvalued, till lost for ever. [...] Where thousands of young fellows have dropped down under its trees, dreaming over Don Juan or the Lotus-eaters; or pulled along, straining muscle and nerve against the Head-Boat; or sauntered beside it in sweet midsummer eves, with some fair face upraised to theirs. (22)

Ouida's novel is not only viscerally keyed into the leisurely and sportive atmosphere of *Tom Brown's Schooldays*, but also directly mirrors *Guy Livingstone* (both discussed below), down to the first-person narrator writing about the muscular hero. Ouida was eighteen when Lawrence's first novel appeared, and she was evidently an avid reader especially of his first two novels. Their literary influence is palpable in her early novels, and not just because character names from *Sword and Gown*, such as Molyneux, Vavasour, and Tressilian, appear in them.

Held in Bondage draws from both of Lawrence's novels by centring on friendships between muscular and dandy heroes who distinguish themselves in hunting, horse racing, womanising, and war as members of the fashionable regiments. Their heroes are physically athletic, and energetic, as well as aristocratic, genial, and proud. Ouida likewise adapts the voluptuous adventuress who threatens that friendship and the bigamy plots which involve previous marriages, although she gives considerably more depth and agency to her female characters. Similarly, *Sword and Gown* sees its (unhappily married) hero Captain Royston Keene frustrated in his attempt to make the pure Cecil Tresilyan his mistress and dying heroically in the Charge of the Light Brigade, Ouida sends her heroes de Vigne, Sabretasche, and narrator Chevasney through that same battle (although the Horse Guards did not, historically, participate). Already however, Ouida improves on Lawrence, who does not describe the charge itself, through her immersive descriptions of

> a feverish exultation; a wild, causeless thought; a fierce tiger-like longing to be at them, and upon them. The ring of the horses' iron hoofs, the chink of the rattling bits, the clashing of chains and sabres, the whistle and screech of the bullets as they flew amongst us from the redoubt, all made music in my ear. God knows how it is, but in such hours as that the last thing one thinks of is the death so near at hand.

> Though men reeled from their saddles and fell lifeless to the ground at every step, and riderless chargers fled snorting and wounded from our ranks; though the guns from the redoubt poured on us as we swept past, and volleys of rifles and musketry raked our ranks; though every moment great gaps were made, till the fire broke our first line, and the second had to fill it up; though from the thirty guns before us poured a deadly fire, whose murderous balls fell amongst us as we rode, clearing scores of saddles, sweeping down horses and men, and strewing the plain as we passed with quivering human bodies, and chargers rolling over and over in their death-agony, – on we rode, down into that fiery embrace of smoke and flame, that stretched out its arms and hissed its fell kisses at us from the Russian line. (321–2)

It is no coincidence she identifies her gallant, heroic masculinity, which comes alive in the heat of battle so closely with "The Six Hundred", then vividly present in the Victorian imagination. As scholars note, the Crimean War (1853–56) and especially the tactical and operational disaster that was the Charge of the Light Brigade during the battle of Balaclava (1854), marked a significant shift in the Victorian public's perception of the common soldier (see Furneaux, 2016: 5–6; also Figes 2011). Reports of the failures of (aristocratic) military leadership like Lord Cardigan, shaped by William Howard Russell's reporting in *The Times* (Brown, 2010: 606–7) into "a campaign more distinguished by blunder than by glory" (Markovits, 2009: 2), led to sympathy, even valorisation by the public at home of the bravery, fortitude, and sacrifice of rank and file, whose lot, in Tennyson's words, was "not to reason why" but only to "do and die" (Tennyson, 1855: 157). Together with the so-called Indian Mutiny of 1857 (see Dawson, 1994), these events on the geopolitical plane gave rise to new military and masculine ideals of national heroes whose prowess was adaptable to both domestic and imperial theatres. As Stefanie Markovits outlines:

"[b]efore the war, the stereotypical soldier was an aristocratic fop. After it, he was a brave pirate" (2009: 4). Intriguingly, in Lawrence's and Ouida's fiction, both those versions coalesce into the *beau sabreur* as a valorised ideal of middle-class soldiers is transferred to the social elite.

Indeed, at the same time there emerged the ideal of "Christian manliness" which Hughes' popular novel enshrined and located firmly in the boys' school (Bristow, 1991: 53). The novel engendered "a new variety of morally responsible and physically strong manliness" which cultivated, on the one hand, "the virtues of the proper gentleman (fair play, team spirit, decorum)" and embraced, "on the other, the values of competition, independence, and a wilful strength of mind" (54, 58). The ideal of gentlemanly chivalry, "deliberately created [...as] a new model for the ruling classes" which would inculcate "the moral qualities necessary to rulers" (Girouard, 1981: 260–1), was inextricably linked to the man of action and soldier hero whose moral superiority and courage predisposed him to exert the same fortitude and benevolent control over colonial spaces. As an actionable national and masculine ideal, the concept would become integral to the burgeoning expansionist politics of New Imperialism, palpably enacted through the so-called Scramble for Africa, and especially British colonial wars fought in Sudan and South Africa, which also became the theatres of popular adventure fiction of the 1880s (see Kestner, 2010; Deane, 2014; Mallett, 2015). It was also closely identified with the boys' school: "Just as the actual public schools of England were increasingly perceived to be entwined with the greatness of its Empire, moreover, the fictional schools of this genre were explicitly invested with imperial consequences, so that the proper education of their schoolboy heroes was presented as the key to the imperial future" (Deane, 2014: 118).

Lawrence's *Guy Livingstone* presents a more violent version of *Tom Brown's Schooldays*, beginning at Rugby but following its stylish, dominant, and recklessly nonchalant heroes into an adulthood peppered with duels, races, flirtation – and demise. As Holly Furneaux notes, it imagines a school of muscular heroics without politics of social reform (2016: 10), but also one where morally flawed men do not end happily. Similarly, Ouida's early dandy heroes are, for all their nonchalance and bravery, also hot-tempered, stubborn, judgemental, and rash, and more than once bring about their own unhappiness, such as when de Vigne marries "the Trefusis" against everyone's council, or nearly forsakes Alma thinking she has absconded with the villain (when she has been kidnapped), or when Strathmore kills his best friend in a duel. Conversely, Ouida also highlights instances of selflessness and gentle care surrounding the battle, for example when de Vigne cares for a dying friend, which Furneaux identifies as equally crucial to the soldierly ideal emerging out of the Crimean War (2). Ouida amplifies this characteristic with Bertie Cecil in *Under Two Flags*. Indeed, in many ways, Cecil marks a subtle turning away from the roguish and flawed de Vigne, Sabretasche, or Strathmore, towards Ouida's ideal hero.

Clubland Dandies

We are introduced to Bertie Cecil in his natural habitat, London's high society, with its parties and picnics, its barracks and bachelor apartments, fashions and flirtations. There is much skilful narration here crafting this hyper-real, glamorous fantasy, such as the brilliantly ironic passage that describes the guardsmen's luxurious social life of post-Napoleonic ennui (Marucci, 2020: 98) in military terms:

> Escorts to Levees, guards of honour to Drawing rooms, or field-days in the Park and the Scrubs, were but the least portion of it. Far more severe, and still less to be shirked, were the morning exercise in the Ride; the daily parade in the Lady's Mile; the reconnaissances from club windows, the vedettes at Flirtation Corner; the long campaigns at mess-

> breakfasts, with the study of dice and baccarat tactics, and the fortifications of Strasburg pate against the invasions of Chartreuse and Chambertin; the breathless, steady charges of Belgravian staircases when a fashionable drum beat the rataplan; the skirmishes with sharpshooters of the bright-eyed Irregular Lancers; the foraging duty when fair commanders wanted ices or strawberries at garden parties; the ball-practice at Hornsey Handicaps; the terrible risk of crossing the enemy's lines, and being made to surrender as prisoners of war at the jails of St. George's, or of St. Paul's, Knightsbridge; the constant inspections of the Flying Battalions of the Ballet, and the pickets afterward in the Wood of St. John; the anxieties of the Club commissariats, and the close vigilance over the mess wines; the fatigue duty of ballrooms, and the continual unharnessing consequent on the clause in the Regulations never to wear the same gloves twice. (Ouida, 1867 [1995]: 70)

Whereas this passage satirises the notion of hardship amidst abundance, Ouida also closely intertwines military and social aspects in her construction of her dandy guardsmen who, as quintessential *beau sabreurs*, excel in both love and war. The same duality and tension between style and vigour also informs Cecil, or "Beauty of the Brigades", whose effeminate characterisation Gilbert and others have thoroughly analysed (Gilbert, 2005; see also Jordan, 1995; Schaffer, 2000; Oulton, 2007; Schroeder and Holt, 2008; Jordan, 2013):

> when the smoke cleared away that was circling round him out of a great meerschaum bowl, it showed a face of as much delicacy and brilliancy as a woman's; handsome, thoroughbred, languid, nonchalant, with a certain latent recklessness under the impressive calm of habit, and a singular softness given to the large, dark hazel eyes by the

unusual length of the lashes over them. His features were exceedingly fair – fair as the fairest girl's; his hair was of the softest, silkiest, brightest chestnut; his mouth very beautifully shaped; on the whole, with a certain gentle, mournful love-me look that his eyes had with them, it was no wonder that great ladies and gay lionnes alike gave him the palm as the handsomest man in all the Household Regiments – not even excepting that splendid golden-haired Colossus, his oldest friend and closest comrade, known as "the Seraph". (Ouida, 1867 [1995], 4–5)

Whereas Cecil's effeminate characteristics have often been read as prefiguring a "Wildean sexual ambiguity" (Sutherland, 1995: xx), that is a decadent homosexuality (Gilbert, 2005: 145; Schaffer, 2000: 127), not only were these frameworks not yet in place in the 1860s, but Cecil, like all Ouida's dandies, is also shown to be a vigorous, muscular hero, and so must be read on his own terms (Oulton, 2007: 38; Jordan, 2013: 55).

As Matt Cook (2003) and Peter Ackroyd (2017) have demonstrated, urban underground cultures and networks of homosexuality have a long history in London, but the sexual pathology of "interior androgyny, a hermaphrodism of the soul" that helped transpose the "sodomite [as] a temporary aberration [into] a species" emerged tangibly only in the 1880s and 1890s (Foucault, 1978: 43), with Richard Freiherr von Krafft-Ebing's *Psychopathia Sexualis* (1886), the Cleveland Street Scandal in 1889, the Wilde trials in 1895, and Havelock Ellis' *Sexual Inversion* (1897). Twentieth-century guardsmen, as dashing figures and national symbols of heroic masculinity, could become part of a homosexual subculture as an erotic fantasy and even moonlight as rent boys or engage in male sexual relationships, although they worked hard to maintain the "imaginary landscape of manliness" (Houlbrook, 2003: 363), but if this was a practise even among Ouida's beloved military men, it is uncertain whether she knew of it. Indeed, while Ouida no doubt inspired later, Wildean figures (Schaffer, 2002; Fitzsimons, 2015), her stakes in masculine homoeroticism were hardly those of a gay man – even if she showed herself somewhat sympathetic. After Wilde's sentencing, she commented: "I do not think the law should meddle with these offences" (Lee, 1914: 158).

Scholarly readings of *Under Two Flags* tend to posit Cecil as the indolent sensation hero redeemed through manly action and so restored to 'proper' manliness (like Mary Elizabeth Braddon's Robert Audley), but it pays to remember that Ouida, while emphasising Cecil's indolence and beauty, also establishes his credentials as adventurous hero of matchless courage early on. For example, she hints at a "certain latent recklessness" (Ouida, 1867 [1995]: 4), assuring us that both Cecil and the Seraph have "the true dash and true steel of the soldier" in them (90), recounting Cecil's near-fatal hand-to-hand combat with a wild boar, or through the steeplechase. Horse racing and horsemanship were, throughout the nineteenth century, masculine realms assimilated into the sportive ideal and closely connected to the military, especially the post-Crimean heroic masculine ideal. As Wray Vamplew and Joyce Kay note, army officers regularly participated in races and steeplechases as gentleman riders, and were encouraged to do so because it "excites that courage, presence of mind and skill in horsemanship without which their glorious achievements of Balaclava and Inkermann would never have been recorded" (*Bell's Life* correspondent, qtd. in Vamplew and Kay, 2006: 376). As Ouida indicates, steeplechases especially were physically dangerous, even deadly, to horses and riders. The incident where Pas de Charge breaks its neck after a difficult fence is no doubt modelled on Becher's Brook at the Grand National in Aintree, a fence notorious as a literal back-breaker and regularly responsible for equine deaths well into the 1980s. Riders equally risked being maimed, crushed, paralysed, or killed (375), so Cecil achieving victory despite his stirrup leather breaking at full speed can be seen as a feat of heroism comparable to and foreshadowing his later escapades in battle.

Homosocial bonds and romantic friendships of the kind observed in Victorian culture by Eve Kosofsky Sedgwick (1985) are central to Ouida's early novels, which "re-write the male romance in order to examine the function of the romantic heroine within the homosocial power structure" (Jordan, 2013: 54). Unlike later, Wildean depictions of male homosexual desire, Ouida at once explores and polices romantic friendship which, while clearly extant between Cecil and the "tall, fair man, with the limbs of a Hercules, the chest of a prize-fighter, and the face of a Raphael Angel, known in the Household as Seraph" (Ouida, 1867 [1995]: 5), cannot be expressed within the framework of "a privileged existence in England", but only in extreme moments, such as under threat of death (Oulton, 2007: 13). Then only, the Seraph may mourn Cecil "with passionate, loving force, refusing to the last to accredit his guilt" (Ouida, 1867 [1995]: 231) or feel his heart "breaking under this doom he could neither avert nor share" (521). Ouida likens these relationships to Biblical friendships (Oulton, 2007: 42) or, in a revised version of her essay on "The New Woman", to the "preferences of the Platonic Age" where "women were not necessary to either the pleasures or passions of men" (Ouida, 1894 [1895]b: 209), thus tapping into centuries-long literary traditions in which idealised male friendships are configured as noble, eternal brotherhoods surpassing the base entanglements of heterosexual romance. When Cecil recognises his servant Rake's loyalty as "a fidelity passing the fidelity of woman" (Ouida, 1867 [1995]: 409), Ouida implies there exists between these comrades in arms a bond that women can neither be part of nor privy to.

In Ouida's earlier novels *Strathmore* and *Chandos*, on the other hand, male friendships turn toxic through the "persecution of the beautiful and effeminate hero by a manly man who, repelled by these qualities, either sadistically punishes him, or kills him" (Jordan,

2013: 55). The irascible Strathmore, tricked by Marion Vavasour, the adventuress he desires, assaults and kills his best friend Bertie Erroll in a duel (Erroll fires in the air), then passionately grieves him. Libertine dandy Ernest Chandos, in turn, is systematically ruined by John Trevenna, his illegitimate half-brother whose sadistic pursuit of dominance is characterised by "a certain savage envy and a certain luscious satisfaction mingled together" (Ouida, 1866 [1879]: 42). His voyeuristic, "homoerotic gaze becomes the vehicle for hostility, competition, class rivalry, and mastery" (Schroeder and Holt, 2008: 56). Ouida here interrogates male homosocial desire as the affective social glue, as Sedgwick puts it, that both undermines and shores up patriarchal structures: "[i]s men's desire for other men the great preservative of the masculinist hierarchies of Western culture, or is it among the most potent threats against them?" (Sedgwick, 1985: 2, 93).

Importantly, Ouida examines male homosocial friendships not only for their own sake, but also to explore how women are placed in relation to them, recognising Sedgwick's claim that, in "any erotic rivalry, the bond that links the two rivals is as intense and potent as the bond that links either of the rivals to the beloved" (31). As romantic interests, women usually act as an acceptable, displaced signifier of their brother or father (much as in Braddon's *Lady Audley's Secret*[1]), or else, by trying to exert agency within a patriarchal social world, they often become – or are forced to become – intruders, competitors, or saboteurs. As Schroeder and Holt illustrate in detail (2008: 33–8, 47–9), Ouida's dandies, particularly in *Held in Bondage* and *Strathmore*, objectify women and value them only for providing the fleeting pleasure of a flirtation that they never intend to become serious. Constance Trefusis (formerly Lucy Davis), who marries de Vigne out of

---

[1] In Braddon's 1862 sensation novel, the hero Robert Audley shares a close, somewhat ambiguous bond with his friend George Talbot, and ultimately marries his sister, who looks much like her brother.

revenge for him leaving her when they were younger, can do so because he is blinded by her sensual beauty: "[y]ou marry her, no doubt, from eye-love; for her luxuriant beauty, which report says is unrivalled" (Ouida, 1863 [1891]: 91). Thus, while Ouida lets her male characters voice misogynistic opinions, or revel in hatred of manipulative women who have entrapped them into a life-long socio-economic bond, she also undermines their position by exposing the power imbalance that governs sexual relationships in a society that commodifies women. Like the women I discuss in Chapter 3, Trefusis and Vavasour know to mobilise their voluptuous beauty to their advantage and so threaten the patriarchal order. The men they seduce are left furious because their sexual agency has been restricted, and they feel cheated out of the social and economic powers they take for granted. To some degree, they are made to share the frustration of having limited agency that women endure – even if not for long. Marion Vavasour subjugates Strathmore with her coquetries, emasculates him by making him abandon his political career, and manipulates him into killing Erroll (whom she perceives as a rival and threat to her power) but there reaches the limits of her possibilities. On discovering her deceit, Strathmore begins to exert a deliberate and cruel revenge, taunting, ruining, and dethroning her by exposing the secret of her illegitimate marriage, refusing to share their guilt, sabotaging her efforts to support herself, even abandoning her to drown during a shipwreck. While he regains masculine dominance and Vavasour loses agency, "she is so mercilessly victimized that she ultimately becomes a sympathetic character" (Schroeder and Holt, 2008: 49). Ouida here exposes a patriarchal double morale still in effect today: "[m]ales rise in spite of their sins; women are condemned to fall" (48). This is not least evident in the novel's culmination in Strathmore's happy marriage to Erroll's oblivious daughter.

Still, Ouida saves her adventuresses from the Fallen Woman's fate. She lets Vavasour repent and find a measure of peace as a nun, and grants Trefusis new success as a Russian prince's mistress: "[w]hile Ouida's attitude makes clear there is nothing praiseworthy about the Trefusis, the relative success of her indomitability, independence, and resilience, clashes with the moral judgement against her" (39). In contrast to Lawrence, Ouida conceives of women's lives as inextricably entangled within male homosocial relationships, but without sharing their privilege of having the freedom of choice or action without consequence.

In *Under Two Flags*, both of Cecil's mistresses, the imperious Lady Guenevere and the rowdy courtesan, the Zu-Zu, take no active part in Cecil's ruination, nor do they take much notice. Indeed, when Cecil's brother Berkeley frames him for a forgery to cover his gambling debt, Cecil refuses to produce his alibi, which is a break-neck carriage ride with Lady Guenevere, to save her reputation. She, having the power to exonerate him, returns blithely to her luxuries: "[s]he sacrificed him for her reputation and her jewels; the choice was thoroughly a woman's" (Ouida, 1867 [1995]: 159).

Instead, the novel focuses more on the homosocial dynamic of elite masculine spaces, such as gentlemen's clubs, smoking rooms, race courses, and military barracks – spaces in and through which the twin ideals of manliness and Englishness were continually shored up and re-affirmed. The "Pall Mall Clubs" which belong to Cecil's social landscape as much as "London seasons, Paris winters, ducal houses in the hunting months" and "yachting with the R. V. Y. Club, Derby handicaps at Hornsey, pretty chorus-singers set up in Bijou villas, [and] dashing rosieres taken over to Baden" (18) were places "where upper-class men forged and cemented their class and gender identities" (Milne-Smith, 2011: 2), and as such "central to a serious examination of nineteenth-century British masculinity under construction" (Black, 2014: 34). As spaces where the gentlemanly ideal of 'public-school origin' was maintained and perpetuated, they were a key component in "fashioning a male elite founded upon the argot of sociability as a way to consolidate male power to serve empire and high capitalism" (28). Staging ground for patriarchy and a counterpart to domesticity, gentlemen's clubs encouraged homosociality and often instilled in its members, as Black notes, a semi-ironic horror of marriage (32), which Ouida alludes to through de Vigne or the Seraph.

Chevasney and de Vigne congregate in smoking rooms to gossip about women such as "The Trefusis" – a use of slang to which Vincent E. H. Murray objected ("men of the *monde* speak of women of the *demi-monde* as if they were horses, with the definite article before their name" (Murray, 1873: 934)), but which no doubt rings authentic and illustrates Ouida's criticism. Similarly Cecil joins his peers to discuss horseflesh in "that sanctuary of the persecuted, that temple of refuge, thrice blessed in all its forms throughout the land, that consecrated Mecca of every true believer in the divinity of the meerschaum, and the paradise of the nargile – the smoking-room" (Ouida, 1867 [1995]: 18):

> A spacious, easy chamber, too; lined with the laziest of divans, seen just now through a fog of smoke, and tenanted by nearly a score of men in every imaginable loose velvet costume, and with faces as well known in the Park at six o'clock in May, and on the Heath in October; in Paris in January, and on the Solent in August; in Pratt's of a summer's night, and on the Moors in an autumn morning, as though they were features that came round as regularly as the "July" or the Waterloo Cup. (18)

Identifying Cecil and the Seraph with London's "Clubland", Ouida understands, means implying "something about a man's lifestyle, about his leisure time, and about his values": "'Clubmen' were a group in society of which contemporaries spoke as a unified whole [...] the men who rode in Rotten Row, shopped on Bond Street, and visited their friends in Mayfair" (Milne-Smith, 2011: 5). This is indeed true for Cecil, who had never been without his Highland shooting, his Baden gaming, his prize-winning schooner among the R. V. Y. Squadron, his September battues, his Pytchley hunting, his pretty expensive Zu-Zus and other toys, his drag for Epsom and his trap and hack for the Park, his crowd of engagements through the season, and his bevy of fair leaders of the fashion to smile on him, and shower their invitation-cards on him, like a rain of rose-leaves, as one of the 'best men'. (Ouida, 1867 [1995]: 12–3)

Whereas Barbara Black notes that in Victorian culture "tension lies between the characteristically earnest gentleman and the glib, elegant dandy, between the muscular and effete conceptions of masculinity that they represent" (2014: 26–7), no such tension exists in Ouida's novel, where Cecil "dressed a shade more perfectly than anyone, and with such inimitable carelessness in the perfection, too" or "made a prima donna by a bravissima, introduced a new tie by an evening's wear, gave a cook the cordon with his praise, and rendered a fresh-invented liqueur the rage by his recommendation" (Ouida, 1867 [1995]: 71).

In the end, however, neither clubs, smoking rooms, nor English barracks succeed as spaces that foster lasting loyalty or sympathy. After Cecil's ruination and flight, when his compatriots believe him killed in a train wreck, his misfortune becomes fodder for gossip over drinks as he is eulogised as a good sport and soon forgotten: "[s]o the De Profundis was said over Bertie Cecil; and 'Beauty of the Brigades' ceased to be named in the service, and soon ceased to be even remembered. In the steeple-chase of life there is no time to look back at the failures, who have gone down over a 'double and drop,' and fallen out of the pace" (173).

Desert Heroes

The closest real-life embodiment of Ouida's Clubland heroes, apart perhaps from her salon guests, was Captain Frederick Burnaby

(1842–85), a gentleman adventurer who joined the Royal Horse Guards in 1859, became Captain in 1866 (Stearn, 2004), and was painted in leisurely repose and dashing uniform by James Tissot in 1870. Whether or not Ouida was acquainted with him is unknown. Still, he, as a guardsman famous for physical strength, courage, and travel to "unexplored" places, uniquely embodies the Victorian masculine ideal of gentlemanly style and military vigour, not least because he died at Abu Klea in 1885 during the failed expedition to relieve general Gordon – another iconic masculine hero – at Khartoum.

Gordon's Khartoum in turn encapsulated, if not catalysed late-Victorian New Imperialist expansionist politics and ideology: the Berlin Conference (1884–85) had formalised the Scramble for Africa, after such key events as the disgraceful end of the First Boer War in 1881 or Britain's assembling of Egypt as protectorate in 1882. Now "Chinese Gordon", already a colonial hero due to his role in the so-called Taiping Rebellion (1850–64), was sent to evacuate Khartoum and leave the Soudan to the Mahdist revolt, but instead decided to fortify the city, incurring a massive media response at home (see Budd, 2009: 198; Villa, 2019: 61). His death at the hands of the Mahdists three days before the arrival of the relief expedition Prime Minister Gladstone had been pressured to send, turned him into a martyr and helped "create imperialism as a mass emotion" (Girouard, 1981: 229). How his demise was mythologised within a national imperial ideal is perhaps best illustrated by George William Joy's 1893 painting, "The Death of General Gordon", which was recreated in 1897 as a display at Madame Tussaud's (see Smith, Brown, and Jacobi, 2016: 114–5).

The events certainly prepared the ground for a muscular manly ideal played out on the imperial plane, not least through increasingly popular adventure fiction, which was configured as masculine literature written by men about the activities of men (Kestner, 2010: 6). H. Rider Haggard, whose most popular novels, *King Solomon's Mines* (1885) and *She: A History of Adventure*

(1886), were published around this time, famously assured his readers that "there is not a *petticoat* in the whole history" (Haggard, 1885 [1951]: 243, original emphasis). Adventure novels and desert adventures therefore responded to and became integral in maintaining the interconnected mental landscapes of masculinity and national imperial identity, which itself was inextricably keyed into boyhood and public-school education (see Bristow, 1991; Deane, 2014; Mallett, 2015). As Luisa Villa (2019) shows, a wealth of popular novels written for boys specifically conjured up the Sudanese desert, among them Rudyard Kipling's *The Light that Failed* (1891), G. A. Henty's *The Dash for Khartoum* (1891) and *With Kitchener in the Soudan* (1903), and Arthur Conan Doyle's *The Tragedy of the Korosko* (1898). The latter two responded to the Anglo-Egyptian conquest of Sudan (1896–99), led by Herbert Kitchener. Imagining conquests of hostile territories, close encounters with the enemy, military prowess, and advocating both chivalric values and fearless courage, these novels glamorised Empire through a fantasy of action (see Villa, 2019: 64–5). Deployed as educational tools portraying a gendered rite of passage, they emphasised masculine camaraderie (66) and "reinforced the links between the language of manliness – energy, duty, leadership – and the language of British imperial power" (Mallett, 2015: 155). Robert Baden-Powell's Scouts movement would transfer these ideals from the page to real life in 1908.

It is especially interesting to consider Ouida's *Under Two Flags*, written two decades earlier, against this methodically gendered and ideologically charged context. How does this desert adventure novel written by a woman and deliberately placed beyond the reach of British colonial interest anticipate, pre-configure, or undermine these future ideologies, considering especially that it emerges nonetheless out of the public-school ideal of chivalrous manliness?

Cecil's arrival in Algiers and his joining of the French army immediately and powerfully contrasts against the ideals outlined above, as well as European stereotypes of the desert as desolate and savage. To begin with, Ouida establishes a beautifully chaotic, lively, romantic vision of the city "with the Mediterranean so softly lashing with its violet waves the feet of the white, sloping town", its "green sea-pines" and "rugged Kabyl mountains", its "straight, white boulevards, as in the winding ancient streets", the Cabash, where "dreamy Arabian legends, poetic as Hafiz" linger, or the sun glowing "on the folds of the French flags as they floated above the shipping of the harbour, and on the glitter of the French arms, as a squadron of the army of Algeria swept back over the hills to their barracks" (Ouida, 1867 [1995]: 159–60). Such a vision of bonbon shops and cafés, cigar shops, newspaper stands, chansons, military drums, and laughter contrasts against French depictions of Algeria, for example by writers Théophile Gautier, Gustave Flaubert, or Pierre Loti – whom Ouida read and reviewed – as haunted, ambiguous, and disorienting (see Goellner, 2018: 16, 37). Whereas such depictions mirrored Algeria's unstable status within a French national and colonial identity (44; see also Middleton, 2015), Ouida establishes her critical perspective through hints at Algiers' "incongruous blending, its forced mixture of two races – that will touch, but never mingle; that will be chained together, but will never assimilate" or "the strange bizarre conflict of European and Oriental life spread[ing] its panorama" (Ouida, 1867 [1995]: 160). Cecil, too, when asked whether he wants to join the Chasseurs, carelessly responds: "'I am more inclined to your foes. [...] In the first place, they are on the losing side; in the second, they are the lords of the soil; in the third, they live as free as air; and in the fourth, they have undoubtedly the right of the quarrel!'" (164) For the French Algerian context at least, which was seen patronisingly by the British press as an administrative failure and as too violent, especially measured against British India (Middleton, 2015), Cecil's chivalry compels him to side with the native Bedouin, whom he sees as disadvantaged, but noble and morally right – perfect champions for the *beau sabreur* against

French greed and inefficiency. In the end, he lets a dice throw decide whether he joins the Arabs or the French army (Ouida, 1867 [1995]: 165), and even as a French soldier he entertains allegiances and even friendships with Bedouin tribes.

Ouida describes that friendship against a luscious, romantic portrait of the Bedouin lifestyle: "Rembrandt in colour, Oriental in composition" (206). After many "hot, desperate struggles" after which "each had watched and noted the other's unmatched prowess, and borne away the wounds of the other's home-strokes, with the admiration of a bold soldier for a bold rival's dauntlessness and skill" (207), Cecil's commanding officer and antagonist Raoul de Chateauroy, "ruthless, inflexible, a tyrant to the core" (208), violates the unspoken mutual respect that has been established by abducting the Sheik's favourite wife, Djelma. Hoping he will be killed by the Sheik's wrath, he sends Cecil to communicate his terms, which Ouida describes in shocking clarity ("she would be made the Marquis' mistress, and abandoned later to the army" (211)). To Cecil, this is an unpardonable humiliation, and he identifies himself with the honourable foe over the officer who has betrayed the moral code to which he adheres: "[s]hame has been done to me as to you. Had I been told what words I bore, they had never been brought by my hand. You know me. You have had the marks of my steel, as I have had the marks of yours" (211). He returns Djelma and secures the tribe's lasting friendship, but his flaunting of Chateauroy's unethical tactics incurs a bitter feud. Chateauroy repeatedly prevents Cecil's promotion and bullies him relentlessly, thereby frustrating the agency and winning of prestige which 1880s adventure fiction presents as central. Indeed, Cecil's heroics earn him trouble rather than commendation, and more than once he is rescued by Cigarette, the intrepid vivandière and co-star of the novel. Altogether, the French Algerian context is not geared towards participation in national feats of glory, not least because all the fierce fighting never leads to lasting change; despite its frequent parades and celebration of French national identity, it is imagined as a space of exile forgotten by others. Resisting assimilation, it retains its own romantic catalogue of imagery, and obeys its own internal logic. In short, Ouida builds up a textbook Victorian heroic masculinity full of vigour and chafing against London society's luxurious ennui, but then sends it into a world where that identity has no purchase. Cecil's heroics, while espousing the chivalrous ideal, remain somewhat self-contained:

> He was a dashing cavalry soldier, who had had a dozen wounds cut over his body by the Bedouin swords, in many and hot skirmishes; who had waited through sultry African nights for the lion's tread, and had fought the desert-king and conquered; who had ridden a thousand miles over the great sand waste, and the boundless arid plains, and slept under the stars with the saddle beneath his head, and his rifle in his hand, all through the night; who had served, and served well, in fierce, arduous, unremitting work, in trying campaigns and in close discipline; who had blent the verve, the brilliance, the daring, the eat-drink-and-enjoy-for-tomorrow-we-die of the French Chasseur, with something that was very different, and much more tranquil. (190)

Although he assumes a French identity as Louis Victor, Cecil himself remains somewhat apart, his identity hybridised and uncertain. He rides like an Arab, smokes like a Zouave, dances like an aristocrat, and fights with elegance (his nickname is 'Bel-a-faire-peur'). But unlike the French soldiers, he does not loot bodies, or steal from the locals, and is rumoured to be English because of his manners.

Indeed, although Ouida saw herself as "more French than English" (Jordan, 2014b), *Under Two Flags* mirrors a British view of French Algeria espoused by the *British Army and Navy Review*'s anonymous serial, "Scenes of Franco-Arab Life" (Jordan, 2013: 64), the *Penny Magazine* or the *Illustrated London News*

(Middleton, 2015). All engaged in pro-Bedouin, anti-French critique, which was that no progress was being made in territorial conquest, no commercial gain or civilisation progress was visible, and that the "French regime in Algeria was excessively and unconscionably violent, obsessed with military glory and the extension of territory, and indifferent to native welfare" (9). One opinion expressed to the *Birmingham Daily Post* in 1861 was that "so long as the possession of Algeria is secured only by the presence of a large standing-army, it may remain in the *occupation* of the French, but it can never become, in the proper sense of the term, a colony to France" (qtd. in Middleton, 2015, original emphasis). In addition, France relied too much on the perception of pageantry and parades, while its administration was corrupted and violent.

Indeed, Ouida openly critiques the French colonial project as a senseless fight over "useless and profitless soil" (Ouida, 1867 [1995]: 445), fought unequally with "all the resource of a great empire against the sons of the desert, who had nothing to oppose to them save the despair of a perishing nationality and a stifled freedom" (505). Such sentiments found no echoes in the British masculine adventure fiction of the 1880s set in Egypt and the Soudan (although they are evident in Karl May's German adventure fiction of the 1890s), but returned powerfully after Gertrude Bell and T. E. Lawrence had mobilised Bedouin allegiances against the Ottoman Empire in the First World War, then very much within a framework of British national interest. John Sutherland notably remarks on *Under Two Flags*' influence on 1920s and 1930s desert adventures, such as P. C. Wren's Foreign Legion adventures *Beau Geste* (1924), *Beau Sabreur* (1926) and *Beau Ideal* (1928), Edith M. Hull's 1919 novel *The Sheik* and its 1921 film adaptation with Rudolph Valentino, as well as several more or less faithful film adaptations (1912, 1915, 1922, 1936, see Sutherland, 1995: xii-xiii). For these, Ouida lays a rich, romantic foundation of pathos mingled with fatalism, valorising the freedom-loving sons of the soil who fight a losing battle against a powerful modern Empire.

Such fatalism is encapsulated in anecdotes such as the one about Rire-pour-tout, who defeats six Arab warriors in single combat, winning honour, fame, and the battle, before dying of his wounds: "Sacre bleu! It was a splendid end; I wish I were sure of the like" (Ouida, 1867 [1995]: 164). Within this framework of heroic fatalism, where battles are fought for an abstract glory that never transcends its immediate context, rather than a tangible teleological outcome or lasting victory, true chivalry and heroism emerge out of personal integrity, shows of courage, or acts of kindness and self-sacrifice, which are their own reward regardless of outward affirmation. Cecil's kindness to Leon Ramon, the dying comrade, his giving away his water to a drummer boy or half his rations to a "murderous, sullen, black-browed, evil wretch" because he is hungry (374), are acts of mercy that mirror accounts of the Crimea recounted by Furneaux (2016: 2), and are no less valiant because they may go unnoticed. On the contrary, they lead by example, as when the young Pipcon, once Cecil's antagonist, whose life he has saved during battle, loyally returns the favour during the battle of Zarâila, and in turn, dies saving Cecil: "[t]his was the sort of loyalty that the Franco-Arabs rendered; this was the sort of influence that the English Guardsman exercised among his Roumis" (Ouida, 1995 [1867]: 287). Cecil's former groom-turned-comrade Rake and his loyalty likewise illustrate Ouida's argument that individual integrity incurs its own rewards, and will, in the long run, reform social groups for the better. As such, Ouida's soldier heroes foreground integrity, courage, and solidarity with fellow men and enact her revered aristocratic habitus in tandem with her democratic ideals. For his comrades, Cecil bears "injustice and indignities" with "resolute endurance" and "undeviating serenity beneath provocation", withstanding "tyranny with such absolute submission for sake of those around him, who would revolt at his sign and be slaughtered for his cause" (489). This self-sacrificing loyalty breaks only when Chateauroy insults Lady Venetia, the woman Cecil loves, and who is, coincidentally, the Seraph's sister. Cecil's chivalry demands he defend her, even if that means assaulting a superior officer. When court-martialled, Cecil bears the sentence with "a calm, weary dignity" (493), tranquil because his conscience is clear. Saved from the firing squad by Cigarette, Cecil's name is cleared and he is free to reunite with the Seraph through Venetia, thus re-affirming male friendships.

While his comrades remember the hero of the battle of Zarâila, Cecil achieves fame and admiration only among his peers and is never promoted because of his feud with Chateauroy. Ouida here places her hero in conflict with military hierarchies and unjust, interpersonal pettiness, rather than with the territory or its natural inhabitants. The masculine imperial ideal expressed through dominance, conquest, or mastery has no currency here: Cecil's heroic feats, however numerous, earn him nothing within Algeria's military politics – instead, he ends up in front of a firing squad, manipulated by his commander. His gallantry remains contained between page and reader, or between him and equally powerless individuals, like his comrades or the Bedouin. Writing outside the 1880s context, in which British geopolitical interests in Africa assembled desert adventure fiction as a national project, Ouida was as yet free of a didactic masculine ideal in the service of Empire. Indeed, the Algerian desert is, unlike the desert in Haggard, Doyle, or P. C. Wren (which shows some influence of Joseph Conrad), not a hostile space to be mastered, but instead a place of inherent beauty and romanticism in which, Ouida emphasises, natives have lived according to their traditions and are now threatened by tyranny, starvation, oppression, and displacement (355). It is a defined place that confounds, defies, and demands immense sacrifices, and which Cecil leaves as his final reward. Here, familiar European hierarchies, paradigms, and conventions cannot be replicated, and accordingly, men are not measured by race or class, but through courage and combat skill, and there arises a fatalist bravado and resigned *carpe diem* cheeriness that somewhat resembles the "we're here because we're here" attitude of First World War soldiers. Similarly, the French soldiers' experiences are more closely mirrored by their Arab foes than their own military commanders, and the latter thus become respected equals: "[t]hey were fine men – diable! – they were fine men" (162).

Indeed, Ouida here rehearses an anti-imperialist anti-militarism she would retain throughout her life and voice in critical essays such as that on French writer Georges Darien (see Ouida, 1897 [1900]). Here, she indicts the military's blind obedience and rigid hierarchies, where minor offences such as "to have lost a regimental article, to have forgotten to salute a superior, [or] to have stopped to drink from a brook on a march" comprise acts "in which only the semi-insanity of perverted authority could see any provocation" (Ouida, 1897: 76). The same critique is played out between Cecil and the vainglorious and tyrannical Chateauroy, against whose chicaneries the *beau sabreur* is obliged to rebel by his sense of honour and compassion, even if that proves almost fatal. Neither he nor his roguish comrades are ever blindly obedient soldiers. Thus, while Ouida certainly valorised the Victorian masculine ideal of chivalry and leadership by virtue of birth and gallantry, she was increasingly and deeply critical of those nationalistic projects in which that ideal was effectively instrumentalised.

Conclusion: Vicarious Adventure

Ouida's *beau sabreurs* exemplify how her work is simultaneously rooted in and rebelling against dominant traditions, types, genres, and gender ideologies. She constantly assembles them into and re-makes them through her own powerful vision – a vision that, while at times puzzling to nineteenth-century readers and contemporary scholars, nonetheless was (and still is) strong enough to fascinate. So, for example, does she intertwine masculine heroes of Crimea fame with scandalous sensation, or craft a masculine adventure hero who both anticipates and rejects the 1880's New Imperialist ideal, not just because she writes him twenty years too early and criticises the colonial effort, but because she writes him at all: she is, after all, one of those useless petticoats summarily presumed to be of no consequence in the masculine genre.

Indeed, scholarship on Victorian masculinity traditionally focuses on masculinity as constructed by men. To such insights and politics, however, Ouida remains an outsider, albeit one who understood how to replicate genre conventions and gendered affectations so persuasively that, for the first years of her career, she was thought to be a "gentlemanly *littérateur*, writing 'brilliant nothings' on a whim", and with military experience (see Jordan, 2013: 56, original emphasis). The fact that she was able to pass and succeed with a style that, allegedly, "never shows a woman's hand" (*Westminster Review*, qtd. in Jordan, 2013: 57), destabilised Victorian essentialist views of binary gender, and exposed the reviewer's double standards, as "critical opinion changed entirely when her sex was discovered" (58). As the *Saturday Review* proclaimed: "when this class [of fiction] comes to be described by a lady the result is at once offensive and incredible" (review of *Under Two Flags*, 1868, qtd. in Jordan, 2011b: 224).

Nonetheless, I argue that Ouida is doing more complex things than simply trespassing on established, binary gender ideals, but instead adapts them towards her own purpose. Her archetypal guardsman hero, "before whom even Queens turned to coquettes and Kings to comrades; careless, caressed, *insouciant*; of all men the beloved or envied; inimitable alike in his grace of person and in the perfection of his taste; passing from the bow-windows of St. James's to the faded and fetid alleys of Stamboul, from the Quartier Breda to the Newski Prospect" (Beerbohm, 1899: 113), establishes a tension between gendered attributes that confused contemporary reviewers as over-stylised, overly sensual, and imbued with feminine habits (Preston, 1886: 48; Corelli, 1890: 362; Douglas, 1921 [1922]: 113; Jordan, 2013: 58–9): "Nobody", said Street, "has met a guardsman like him" (1895: 168). Instead of anticipating 1880s and 1890s sexological theories in which ambivalence translates to inversion, however, Ouida's *beau sabreur* combines conventionally masculine and feminine attributes such as style, romance, and derring-do, and in her hands becomes a figure onto which fantasies of both kinds could be projected and so become, potentiality, de-gendered.

Indeed, Ouida's own life exhibits little of what one might call "traditional femininity" in a Victorian context, and she evidently struggled to identify with any such model. Brought up on her father's stories about "Paris salons, beautiful princesses, fascinating counts, gallant warriors, thrones well lost for love, and machinations of wicked courtiers" (Bigland, 1951: 17) and self-educated after models of royal court life and adventurous masculinity (Jordan, 1995: 77; Moore, 2011: 485), Ouida cross-identified strongly with "masculine codes of culture and thought" (Yates, 1879: 245). She was fascinated by socially institutionalised male friendships that existed in and through spaces such as London's Clubland and the military, she never forged close female friendships (indeed, she banned women from her salon), and she shows a keen awareness that the patriarchal marriage market encourages women to market themselves through their sexuality and in competition with each other. As such, diagnosing *Under Two Flags* in particular as some fetishistic attempt to compensate Louis Ramé's loss, in which she projects herself onto Cigarette and Lady Venetia (Sutherland, 1995: xvii, Schroeder and Holt, 2008: 15) risks (patronisingly) obscuring the nuanced insights at play in her work. For one, why, after four full-length novels about *beau sabreurs* engaged in intrigue and war, which a Victorian public found imminently convincing, would we assume she projected her romantic fantasies only onto the female characters?

After all, the appeal of the adventure novel, as Mallett explains, is the promise of agency: "[p]ast and future yield in importance to the present; what counts is the necessary and immediate action, isolated from the wider context of life. [...] [One] of the pleasures offered by the adventure story is the chance to explore, unseen and unembarrassed, fantasies of a more powerful self, regardless of whether they are achievable in reality" (2015: 153). Hence Ouida, who had to support her fatherless family at twenty-two and who examines and re-negotiates women's relationships with a patriarchal culture time and again throughout her work, may very well have explored masculinity, especially one open and malleable towards effeminate attributes, as a vicarious fantasy.

Ouida here pioneers a widespread phenomenon of today's participatory culture, namely that of women exploring male homoerotic relationships in fan works and erotica (Jenkins, 1992 [2013]; Stanfill, 2021), where ambivalently gendered men supposedly speak doubly to female audiences, that is as objects of desire and as "displaced selves" that represent agency and independence denied to the female reader in contemporary society (Matsui, 1993: 178; McLelland, 2000). Thus, as Carl van Vechten noted, "she painted portraits of men she desired to embrace" (1926: 52), but Ouida also clearly recognised and explored male homosocial relationships as partnerships between equally active and vocal participants which afforded solidarity, loyalty, and even emotional intimacy that could not be fostered between men and women to the same extent due to the unequal power hierarchies and social codes of the era. Not only were heterosexual courtships heavily policed and ritualised, but women's passively configured role (then and even today, see Neville, 2018) hardly encouraged claiming their sexualities and bodies, let alone voice their desires. Thus, as Ouida's adventuresses (and later novels) exemplify, heterosexual romances remain fraught with tension, anxiety, and mutual deceit. In line with one of the sensation novel's central themes, men and women are shown "as being foreign countries to each other" (Pykett, 1992: 50).

Ouida's dandy heroes then embody romantic and attractive ideals about masculine gallantry, courage, and style, but they, like her fiction in general, may also serve as vicarious fantasies that allow (imagined) access to spaces of agency and adventure. Ouida identified male homosocial allegiances, based on gender and class and institutionalised across social geographies, as significant obstacles to female self-direction, but also, as her salon exemplifies, longed to participate in them. In her fiction, this tension plays out through her dandy soldiers, who navigate so much of her glamorous world with effortless ennui, and the adventuress wearing herself out in her struggle against a patriarchal society. Like the present-day phenomenon of heterosexual women writing male romance, Ouida's guardsmen possibly represent less an exploration of authentic male (potentially queer) identities and more a twin projection of fantasies about heterosexual attraction and personal agency.

CHAPTER 2

Soldiers and Spies: Women in Masculine Spaces

Introduction: Feminine Heterotopias

> She was pretty, she was insolent, she was intolerably coquettish, she was mischievous as a marmoset; she would swear, if need be, like a Zouave; she could fire galloping, she could toss off her brandy or her vermouth like a trooper; she would on occasion clinch her little brown hand and deal a blow that the recipient would not covet twice; she was an *enfant de Paris* and had all its wickedness at her fingers; she would sing you *guinguette* songs till you were suffocated with laughter, and she would dance the cancan at the Salle de Mars, with the biggest giant of a Cuirassier there. And yet with all that, she was not wholly unsexed; with all that she had the delicious fragrance of youth, and had not left a certain feminine grace behind her, though she wore a vivandiere's uniform, and had been born in a barrack, and meant to die in a battle; it was the blending of the two that made her piquante, made her a notoriety in her own way; known at pleasure, and equally, in the Army of Africa as "Cigarette", and "L'Amie du Drapeau". (Ouida, 1867 [1995]: 175–6)

No consideration of Ouida's work can pass over Cigarette, the formidable young vivandière, Bertie Cecil's counterpart, and perhaps Ouida's most fascinating and puzzling creation: "a cross-dressing, sunburned, short-haired adolescent girl who vigorously promotes everything forbidden by the aristocratic code: radical democracy, violence, lawlessness, and unrestrained sexual and personal liberty" (Schaffer, 2000: 126). Scholarship has oft examined how *Under Two Flags'* ambivalently gendered and racially hybrid tomboy collapses binary gender orthodoxies (Jordan 2011b; Gilbert, 1999; Schroeder and Holt, 2008), positioned the smoking, gambling, free-loving heroine as a proto-New Woman (Gilbert, 1999; Schroeder and Holt, 2008: 74–7), and commented that Cigarette is, ultimately, doomed to be safely neutralised through her redemptive death, "a death that both salvages and disposes of this troublesome character" (Schaffer, 2000: 126).

This chapter expands on those readings by arguing that Cigarette's self-sacrifice to save Cecil from the firing squad is also heroic, because it is a soldier's death, and that there is more complexity to unearth. It considers in depth Ouida's 1867 heroines, Idalia (of the so-titled novel), and Cigarette, both of which threaten the heroes' "masculine authority, and whose source of power is not so much [their] sexuality but [their] ability to hold [their] own in an exclusively male sphere" (Jordan, 2011b: 226). Indeed, both Idalia, the femme fatale spy inspired by Risorgimento politics who finds independence and redemption, and Cigarette, the soldier-heroine who becomes a decorated war hero, are remarkable insofar as they fully inhabit, even reign over, the male homosocial spheres of espionage and war. Unlike Ouida's earlier adventuresses, these two are not positioned as interlopers to male friendships but navigate this sphere competently enough to repeatedly save the male hero, who enters as a newcomer and outsider.

I specifically interrogate why and how Ouida's vision of sexually independent female identities unfolds in – but is also contained by – heterotopic spaces which, in Foucault's estimation, function as "a kind of effectively enacted utopia in which the real sites, all the other real sites that can be found within the culture, are simultaneously represented, contested, and inverted" (Foucault, 1984: 3). Idalia's and Cigarette's remarkable independence may only unfold in spaces not governed by normative social codes, which is why I round off this chapter with a brief consideration of Folle-Farine, of the so-titled 1871 novel. Like Cigarette, Folle-Farine is a tomboy navigating a complex coming of age, struggling with and rebelling against the transition from tomboy innocence to womanhood – more specifically, the awareness that her female body becomes socially coded and sexualised through the male gaze. Where Idalia successfully instrumentalises her sexuality to instigate political manoeuvres, Cigarette and Folle-Farine remain blissfully unaware and so are unencumbered by it until made aware by a male character. Still, in the heterotopic, undefined, lawless spaces of espionage and war, both Idalia and Cigarette seduce and roam freely, without 'falling', whereas Folle-Farine, who lives in the French countryside, is weighed down by misogynistic prejudice long before she trespasses.

I argue therefore that Ouida, understanding a fundamental paradox of female identity, here mobilises heterotopic, masculine spaces to disentangle and debate the differences and interconnections between femaleness, that is the state of existing in a biologically female-coded body, and femininity, that is the socially constructed superstructure imposed on that body especially as it reaches maturity, including projected expectations of how that body performs in society. Indeed, Cigarette's struggle begins when Cecil calls her "unsexed", effectively disqualifying her as a viable romantic interest because, to him, she falls outside of the category of her own sex. The narrative, however, repeatedly challenges and undermines Cecil's assessment, as indeed her introduction assures us of her "feminine grace". All three heroines are brought into conflict with their independent identity through their romantic desire for the hero, who in turn functions as a mouthpiece of social expectation and in some way threatens their heterotopic freedom. So, as this chapter explores, does Ouida not only use heterotopic masculine spaces to challenge social norms and open up a nuanced debate about femininity as codified and legible meaning imposed on female bodies, but she also articulates a core problem of feminist fiction, and not least the New Woman (see Beller, 2020), namely that the heroine's "love (the force of her feminine side) requires that she give up her freedom and independent identity" (Schroeder and Holt, 2008: 77).

The Femme Fatale

Scholarship on spy fiction has identified the genre as a masculine domain rooted in "an amalgamation of the imperial adventure tale and the detective novel", where confrontations between individual and state are negotiated through "orthodoxy and heresy played out in a twilight world of *secrecy*" (Bloom, 1990: 1; 3–4, original emphasis), or else as an Edwardian successor to post-1870 invasion narratives (Stafford, 1981). Joseph Conrad, John Buchan, and William Le Queux are usually named as its originators. But the debonair, cosmopolitan gentleman-spies whom David A. T. Stafford finds in Le Queux's popular fiction have clear antecedents in Ouida's gallant heroes, not least because they are dashing, summer in European glamour capitals, befriend "half a dozen sovereigns", or hold "a commission in the cavalry" (1981: 491, 490). More than that, political intrigue and revolution were part and parcel of a European popular imagination throughout the nineteenth century, including for example the 1848 revolutions, Russian Imperialism, and Greece's independence from the Ottoman Empire. The 1860s particularly saw the Austria-Hungarian Compromise and the ongoing Italian Risorgimento, both of which palpably inspired Ouida's *Idalia* (1867): "[i]ncidents of the war of Italian independence," notes Preston, "are very effectively worked in with the *dénoûment* of several of Ouida's earlier and more exuberant romances, *Idalia* among them" (1886: 51).

Indeed, episodes such as *Chandos*' (1866) rebellion against Austrian occupiers in Venice, or the viscerally narrated battle scene in *Pascarèl* (1874) gave Ouida the opportunity to express both her love for Italy and her fiercely democratic ideals. "She was born", diagnoses Preston, "like all the restless and imaginative souls of the 'forties', to the ardent and confident belief in a *cause*: and that was the cause of civil freedom, [...] the emancipation of 'Europe's oppressed peoples' from the supposed tyranny of their effete kings – the cause of which [Lajos] Kossuth and [Giuseppe] Mazzini were the prophets, [Alphonse de] Lamartine the poet-laureate, and [Guiseppe] Garibaldi the doughty champion" (51). In *Idalia*, that cause provides the enthralling background not for battles, but a glamorous, cosmopolitan, and secret world hidden among Parisian opera balls, restaurants, and private apartments, where the titular heroine may assemble "the Prince of Viana, a Neapolitan; the Count Phaulcon, a Greek; the Graf von Lilmarc, a Hungarian; the Marquis de Beltran and the Marechal d'Ivore both of Paris; and one Englishman, Victor Vane" (Ouida, 1867 [1902]: 91) at three in the morning over hookahs and hothouse flowers. Her co-conspirators are the anti-Austrian, Venice-born courtier Vane, who adopts "politics – or, perhaps, to give them their true and naked name, conspiracies – as the scaling-ladder for his own advancement" (86), and the callous republican Phaulcon, with whom Idalia has a dubious relationship (it turns out he is her father), and who belongs "to the Bohemian class of Free Lances, the Chevaliers d'Industrie of politics, the wild lawless Reiters of plot and counterplot, of liberalism and intrigue, who [...] are the arch disturbers of continental empires, where the people recognise at the bottom of all their schemes and crimes the germ and memory of one great, precious, living truth and treasure – Liberty" (80). Far from gallant fighters for freedom, however, they are painted as unscrupulous and power-hungry, carelessly debating murder over macaroons: "[i]n these days confederates meet over liqueurs and cigarettes, instead of in subterranean caverns; and conspirators plan their checkmates in a coffee-room, an opera-box, or a drive to an imperial stag-hunt, instead of by midnight, under masks, and with rapiers drawn" (79–80).

Here, the heterotopic world of espionage is entirely congruent with high society – a concept familiar to every modern watcher of James Bond films – as both are loci of socio-political power and as such full of incendiary potential. Over this hidden-in-plain-sight world, which "spreads more widely and finely beneath society than society dreams, stretching from Paris to Caucasus, and from the Quadrilateral to the Carpathians, [occupied] in [...] restless scheming for the future, and [...] plans for the alteration of the map of Europe" (86–7), Idalia, Countess Vassalis, reigns supreme as haughty seductress, whose charms are instrumentalised to persuade and manipulate powerful men. She is positioned as a *femme fatale* whose sexuality proves more enticing than political ideals: "Miladi's loveliness", said Vane, "has done more for the cause than half our intrigues" (84). Indeed, Idalia's feminine grace – or the performance thereof – "the patrician ease, the silver wit, the languor and the laughter, the dignity and the nonchalance, the brilliance and the eloquence" (90) are considered to be just as dangerous and powerfully pivotal in European politics as "the White Coats in Venice, the Muscovites in Warsaw, or the state of siege in Galicia" (87). She wields power in this masculine sphere not despite her gender, but because of it, seemingly undermining established power structures.

It is certainly no coincidence that Idalia is called 'Miladi'. Allusions to Marie de Rohan, "the arch-intriguer" Buckingham, and "the Iron Cardinal" (89) hint at Alexandre Dumas père's *The Musketeers* (1848) as an inspiration. Indeed, Preston identifies Ouida as successor to the adventure romance of Walter Scott, Dumas, Victor Hugo, and George Sand, and her "almost endless variety of striking figures and picturesque situations, combined with an independence of conventionalities, whether moral or literary, which moves one to something like awe" (1886: 50) are remarkably reminiscent of Dumas' own, visual style, which abounds with effortless gallantry, resourceful bravado, high drama, passion, imprisonments and escapes, "gothic thrills and a *frisson* of sadism" (Coward, 1991: xi). *Idalia*, too, features dastardly ambushes in high Moldavian ravines, lecherous clergy, desolate prison cells, Italian brigands, and daring escapes, which were perhaps inspired by *The Count of Monte Christo* (1844).

What is most remarkable about Ouida's adventure romance is that its pivotal character is a heroic woman and that the hero's role consists largely of standing loyally by her. Erceldoune, the gallant Englishman, though also a well-travelled State messenger for the Foreign Office, is only on the periphery of Europe's nebulous spy networks when, carrying out a mission in Wallachia, he is ambushed by Phaulcon, shot, and left for dead. Idalia saves him, he falls in love with her. His desperate search for her, which has been read as emasculating (Schroeder and Holt, 2008: 68), draws him into the machinations at the Risorgimento's heart, in which Idalia has become a key player wanted by King Francis II's followers. Idalia, betrayed by the scorned Vane, is captured, imprisoned, and sexually harassed by the unscrupulous Monsignore Villaflor, but she defies and angers him, withstanding his invitations to 'buy her freedom' and his threats of rape with "pitiless serenity", "dauntless scorn", and "royal defiance" (Ouida, 1867 [1902]: 295, 297, 301). Not only does she not plead feminine frailty ("'I take no refuge in the shield of my sex's weakness'" (302)) and refuse to give up her political secrets, but she exhibits heroic emotions, such as selflessness, courage, and pity for her fallen comrades – actions and characteristics usually reserved for male heroes. This importantly frames Erceldoune's rescue of her, an act of honour and bravery that reclaims his virile masculinity, as him rising to her level and so earning her love. Her strength of character need not be sacrificed for romantic love. Indeed, when Erceldoune, misunderstanding her relationship with Phaulcon, broken-heartedly leaves and is captured and tortured by the king's brigands, Idalia gives herself up to save him – positioning him, unusually, as the damsel in need of rescue.

Idalia exhibits the virtues of Ouida's proud, beautiful, aristocratic women – "the exquisite witchery, the polished insouciance, the careless disdain, the cultured fascination of a woman of the world" (90) – but differs from both her earlier adventuresses and her later Femme Galantes in that she grows tired, even ashamed of the sexual power she wields. Naturally, as the heroine, she only ever wields the promise of her favours and is never compromised herself (either by love or declarations of passion). But Idalia is not driven by vanity. She is ruthless ("[a]ll power had irresistible fascination for me, and I learned to use mine pitilessly" (406)), but her coquettish manipulations are never in service of personal triumph or play, she assures Erceldoune, but always for the cause she believes in: "I loved freedom; I loved the peoples; I rebelled against the despotism of mediocrities, the narrow bonds of priesthoods; I had the old liberties of Greece in my veins" (405). Not only is Idalia allowed to be ambitious and idealist, but through her feminine performance at least, she wields actual political power: "I have held in my time, indirectly, more power than many a minister whose name is among the rulers; the world does not know how it is governed, and it does not dream how kings have dreaded and statesmen sought to bribe me" (407). However, she increasingly understands she has been manipulated by Phaulcon and is caught up in the power play of men who are "desperate, insatiate, unscrupulous, guilt-stained gamesters, who [stake] a nation's peace to win a gambler's throw" (406). She grows disillusioned and dissatisfied both with the movement and her role in it, especially as she understands the superficiality of men's desire for her:

> I luxuriated in the sense of my own power, in the exercise of my own fatal gifts; but I scorned from the bottom of my heart the men who were fooled by such idle things as a girl's glance, as a woman's smile. If the gold gleam of my

hair ensnared them, I could not but disdain what was so easily bound; if they were spaniels at my word, I knew they had been, or they would be, as weakly slaves of any other who succeeded me, and as easily subjugated by a courtesan as they were by me, when I chose to use the power. [...] I thought very scornfully of love. I saw its baser side, and I held it a madness of men by which women could revenge a thousandfold the penalties of sex that shut us out from public share in the world's government. (408–9)

Idalia here shows herself conscious of the fact that she wields her sexual power as a substitute for political power, and has grown weary of what amounts to self-commodification, yearning instead for the 'true' values and emotions of liberty and love. The latter of course presents itself in Erceldoune, and when the novel ends with Garibaldi's conquest of the Kingdom of the Two Sicilies in 1860 and her father's death in it, a redeemed Idalia sails into the sunset, newly free. Phaulcon's death, as Schroeder and Holt note, marks "the demise of patriarchal authority in Idalia's life" and allows her to enact "a fantasy of transcendence, withdrawing entirely from their society to rule over a separate space free from [...] cultural determination" (2008: 69). Idalia's struggle for autonomy and self-empowerment is so mirrored in the political struggles and the ideals for which she fights, and she is remarkable both among Ouida's work and Victorian literature at large for being a destroyer of men and kingdoms, a heroic supporter of liberty, and a successful romantic heroine, all at once.

In some aspects at least, this thoroughly unusual heroine may have had a real inspiration: the infamous Countess Castiglione. Born in 1837 into Florentine aristocracy, and so only two years older than Ouida herself, Virginia Oldoïni was married at sixteen to Fransesco Verasis, Count di Castiglione. At nineteen, she was sent to Paris by her cousin, Count Cavour, minster to Victor Emanuele II of Savoy, then King of Sardinia and Piedmont, and a leading figure in the Risorgimento. Oldoïni was renowned for her beauty. Princess Metternich, wife to the Austrian ambassador, Empress Eugénie's confidant, and by no means a fan of Oldoïni, admitted: "I have never in my life seen such beauty and I do not expect to see its like again" (qtd. in Montesquieu, 1913: 26). Keenly conscious if this, Oldoïni became notorious among court society for extravagant costumes, choreographed entrances, and endless self-staging, for example by posing like a statue to be admired. She seldom spoke to women and greeted male admirers with haughty indifference (Apraxine, 2000: 23). Sent to curry Napoleon III's support for Italian unity, she became the Emperor's mistress in 1856. Oldoïni consciously instrumentalised her beauty and was deeply invested in her own sexual power, as the more than 400 photographs taken of her by royal photographers Mayer & Pierson show. These intriguing images testify not only to a narcissistic nature, but also to a virtuosity in self-staging, and an intuitive understanding that her power emanated from her beauty, and her sexualised body (Solomon-Godeau, 1986).

Indeed, while the photographs were not publicly accessible apart from those shown at the 1867 Exhibition (Gere, 1998: 25), Oldoïni shares her notoriety and exploration of her sexuality-as-power with many Ouida heroines, and her (potentially imagined) role in pro-Italian politics with Idalia in particular. More than that, Countess Verasis (Oldoïni) sounds not a little like Countess Vasalis (Idalia). Lastly, the novel half takes place amid the Risorgimento's turmoil in Italy, and half in Paris, where Idalia seduces powerful men to her cause. It is, then, easily imagined that Ouida drew inspiration from Oldoïni – or the myth that surrounded her.

Idalia is not Ouida's first, nor her last, high-society seductress navigating the interconnectedness between female sexuality and social power, but she is the only one who attains that power in the heterotopic masculine sphere of espionage and politics, becomes a libertarian hero, and who rejects her (tarnished) social power for a romantic happy ending. As such, she provides an especially interesting foil to *Under Two Flags*' Cigarette.

The Soldier

The vivandière was by the 1860s a romanticised figure, having gained prominence through the Crimean and the American Civil War. Ouida might have been inspired by an article in the *Illustrated London News* from 1859 (see Gilbert, 2005: 144), ostensibly concerning the Franco-Austrian War of that year, or by Gaetano Donizetti's *opéra comique*, *A Daughter of the Regiment* (1840, see Marucci, 2009), as indeed this is what Cigarette is called. Ouida herself may have contributed to the figure's notoriety, seeing that W. S. Gilbert adapted Donizetti in 1867, just after *Under Two Flags* had been serialised, and notably "converted all the soldiers [...] into gorgeously attired Zouaves" ("Review of *La Vivandière*", 1868). Cigarette, however, differs vastly from the operetta's Maria, the sentimental orphan figure to be recuperated under patriarchal protection. On the contrary, Cigarette is a free agent and a soldier in her own right.

Introduced as a wayward, youthful, and boyish waif with bronzed skin, a "kitten-like face", short hair, and scarlet rosebud lips (Ouida, 1867 [1995]: 175), she combines tomboyish esprit and natural sensuality. Constantly compared to animal wildness, from kittens and leopards to hawks, hares, and chamois, she lives "a dashing, dauntless, vivacious life, just in its youth, loving plunder, and mischief, and mirth; caring for nothing; and always ready with a laugh, a song, a slang repartee, or a shot from the dainty pistols thrust in her sash" and exudes a "devil-may-care nobility, and of a wild grace that nothing could kill" (179). She emblematises the (imagined) Oriental, lawless vivaciousness of French Algeria: free and ready to love or kill, without much attachment to either, to dance or smoke, and move around alone, Cigarette enjoys an exotic independence denied her European counterparts – even a femme fatale like Idalia.

But Cigarette is more than a tomboy. Although often compared to "a handsome, saucy boy", the novel's narrative voice frequently reminds us also that Cigarette is "feminine with it all – generous and graceful amid all her boldness" (180). Indeed, she always retains what Ouida deems a female character and is positioned in traditionally female roles towards the soldiers: they are both her lovers and her charges. She cares for wounded soldiers with selfless love, is generous, loyal, and charitable, but also calls them her "gros bebees" and keeps them in line with ribald mockery ("[y]ou call him a misanthrope?" she cried disdainfully. "And you have been drinking at his expense, you rascal?" (200)). Whereas her maternal self-understanding has little to do with domestic Angels as imagined by Coventry Patmore or John Ruskin, she is nonetheless earnestly caring and protective towards her unruly soldiers. For example, when she makes Cecil promise not to defy Chateauroy's orders, because it would inspire rebellion and cost lives. As such, Cigarette and Cecil exert similar influences: he reforms soldiers by leading by example, and she by holding them accountable – including Cecil. As such, while not conventionally feminine, she is appreciated for what she is: "[h]er own sex would have seen no good in her", diagnoses Ouida, "but her comrades-at-arms could and did. Of a surety, she missed virtues that women prize; but, not less of a surety, had she caught some that they miss" (181).

Although considered intrinsic to the French army, Cigarette (unlike Cecil) is positioned outside or even above its hierarchies: "Cigarette was, in her fashion, Generalissima of all the Regiments of Africa" (238). A street-smart, "resolute little democrat" (261), she has no regard for hierarchies or luxury, and "would have 'slanged' the Emperor himself" (189). She embodies Ouida's democratic ideals: "[t]he holiness of an impersonal love, the glow of an imperishable patriotism, the melancholy of a passionate pity for the concrete and unnumbered sufferings of the people were in her, instinctive and inborn" (379). Her undiscerning movements across military infrastructures translate into physical mobility:

"[s]he loitered in a thousand places, for Cigarette knew everybody; she chatted with a group of Turcos, she emptied her barrel for some Zouaves, she ate sweetmeats with a lot of negro boys, [...] she drank a demi-tasse with some officers at a cafe" (185). She is accustomed to entering Chateauroy's villa unannounced and through the window, and to sharing wine and cigars with his officers, as well as climbing and leaping across casements, ledges, and rooftops, always in step with Algiers' ebb and flow:

> [She] sprang, with a young wildcat's easy, vaulting leap, over his head, and over the heads of the people beneath, on to the ledge of the house opposite, [...] with an airy pirouette on the wine-shop's roof that would have done honour to any opera boards, and was executed as carelessly, [...] let herself down by the awning, hand over hand, like a little mouse from the harbour, jumped on to a forage wagon that was just passing full trot down the street, and disappeared; standing on the piles of hay, and singing. (258)

In such cinematically envisioned scenes, Cigarette is literally above convention. She also lives alone with some veteran mascots in a garret, and so fully inhabits the heterotopic, heterogenous space of French Algeria on her own terms. Like Idalia, she holds more power than the male hero. This becomes evident when Cecil tries to sell carved figurines to a local vendor to buy ice for a dying comrade, but is refused, and Cigarette secretly bullies the vendor into purchasing the figurines with her money. More viscerally, when Cecil is ambushed by four drunken Arab riders, Cigarette saves his life by shooting three, then reports the incident herself so as to spare him from unfair superiors.

In turn, while Cigarette has the power and agency to save Cecil's life, he (unknowingly) has the power to trouble hers simply by calling her "unsexed" (203). Before considering that indictment's impact, however, it is important to establish Cigarette's relationship with her sexuality. She is sexually independent, her wild grace aligned with a natural, instinctive charm rather than the performance of a social register of femininity. When she dances in a tavern, conjuring up comparisons with "a Bayadere" or a "Nautch girl" (Ouida, 1867 [1995]: 193), such an Oriental register might contribute to her reception by (male) readers as a sexual fantasy (Schroeder and Schroeder, 2011: 241–2), but, whereas this might indeed have been readers' response, importantly, Cigarette's relationship with the male gaze within the intradiegetic world is vastly different. Unlike Idalia, who leverages men's desire into political power, Cigarette's sensuality is "untutored and instinctive in her as its song to a bird" (Ouida, 1867 [1995]: 193), and although bewitching, indolent, and voluptuous, is also hers to bestow or withhold. She dances joyously and alone, to be looked at by the soldiers, who know not to join her unless she gives a sign, or else she stops or violently rebukes interruptions with "a blow of her clenched hand" (194). She cannot be bribed to dance, would indeed "refuse point-blank a Russian Grand Duke" (193), but dances to cheer battle-weary troops. As such, her youthful spirit and female body are gifts to be dispensed as reward or solace, exposed to the male gaze when and how she chooses, given out of compassion more often than caprice, and not as a commodity for exchange value. Cigarette enjoys the attention, but her dancing has nothing to do with the power she wields. Within the heterotopic space of soldiering, she so retains more agency over her body than most Ouida heroines and is even allowed to enjoy her sensuality during the "dance-delirium" (193), blissfully unaware of gendered meta-narratives that demand decorum or passivity.

Against this backdrop, Cecil's comment, made in comparison with a (dead, absent) Arab woman and her "sweet, silent, tender grace" enrages Cigarette: "'[u]nsexed? Pouf! If you have a woman's face, may I not have a man's soul? It is only a fair exchange'" (203). She here undermines his diagnosis by calling attention to Cecil's gender performance as equally ambiguous, and the novel seems to ask the following questions: what then, to Cecil, is 'sexed'? Why is this his verdict to bestow? And why may he 'pass' while she 'fails' out of "the prevailing gender economy of marriageable females" (Schroeder and Holt, 2008: 76)? As Cigarette falls in love with Cecil, his inability to recognise her vigour and fortitude as beautiful, and indeed his patronising pity for her instigate not only defiant wrath but a profound identity crisis in the heroine. Comparing herself against the "costly, delicate, brilliant-hued, hothouse blossom" Lady Venetia (Ouida, 1995 [1867]: 254), whom Cecil loves, Cigarette recognises (aristocratic) femininity as a catalogue of "courtly negligence, [...] regal grace, [...] fair, brilliant loveliness, [...] delicious, serene languor" and "all she had missed" (269). Seeing this difference between her own, natural tomboy liberty and the femininity Cecil understands and covets comprises a loss of innocence for Cigarette and prompts an ongoing, though defiant, struggle.

Cecil, a mouthpiece for his class and gender, cannot grasp her beyond the narrow parameters of the gender catalogue he knows, cannot acknowledge her as the beautiful, courageous, complex person the text presents her to be, let alone as a hero in her own right: "Cecil thought that a gallant boy was spoiled in this eighteen-year-old brunette of a campaigner; he might have gone further and said that a hero was lost" (260). More than that, feeling merely "an involuntary pity" (277), he sees her as a future tragedy, as a predestined Fallen Woman: "[b]ut when the bloom should leave her brown cheeks, and the laughter die out of her lightning glance, the womanhood she had denied would assert itself, and avenge itself, and be hideous in the sight of the men who now loved the tinkling of those little spurred feet" (259). His perception always relates her to the male gaze: it is either her inability to charm him as a viable romantic partner or her impending failure to please the men who now adore her that makes him deny her the epithet of 'feminine' altogether.

In itself, this is not an extraordinary reaction to gender ambiguity in Victorian literature. However, Ouida crucially undermines and exposes Cecil's double standards (see Gilbert, 1999: 176). She repeatedly lets Cigarette react to Cecil's patronising indifference with passionate irritation, she even thinks of shooting him, and defiantly rejects his pity: "'[n]one of your pity for me! Buffeted about? Do you suppose anybody ever did anything with me that I didn't choose?'" (Ouida, 1867 [1995]: 251). The novel continuously affirms Cigarette as "however unsexed in other things, [... she is] thoroughly feminine" (259), asserts "that girls who were 'unsexed' could keep enough of the woman in them not to be neglected with impunity" (254), and attributes to her "the allurement of a woman's loveliness, bitterly as she disdained a woman's charms", while reminding us that Cecil, with his various mistresses about whose fates he never worries, is "a man on whom [female] beguilement usually worked only too easily and too often" (277). Lastly, the dying painter Leon Ramon disagrees with Cecil, voicing the soldiers' collective perception: "'[s]pare me the old world-worn, threadbare formulas. [...] There will always be a million of commonplace women ready to keep up the decorous traditions of their sex, and sit in safety over their needles by the side of their hearths. One little lioness here and there in a generation cannot do overmuch harm" (309). Ramon so disarms Cecil's European aristocratic gender politics which, as the first chapter explored, have no purchase here.

The incident with the four riders already suggests that Cecil misunderstands and underestimates Cigarette, but it is the battle of Zarâila which proves her to be a "chivalrous soldier" in her own right (259). In the desert, Cecil's regiment is ambushed by enemies, and despite his heroic fighting, which Ouida orchestrates with cinematic skill, the army seems lost until Cigarette leads in reinforcements:

> Above the din, the shouts, the tumult, the echoing of the distant musketry, that silvery cadence rung; down into the

midst, with the Tricolor waving above her head, the bridle of her fiery mare between her teeth, the raven of the dead Zouave flying above her head, and her pistol levelled in deadly aim, rode Cigarette. The lightning fire of the crossing swords played round her, the glitter of the lances dazzled her eyes, the reek of smoke and of carnage was round her; but she dashed down into the heart of the conflict as gayly as though she rode at a review – laughing, shouting, waving the torn colours that she grasped, with her curls blowing back in the breeze, and her bright young face set in the warrior's lust. Behind her, by scarcely a length, galloped three squadrons of Chasseurs and Spahis; trampling headlong over the corpse-strewn field, and breaking through the masses of the Arabs as though they were seas of corn. (357)

After a heroic entrance, she rides up to Cecil ("'[w]ell struck! The day is turned! Charge!' She gave the order as though she were a Marshal of the Empire" (357)), and they fight side by side. Later, she is celebrated and decorated with the Croix de Guerre, but before that, she once again displays her psychological complexity when she saves and cares for the wounded, unconscious Cecil in a tent off the battlefield. Here, albeit hidden and secret even from him, she shows tenderness and vulnerability to which she is otherwise too proud to admit. Her gendered identity, which "fiercely contemned womanhood" is troubled by her romantic love, which asserts itself as feminine: "she was thoroughly woman-like in her passions and her instincts" (363). In the tent's seclusion, "she let his head lie on her lap", "moving her hand softly among the masses of his curls [...]. Her face grew tender, and warm, and eager, and melting with a marvellous change of passionate hues" (364):

> She loved to see him lie there as though he were asleep, to cheat herself into the fancy that she watched his rest to wake

it with a kiss on his lips. In that unconsciousness, in that abandonment, he seemed wholly her own; passion which she could not have analyzed made her bend above him with a half-fierce, half-dreamy delight in that solitary possession of his beauty, of his life. (364)

But Cigarette also understands that Cecil does not love her, and resents his influence over her independent spirit: "a thousand changes swept over her mobile face. It was one moment soft, and flushed, and tender as passion; it was the next jealous, fiery, scornful, pale, and full of impatient self-disdain" (366). Her love renders her vulnerable not just emotionally, but socially – it threatens her identity as a proud, self-sufficient agent:

> At a word of love from him, at a kiss from his lips, [...], she would have given herself to him in all the abandonment of a first passion, and have gloried in being known as his mistress. But she would have perished by a thousand deaths rather than have sought him through his pity or through his gratitude. (371)

Staying with Cecil instead of joining the celebrations in her name and enduring the physical discomfort of being "bruised, stiff, tired, [...] her rounded, supple limbs [...] aching, her throat [...] sore with long thirst" (367), she displays both feminine devotion and selfless soldierly camaraderie, not least when she warms him with her tunic and calls that being "*en bon soldat*" (368). Like Idalia, Cigarette endures physical hardships and danger, displays solidarity with fellow soldiers, and is allowed not only to save the hero, but to claim masculine-coded heroism within the heterotopic space of battle: "[t]he divine fire of genius had touched her, and Cigarette would have perished for her country not less surely than Jeanne d'Arc" (379).

The novel never negates Cigarette's femaleness, and in fact

asserts it, even as it likewise affirms the gulf between Cigarette and traditional femininity. Trying to confront Venetia, Cigarette is cowed by "the grace, the calm, the beauty, the nameless, potent charm" of "her superb rival" (468):

> She felt [...] as though she were some very worthless, rough, rude, untaught, and coarse little barbarian, who was, at best, but fit for a soldier's jest and a soldier's riot in the wild license of the barrack room or the campaigning tent. It was only the eyes of this woman, whom he loved, which ever had the power to awaken that humiliation, that impatience of herself, that consciousness of something lost and irrevocable, which moved her now. (454)

It is interesting that Ouida, who lauds Cigarette's "immunity from the weakness of her sex", that is, her lack of "meanness nor selfishness" (453), likewise does not invalidate the social power of Venetia's aristocratic femininity, and the confrontation exemplifies Ouida's paradoxical aristocratic values and democratic ideals. Despite her proud scorn, Cigarette secretly envies that femininity as something escaping her, something that has currency beyond her own world, within Cecil's social imaginary and his affections. But just as his heroic masculinity barely translates into power in Algeria, so does Cigarette's wayward womanhood fail to transcend the heterotopia of war. Within it, she ("a child in years and a woman at heart" (387), that is a young woman on the brink of sexual maturity) wields incomparable freedom, agency and courage, being uniquely "bewitching, dauntless, capricious, unattachable, unpurchasable, and coquettish" (252), but that liberty is conditioned on her youth and confined by the exceptional, exotic social and geographic parameters of French Algeria.

When she finally races across the desert to save Cecil from the firing squad, she is apprehended by enemy Arabs (survivors of

Zarâila), who "longed to draw their steel across the fair young throat, to plunge their lances into the bright, bare bosom, to twine her hair round their spear handles, to rend her delicate limbs apart" (513). Despite this sexually-coded violent fantasy, even they consider her a de-gendered soldier: "she was neither child nor woman to them; she was but the soldier who had brought up the French reserve at Zarâila" (512). Respecting her noble mission, they – showing their own generosity – free her and give her a fresh horse, testifying that her power within this space, which obeys its own rules, transcends her gender.

Ultimately, Cigarette throws herself in front of the firing squad and dies sacrificing herself for Cecil in a supreme act of love with which Venetia will always compete unsuccessfully (see Gilbert, 2005: 158). However, while her demise has often been read as recuperating Cigarette into a conservative Victorian ideology, as it "violently expurgates the discontented woman from the narrative in a manner ultimately in keeping with prevailing concepts of self-sacrificial femininity" (Schoeder and Holt, 2008: 77), I want to emphasise that she also dies, as foreshadowed throughout, as a soldier in battle. She saves Cecil yet again, having mobilised all her military power to obtain his pardon, and all her physical and martial prowess to reach him in time. Her violent self-sacrifice, after all, unfolds within the homosocial military world, and so mirrors that of Pipcon, or Cecil's faithful servant Rake. Cigarette remains, to the last, Cecil's comrade in battle, and is buried and remembered as a "soldat de la France" (Ouida, 1867 [1995]: 528).

Her death may safely contain her and neutralise unresolved gender ambiguities, but it is also a victory of sorts. "As a woman who defies prevailing gender codes and refuses to participate in her own commodification as marriageable material", Schroeder and Holt diagnose that Cigarette "will remain forever outside the hearth of Western society's domestic economy" (2008: 76). Ouida conjures up a vision of female agency free from outward sexualisation, one that is, by necessity, female without being traditionally feminine, but also recognises the limits of such adolescent tomboy freedom as its intersection with a culturally defined femininity. In Algeria, Cigarette moves freely across social, military, urban, and gendered infrastructures, and is free to define herself until she encounters Cecil's (male, Western, aristocratic) cultural gaze, intent on defining her from without, measuring her up, tallying her 'failures' to meet its own, gendered ideal. Cecil's inability to assimilate her into familiar structures translates into dismissive, benevolent pity, and Cigarette's identity crisis pits her innate pride and independence against her romantic desire for his approval. In the end, her dilemma is resolved through an act that reconciles her love with her agency as a soldier and allows her to stay eternally herself: young, unclaimed, and a hero.

The Martyr

Ouida similarly examines femininity and its social baggage in *Folle-Farine* (1871), albeit not in a heterotopic space of espionage or war where social parameters may be at least partially suspended or subverted, but explicitly in and through the normative social world. Pamela Gilbert delivers a persuasive, in-depth analysis of this novel's heroine, which I will therefore only briefly contrast against Cigarette. Folle-Farine, named after flour dust, is also a hybrid, Orientalised tomboy, an illegitimate half-"gypsy" child (Ouida, 1871 [1872]: I, 45) so vilified and abused by the overly superstitious French peasants that she willingly allies herself with the (imagined) devil. As Gilbert notes, the novel thus enacts Faust's nature in Gretchen's circumstances through Folle-Farine's coming of age (Gilbert, 2005: 160), which entails a crushing awareness of how her sexuality commodifies her.

Like Cigarette, she is aligned with animals and nature, and so retains a rebellious, and to Ouida, noble, wildness. It is this undomesticated ignorance of social gender that lets her withstand her grandfather's sadistic, and sexually connoted abuse: "[t]here was a liberty in her that escaped his thraldom; there was a soul in her that resisted the deadening influence of her existence" (Ouida, 1871 [1872]: I, 141). She silently endures his flogging, "insensible of humiliation because unconscious of sin", cleaving to "silence and fortitude and strength [as] the greatest of all the virtues" (I, 138), and so retains a certain liberty through her refusal to engage. Indeed, through a paradoxical decoupling of mind and body, Folle-Farine resists her oppressive circumstances: while the patriarchal figure of her grandfather performs "the cultural impulse to fetishize and dehumanise the youthful female body", Folle-Farine, fortified through her ignorance and allied to a different moral order, enacts Ouida's "glorifying [of] female sexuality as an almost sacred province ultimately impervious to male degradation and thus representative of female resilience" (Schroeder and Holt, 2008: 104–5). Whereas her community considers her a valueless person, her disengagement from the social marketplace is her strength (see Gilbert, 2005: 162–4). In this, she mirrors Cigarette's heterotopic liberty on a microcosmic scale.

However, like Cigarette's, Folle-Farine's innocence is troubled and ultimately lost through the comments of a man. When Arslan, the selfish but beautiful painter, tells her she is beautiful, Folle-Farine learns of her sexuality and its potential exchange value through the male gaze. This bittersweet awareness, Ouida implies, is how she matures to womanhood: "[l]ike Persephone she had eaten of the fatal pomegranate seed, which, whether she would or not, would make her leave the innocence of youth ... and draw her footsteps backward and downward to that hell which none, – once having entered it, – can ever more forsake" (Ouida, 1871 [1872]: I, 326). Whereas this awakening, coupled with her falling in love with Arslan, gives her the strength to defy her grandfather ("[h]er body had grown sacred to her because a stranger had called her beautiful, and [...] her life for the first time had acquired a worth and dignity in her sight because one man had deemed it fair" (II, 9), her sexual awakening is largely pessimistic, as she grows aware of her femaleness as a stigma: "[p]aradoxically, beauty and sensuality meant for women both empowerment and subjugation through commodification" (Schroeder and Holt, 2008: 108).

Folle-Farine becomes the unwilling participant in a game she cannot win. Throughout the novel, she defends her purity from men's objectification, caught in a gendered role defined by desires projected onto her from outside (Gilbert, 2005: 171). Ouida portrays the male gaze throughout as invested with sadistic desires "to hurt, to please, to arouse, to study, to portray" (Ouida, 1871 [1872]: II, 82), that is to possess, manipulate, or destroy the female body and soul, and unlike Cigarette, Folle-Farine is ultimately consumed by that gaze (conversely, in subjecting Folle-Farine to the superstitious torture of the village women, Ouida also implicates women as agents of patriarchal oppression [see Schroeder and Holt, 2008: 112–3]). So doomed by her gender (Gilbert, 2005: 161), Folle-Farine becomes entangled in the gendered economy. In her attempt to support the (unworthy) man she loves, she leverages her only capital – herself – to the wealthy Sartorian and becomes his mistress.

However, Ouida complicates the stereotypical role of the Fallen Woman through the disentangling of her heroine's body and mind. Folle-Farine yields the former, "vacates" it, as Gilbert notes, and retains her essence elsewhere: "even though her body submits to the laws of exchange, she remains outside the system" (Gilbert, 2005: 165). Through complete self-negation and selfless suffering, Folle-Farine achieves the paradoxical, but characteristically Ouidean victory of withholding herself from the gendered economy. Understanding that claiming her feminised, sexualised body entraps her in the unequal power dynamics of the social marketplace, Folle-Farine maintains her purity and freedom only by never 'becoming' a woman, either as an 'unsexed' child-tomboy or in the ultimate freedom of death.

Folle-Farine mirrors Cigarette's struggle with a female coming of age as a bittersweet loss of innocence. Both find liberty in their wild, unsocialised youthfulness but are undone by their love for men who represent the normative order. Whereas, however, the vivandière achieves agency and even heroism in the lawless, far-away sphere of colonial war, Folle-Farine fights a losing battle against the deeply entrenched, European economy of spectacle into which women enter as commodities, and so pre-figures a theme that emerges regularly in Ouida's fiction going forward.

Conclusion: All is Fair in Love and War

Idalia and *Under Two Flags* are Ouida's most swashbuckling novels. Although scenes of war and revolution, often inspired by the Risorgimento, feature throughout her work, these novels most resemble adventure romances in the style of Dumas *père*, and so it is especially remarkable that she places successful female heroines in their centre. Her empowered female spies and soldiers, however, are by no means only fictional and drew inspiration from real, ongoing politics, high society agents such as Virigina Oldoïni, and French vivandières. Ouida here mobilises heterotopic spaces of war and revolution to disentangle her heroines from normative social forces, and crafts both a proto-spy novel and a proto-desert adventure, both of which subsequently evolved as traditionally masculine and masculinist genres. Cigarette and Idalia achieve what, in the fiction of both the nineteenth and twentieth centuries, has been commonly granted to men, especially in these genres: agency, consequence, and heroism. They so affirm Mallett's previously cited diagnosis, namely that the adventure genre facilitates "fantasies of a more powerful self" (2015: 153), and do so two decades before the genre solidified into largely glorifying male exploits in colonial spheres.

Indeed, in Ouida's hands, Other spaces provide realms in which femaleness and femininity may momentarily be decoupled and female heroines for a time master their sexualised bodies, influence world-changing events, and realise their most powerful selves. The aspect of romance, with which readers like Preston (above) identified Ouida along with Dumas *père*, Hugo, Sands, or Scott, here plays a crucial role. René Doumic, writing about Octave Feuillet, whose relationship with Ouida's fiction will be explored in the next chapter, defines romance as follows:

> It is the taste for the extraordinary; it is also the impatience in supporting the yoke of reality, a longing to forsake the trodden paths, a belief that happiness exists only outside the established rules, and that life is not worth living except in those fiery moments which break up its monotony and platitude. The imagination in revolt against reason escapes toward the rare, the exceptional, the difficult, the impossible. (1899: 26)

He here captures not only Ouida's exuberant imaginative style but also her rebellious, libertarian politics, which "[bring] us into conflict with the implacable order of things": "[r]omance is the badge of unhappiness; the souls a prey to its influence are perpetually unsatisfied and disconsolate. They have asked from life what it cannot give; they have gone out to meet its inevitable disappointments" (26, 31).

Idalia and Cigarette, both fiercely democratic idealists, exemplify this: their extraordinary, swashbuckling exploits challenge established orders and reveal Ouida's narrative style and her politics as intrinsically entwined, but are also inescapably entangled in that order through their gender. While they move as far out of reach of Victorian gender norms as Ouida can imagine, they can never fully escape them. Idalia's access to power is tainted by its exploitation of male desire and subject to their self-aggrandising machinations, and Cigarette's liberty comes at the cost of her romantic love – and her future. Their exceptional endeavours strain beyond "the established rules" but are ultimately also thwarted by them. Established Victorian gender notions cannot fully confine or define these ambiguous heroines, but they become an antagonistic force, and as Folle-Farine exemplifies, the closer these heroines move to the European social order, the faster they are drawn in and re-defined by it. Meeting life's "inevitable disappointments", all three women are made to understand that how they understand themselves as natural beings differs from what society projects onto them, and they can only transcend their projected-onto female bodies through radical escapes.

Revolution and war therefore provide imaginative spaces in and through which Ouida's female heroines may participate in swashbuckling adventure romances and realise idealistic longings for freedom, even as they throw into relief the (gendered) limits of that endeavour. In (albeit briefly) appropriating the genre as a viable vessel for exploring democratic politics in tandem with gender as an inescapable category, Ouida demonstrates the potential of adventure as a female, even feminist, genre.

CHAPTER 3

French Novels and Femmes Galantes: Agency, Cosmopolitanism, Spectacle

Introduction: Second Empire Legacies

Ouida was notorious for writing unconventional, even scandalous women, especially, as this chapter shows, those who have cultivated "adultery as one of the fine arts" (Ouida, 1876 [1892]: 82). Taking up Gilbert's question of why this was tolerated (2005: 143), Jane Jordan has shown that, by French and English critics and readers, and indeed by herself, Ouida was perceived to be writing "*Romans français écrits en anglais*" (qtd. in Jordan 2014a: 77, see also Jordan 2009b, 2014b), that is French novels written in English. Whereas French publishers especially likened her to George Sand, this was by no means a compliment coming from British reviewers, for whom the more sexually explicit French literature exerted dangerous, morally deplorable influences (see Atkinson, 2017: 141).

With her frank depiction of infidelity, Ouida was considered to embody "many of the characteristics of the worst kind of French literature" ("*Signa*", 1875: 831) or to mirror "some of the more disreputable modern French novels" ("Novels of the Week", 1885: 803). One review, critiquing Ouida's *Moths* (1880) and Zola's concurrently published *Nana* (1880) in tandem, ascribed to Ouida's fashionable society and Zola's underworlds the same coarse exploration of vice, only hers was "disguised by rank, by wealth, by culture, or by fashion" (Fiske, 1880: 83). It denies her "claim to the title of English-woman" and classes her with the un-English, "foreign purveyors of infection" (87).

To Ouida, such outrage was a badge of honour. In the novel itself, she claims to have "out-Zolaed Zola" (Jordan, 2014a: 72) when the villainous Prince Zouroff, appraising the Femme Galante Lady Dolly's lurid schemes, exclaims: "'Zola will want a lower deep before long, I suppose; he will do well to leave his cellars for the drawing-rooms'" (Ouida, 1880 [2005]: 431). In her programmatic essay "Romance and Realism" (1882 [1895]), Ouida rejects English realism as tedious and contrived and, in letters to Marie Corelli, she embraces her half-French heritage, declaring herself "very little English" (qtd. in Jordan 2014a: 73). What conservative reviews praised as English literature's "powerful agency of reform and purification" (Fiske, 1880: 87), Ouida dismissed as absurd moral fetishes: "[the] French brain in me", she claims, "has always rendered me so utterly indifferent to the 'prurient Puritanism' of the English hostility to all forms of genius" (qtd. in Jordan 2014a: 73). So, in addition to reading and reviewing French authors such as Alphonse Daudet, Guy de Maupassant, Pierre Loti, or Anatole France herself, and being frequently published in French translation, Ouida purposefully capitalised on her 'Frenchness', and aligned herself with a French literary tradition to stage revolts against English morals.

However, this chapter argues that there are additional, hitherto un-explored influences on, and contexts for, the 'Frenchness' of Ouida's work and that they are central both to her conception of society as commodity culture, and her ability to depict sexually liberal female characters. She herself declares, in "Romance and Realism": "[t]he influences of the Second Empire are still with us all over Europe, but in English literature, this is neither accurately traced nor truthfully acknowledged" (Ouida, 1882 [1895]: 308). Indeed, Ouida's re-imaginations of Second Empire high society did not stop with Countess Castiglione. Conceiving of Europe as a cosmopolitan, interconnected social sphere, she draws on the figure of the Parisian courtesan in order to explore and interrogate female power and ultimately craft her most notorious creation, the happy high society adulteress she terms, in *In A Winter City* (1876), the "Femme Galante":

> The Femme Galante, who has neither the scruples nor the follies of poor Frou-frou, who neither forfeits her place nor leaves her lord; who has studied adultery as one of the fine arts and made it one of the domestic virtues; who takes her wearied lover to her friends' houses as she takes her muff or her dog, and teaches her sons and daughters to call him by familiar names; who writes to the victim of her passions with the same pen that calls her boy home from school; and who smooths her child's curls with the same fingers that stray over her lover's lips; who challenges the world to find a flaw in her, and who smiles serene at her husband's table on a society she is careful to conciliate; who has woven the most sacred ties and most unholy pleasures into so deft a braid, that none can say where one commences or the other ends; who uses the sanctity of her maternity to cover the lawlessness of her license; and who, incapable alike of the self-abandonment of love or of the self-sacrifice of duty, has not even such poor, cheap honour as, in the creatures of the streets, may make guilt loyal to its dupe and partner. Beside her [...], Marion de Lorme were honesty, Manon Lescaut were purity, Cleopatra were chaste, and Faustine were faithful. (Ouida, 1876 [1892]: 82–3)

Such similarities were not lost on readers. A. K. Fiske, already quoted above, complained that "'Ouida' has a very bad opinion of the women of society. She considers them no better than that *demi-monde* which Zola has seen fit to describe for the edification of the prurient" (1880: 84), and G. S. Street remarked on "certain ladies of the Second Empire, whose histories Ouida seems to have studied" (1895: 171). This chapter outlines how such ladies, namely celebrity courtesans such as Marie Duplessis, Blanche d'Antigny, Cora Pearl, Esther 'La Païva' Lachmann, Apollonie Sabatier, Céleste Mogador, and Valtesse de la Bigne, among others, figure into Ouida's continued fascination with and negotiation of female agency. If Idalia, Cigarette, and Folle-Farine struggle with learning that their bodies are being appropriated into powerfully gendered social dynamics, Ouida's courtesans and Femmes Galantes are fully aware of this and learn to instrumentalise their beauty as capital. I argue that they are inspired by real women such as the above, who highlighted and re-appropriated patriarchal power structures in and through which female bodies and lives were commodified. I examine their literary counterparts in Alexandre Dumas *fils*' *La Dame Aux Camélias* (1848) and Émile Zola's *Nana* (1880), comparing these with Ouida's commentary in *Under Two Flags* (particularly her depiction of the courtesan the Zu-Zu) and *Puck* (1870, depicting the career of Avice Dare, later Laura Pearl). Despite her ambivalent portrayal of the courtesan, Ouida here configures female agency as entangled in, and even contingent on, a social economy of spectacle, the entry fee of which is (female) self-commodification. This understanding lastingly informs her conception of the Femme Galante who, like the celebrity courtesan, attains cosmopolitan glamour, travel, luxury, and sexual liberty by playing this economy of spectacle to her advantage, but at the cost of her virtue and integrity.

The other influence on the Femme Galante that I suggest provides insight into the literary and social milieu with which Ouida was identified, is the work of now-obscure but then well-known French novelist Octave Feuillet (1821–90). Favoured by the Empress Eugénie's circles and considered to embody a 'typically Parisian' social spirit, Feuillet's high society romances illustrate that Ouida's Femme Galante, in novels such as *In a Winter City* (1876) and *Moths* (1880) has antecedents and echoes in certain, coldly seductive female characters of contemporary French (popular) literature.

Are they cannibals, these women?

No figure embodied the Second Empire's licentious opulence more than the courtesan. Whereas nineteenth-century Paris knew several classes of professional mistresses such as the *grisette* or the *cocotte*, it was the *lionne* whose glamour and social influence rivalled that of Empress Eugénie and her set. The top dozen *lionnes* formed *la garde* (Rounding, 2003: 20), celebrities whose iconic beauty led fashions and galvanised the media, and who attained riches by becoming living spectacles. Patronising Paris fashion houses such as Charles Frederick Worth or Emile Pingat, parading through the Bois de Boulogne alongside the social elite, caricatured and written about in prominent newspapers like *Gil Blas*, immortalised in novels and operas, embedded in popular entertainments from the Bal Mabille and the Hippodrome to the Paris Opera, and inspiring fashions from hairstyles to novelty dishes such as that dedicated to Cora Pearl by celebrity chef Auguste Escoffier (Authier, 2015: 24), these women dominated the public consciousness as they shaped and were shaped by the bourgeois mass media. As such, they were, as Michael D. Garval remarks, "bound up with the rise of commodity culture, including the development of department stores, and of the fashion, advertising, and entertainment industries" (2012: 54).

However, while notorious for their imagined promiscuity, *lionnes* were often also performers (actresses, dancers, and equestriennes) and hostesses of dinners and influential salons: Appolonie Sabatier, who inspired Charles Baudelaire's *Les Fleurs du Mal* (1857), hosted Théophile Gautier, Gustave Doré, Victor Hugo, and Édouard Manet, whereas La Païva, whose luxurious hôtel on the Champs-Élysées[1] hosted Gustave Flaubert, Émile Zola, Eugène Delacroix and the Goncourt brothers, and maintained pan-European friendships like that with Richard Wagner (Richardson, 1967; Rounding, 2003; Authier, 2015). As such, their reach extended far beyond Paris. Blanche d'Antigny, for example, was mistress to the Russian police chief and the Egyptian Khedive, but most *lionnes* participated in and became icons of, a cosmopolitan European high society by frequenting summer capitals with Grand Dukes or gambling away fortunes in Baden Baden.[2]

Baden Baden emerged in the 1860s as a cultural nexus of a Europe newly connected by trains and rising mass media and provided an important imaginative backdrop for both real and fictional *lionnes* as worldly cosmopolitans. Outfitted by Edouard and Jaques Bénazet with entertainment venues in an operatic Parisian style (the Casino, Kursaal, theatre, and race course), Baden transformed from a spa town into a pleasure capital and hosted eminent politicians (from the emperors of France, Germany, Austria, and Russia to kings and diplomats) and the fashionable elite alongside composers, musicians, artists, thinkers, and writers, such as Clara Schumann, Pauline Viardot, Hector Berlioz, Jacques Offenbach, Victor Hugo, George Eliot, Wilkie Collins, Richard Wagner, Ivan Turgenev, Fyodor Dostoevsky, Leo Tolstoi, and many more. It embodied an emerging, pan-European cultural marketplace in which art, culture, and commerce were newly reconfigured (see Figes, 2019: 42). Ouida, too, imagines Baden in *Under Two Flags* as world stage where multilingualism, fashion, art,

---

[1] Built between 1856 and 1866, the beautifully conserved Hôtel de la Païva now houses a gentlemen's club. It is a testament to the *lionne's* taste and wealth.

[2] The second generation of *lionnes*, such as Liane de Pougy, Carmen Otero, or Cléo de Mérode, rising to prominence at the *fin de siècle*, would patronise Monaco and the French Riviera.

and conspicuous consumption embody new forms of sociability, behavioural codes, and shared spaces, and a "more relaxed sexual morality that stemmed from the self-conscious distancing from an older small-town bourgeoisie obsessed with the narrow social and moral horizon of 'home'" (Evangelista, 2021: 16–7):

> Baden was at its brightest. The Victoria, the Badischer Hof, the Stephanie Bauer were crowded. The Kurliste had a dazzling string of names. Imperial grandeur sauntered in slippers; chiefs, used to be saluted with 'Ave Caesar Imperator', smoked a papelito in peace over 'Galignani'. Emperors gave a good-day to ministers who made their thrones beds of thorns, and little kings elbowed great capitalists who could have bought them all up in a morning's work in the money market. [...] Statesmen who had just been outwitting each other at the hazard of European politics laughed good-humouredly as they laid their gold down on the colour. Rivals who had lately been quarrelling over the knotty points of national frontiers now only vied for a twenty-franc rosebud from the bouquetiere. [...] Brains that were the powder depot of one-half of the universe let themselves be lulled to tranquil amusement by a fair idiot's coquetry. And lips that, with a whisper, could loosen the coursing slips of the wild hell-dogs of war, murmured love to a princess [...].
> (Ouida, 1867 [1995]: 99)

Lionnes like Marie Duplessis and Cora Pearl, who both frequented Baden, were intrinsic to this glamorous, cosmopolitan, and sexually promiscuous sphere. Indeed, Ivan Turgenev's 1867 novel *Smoke*, set in Baden, opens with the following commentary: "[e]ven the blackened and whitened visages of the Parisian demi-monde could not destroy the general impression of bright content and elation, while their many-coloured ribbons [...] recalled the intensified brilliance and light fluttering of birds in spring, with their rainbow-tinted wings" ([1906]: 1). Ouida likewise populates her Baden with a *demi-monde* participating in, and embodying, spectacles of luxury and conspicuous consumption, showing that their 'Parisian' domain extended to European capitals and summer destinations:

> The supreme empires of demi-monde sent their sovereigns, diamond-crowned and resistless, to outshine all other principalities and powers, while in breadth of marvellous skirts, in costliness of cobweb laces, in unapproachability of Indian shawls and gold embroideries, and mad fantasies and Cleopatra extravagances, and jewels fit for a Maharajah, the Zu-Zu was distanced by none. (Ouida, 1867 [1995]: 99)

The Zu-Zu, Bertie's mistress, whose "little toy trap, with its pair of snowy ponies and its bright blue liveries" with which she drives "so desperately through his finances" (52) reflects Cora Pearl's "sky-blue calèche, yellow livieries, and 'café-aut-lait' coloured horses" (Richardson, 1967: 27–8), also serves as Ouida's commentary on the male-authored narratives of the time, especially Dumas *fils*' *Dame aux Camélias*.

Inspired by Dumas' own, non-transactional and hence short-lived affair with Duplessis, the novel lastingly configured the courtesan narrative as one of the entrapped innocent woman doomed to an early, tragic death before the virtuous male hero can rescue her.[3] This patriarchal meta-narrative of reigning in the "promiscuous, greedy, potentially dangerous" courtesan whose self-directed existence as a woman in the public sphere threatened "bourgeois

---

[3] I also analyse both Dumas' and Zola's novels in my *Victorian Popular Fictions* article on Baz Luhrman's *Moulin Rouge!* (2001) in order to explore how the appropriation of celebrity courtesans' lives in male-authored narratives have shaped popular memory and neo-Victorian re-tellings.

order, morality, health, and finances" (Garval, 2012: 49; see also Gledhill, 1992; Anderson, 1993; Bell, 1999; Bernheimer, 1998; Nead, 1988), has been echoed across Verdi's *La Traviata* (1850) and Puccini's *La Bohème* (1896), and even Baz Luhrmann's *Moulin Rouge!* (2001). The novel foregrounds Marguerite Gautier's, the fictionalised Duplessis', redemptive death, as well as the exhumation and melodramatic scrutiny of her dead body by her lover Armand (Dumas's stand-in). In prioritising his grief, his jealousy of her patrons, and his moral edification of the naive "virgin who had been turned into a courtesan by the merest accident of chance, and a courtesan whom the merest accident of chance could have turned into the most loving, the most pure of virgins" (Dumas, 1848 [2000]: 60–1), it entirely negates Gautier's/Duplessis' agency. Whisked away from the temptations of luxury, Marguerite childishly marvels at butterflies and dreams of Armand's pure love, but, realising their life is financially unsustainable, she returns to Paris and writes to Armand from her deathbed that she sacrifices herself to his reputation. Revolting against this conservative and sentimental portrayal, Ouida snidely comments:

> As for the pathetic pictures that novelists and moralists draw, of vice sighing amid turtle and truffles for childish innocence in the cottage at home where honeysuckles blossomed and brown brooks made melody, and passionately grieving on the purple cushions of a barouche for the time of straw pallets and untroubled sleep, why the Zu-Zu would have vaulted herself on the box-seat of a drag, and told you "to stow all that trash"; her childish recollections were of a stifling lean-to with the odour of pigsty and straw-yard, pork for a feast once a week, starvation all the other six days, kicks, slaps, wrangling, and a general atmosphere of beer and wash-tubs; she hated her past, and loved her cigar on the drag. The Zu-Zu is fact; the moralists' pictures are moonshine. (Ouida, 1867 [1995]: 54)

Ouida, setting out to out-Dumas Dumas, here rejects moralistic meta-narratives that safely re-integrate the courtesan into traditional gender roles and so subdue her subversive potential, but she far from endorses the figure. Instead, as *Puck* (1870) illustrates, the *lionne* emblematises – and, ostensibly, indicts – a morally corrupt, spectacle-hungry society in which vice and self-commodification lead to success, but virtue and honour cannot survive. Told from the perspective of a Maltese dog, the novel chronicles the rise of peasant girl Avice Dare to subtly-named London actress, Laura Pearl, to Parisian celebrity courtesan Cléopâtre and finally Marchioness of Isla who ruins her lover, the theatre patron and bachelor hero Vere Beltran, as well as the pure heroine Gladys. Whereas Ouida continuously portrays Pearl as vain, greedy, and ignorant, and indeed with a "misogyny that suggests a profoundly conflicted approach to female desire" (Schroeder and Holt, 2008: 84), her attitude towards women – and it is never clear whether that applies to all women or a certain kind of normative femininity from which Ouida sees herself exempt – is ultimately ambivalent. "You see", opines Fanfreluche, Puck's worldly friend,

> all their girlhood through, they lived hardly; and were beaten and worked, and half-starved; and thought a scrap of bacon or a scrag of mutton a feast for the gods; and could hardly pin their rags together enough to look decent, or keep the wind and the rain from their shivering bodies. Well! – when they come into this world, and are dressed like empresses, and stuff sweetmeats all day long, and drive hither and thither, and eat and drink of the best earth gives, why naturally they can't have enough of it. (Ouida, 1870: I, 137)

As with the Zu-Zu, in both *Puck* and *Tricotrin* (1869), in which the young Viva attains wealth and status through strategic marriages, Ouida depicts these women's deadening lives in poverty, the absolute lack of agency or perspective of lives characterised by hunger and abuse, and their stark contrast to high society life with some degree of insight. In *Tricotrin*, Viva's rise to influential socialite parallels Dare/Pearl's journey as a courtesan: both women aspire to luxury, consequence, and participation in a cosmopolitan sphere ("'A woman!'", exclaims Viva, "'Because one will be a woman must one never see the world?'" (Ouida, 1869: 48)), and both women recognise that, in a patriarchal commodity culture, their only capital is their young, beautiful self. To attain any sort of social power, these women commodify themselves – Viva through her marriage, Avice and the Zu-Zu on stage – to attract wealthy patrons; all three sell themselves to the highest bidders. As such, while Ouida portrays these women as heartless, vain, and selfish, she also recognises the lack of options open to them. Notably, she also re-iterates "the failure of marriage as a form of self-fulfilment for women" by suggesting it as little more than a means to attain status (Schroeder and Holt, 2008: 82), and in so doing erodes the boundaries between the *haute* and *demi-monde*. Both, in her vision, are equally materialistic and transactional. Both allow certain women to leverage its power structures to their advantage, and turn self-commodification into a means of empowerment: "Dare's slavery to a culture of spectacle is self-imposed through her willingness to fetishize her own body, a strategy which allows her in turn to make slaves of her spectators" (71).

Nowhere is this more evident than in Beltran's theatre, which, although in London, is infused with expressly Parisian qualities. Not only does the theatre adapt French plays, which allows for Ouida's satiric commentary on both the piracy and censure that it involves (Ouida, 1870: I, 234; Atkinson, 2017: 279–81), but it features young, ballet-dancing chorus girls looking to attract wealthy patrons – an important 'career step' both for the fictional Avice and real *lionnes*. Cléo de Mérode, for example, (in)famously transformed from chorus girl to celebrity dancer and model after receiving adulations from King Leopold II of Belgium (Garval, 2012: 44–6, Guigon 2012: 82–3). Decades earlier, Ouida illustrates and transfers to London the long-standing tradition in which the Paris Opéra's *ballet du corps* was known, among certain gentlemen, as a "national harem" (Capon and Yve-Plessis, 1906: 26; see also Berlanstein, 2001: 33) or "libertine haven" (Willy, 1904: 253–4). Indeed, Beltran's fellow managers openly acknowledge that their audience comes to gaze at the girls and prefers "good ankles and bad puns" to intelligent actors: "'[p]ray don't attempt to return to high art while you've those forty pairs of fine legs and the Pearl's cellar-flap dancing'" (Ouida, 1870: I, 159). Here, as Schroeder and Holt note, Ouida's interrogation of the relationship between art and commerce, and the commodification of art, intensifies and is revealed to be inextricably gendered (2008: 81–2; see also King, 2009; King 2013a). In addition, in suggesting that "it was well understood that [the play's] chief attraction [...] would lie in the fact of its being written chiefly to exhibit a soulless, shameless, mindless woman, who had a fairer face and a more notorious infamy than any other" (Ouida, 1870: I, 306), Ouida also draws (albeit unkindly) on real *lionnes* such as Blanche d'Antigny, who starred in Offenbach's operettas (Richardson, 1967: 11–2), or the real Cora Pearl, who in 1867 scandalised Pairs as a scantily-clad Cupid in Offenbach's *Orphée aux Enfers*, with diamond-studded boots (Richardson, 1967: 31–2; Rounding, 2003: 242–3). Laura Pearl, too, exposes herself in dazzling costumes to the audience's male gaze as an object for pleasurable consumption, gaining notoriety while Beltran, whose reputation is untarnished, gains actual profit. However, Avice/Pearl becomes powerful enough to turn these power structures to her advantage, first by stealing from him, then by instigating riots and ruining Beltran's theatre simply by withholding herself and her body (and instead absconding to Paris with a new lover). As a *lionne*, it is now she who consumes her patrons, "chopping up men's fortunes and souls in double quick time" and "eat[ing] up a hundred men a quarter", prompting

Puck to ask: "'[a]re they cannibals, these women?'" (Ouida, 1870: I, 142, 116).

Ouida here discusses complex relationships between celebrity and media, self-commodification and social power, and identifies the courtesan as a figure who "anticipates the paradoxical place of celebrated feminine beauty within our mass visual culture, between commodification and creative self-fashioning, exploitation and empowerment" (Garval, 2012: 4; Schroeder and Holt, 2008: 71). Indeed, characters like the ballet girl Nell or Puck himself find themselves equally commodified, but without agency or power. Puck, handed from owner to owner, becomes a spoiled lap-dog, abused performer, and street dog, mirroring Avice's journey as actress and *lionne*, at least while she is dependent on wealthy men's desires and whims: "'I who write", he proclaims, "have I not been purchased by their money and made captive to their power?" (Ouida, 1870: I, 190).

Whereas Ouida here seems to recognise and denounce the power structures of commodity culture, in this novel at least, she also remains steadfastly blind to its patriarchal aspects. Characteristically and paradoxically, she fervently defends and glamorises those who shore up, and profit from, a patriarchal economy of spectacle, such as the aristocratic gentleman (here, Beltran) – indeed prompting an anonymous reader to pencil "[d]ear Ouida, always an excuse for the men!" into my copy of the novel. Ouida instead suggests that social power, where not given by birth, is available only to the most ruthless. This is also no doubt why Avice is repeatedly shown to be wantonly cruel to dogs and horses (the cardinal sin to Ouida, who kept up to thirty dogs and championed animal rights), whereas the real Cora Pearl was known as a skilled equestrienne who was, ostensibly, "kinder to her horses than her lovers" (Arsène Houssaye, qtd. in Richardson, 1967: 27).

Pearl, born Eliza Crouch in Plymouth, was likely a survivor of sexual assault, and her memoirs suggest she considered herself to be taking revenge on men, to exploit them as she had been exploited (Rounding, 2003: 208). Courtesan-authored novels and memoirs, as counter-narratives to salacious or sentimental male-authored fiction, often emphasise the physical hardships and dangers of their profession, showing themselves painfully aware of their precarious position within the patriarchal sexual economy. Céleste Mogador, in an autobiography written to aid her in a legal case against her deceased husband's powerful family, sympathetically chronicles the physical demands of becoming a star dancer and equestrienne (Mogador, 1854 [2001]; Marrone, 1997; Nagem, 2001). Liane de Pougy's auto-fiction speaks back to Dumas *fils* and Zola alike, suggesting through narrating her affair with heiress and salon-hostess Natalie Clifford Barney that queer female desire trumps a young man's attempt to rehabilitate the fallen woman, or by portraying the courtesan's vulnerability to violence and humiliation by her suitors (De Pougy, 1901 [2021]; Sullivan, 2016: 45). Indeed, Cora Pearl was assaulted by a bankrupted lover in 1872, when Alexandre Duval entered her home with a gun, intent on killing her, but accidentally shot himself. While he survived, she, blamed for the incident, was exiled from Paris. Contrary to male-authored fiction, courtesan narratives

> bear witness to the physical and emotional toils inflicted upon [courtesans] by their clients and protectors and underscore the gumption it takes for these women to market themselves and perform in front of hostile audiences. While texts like *Nana* often portray the ascent of the demi-mondaine as precipitous, the courtesan novels indicate that achieving fame, wealth, and notoriety often took years of hustling under difficult financial and social conditions. (Sullivan, 2016: 44)

Ouida's depictions of courtesans show themselves aware of such hardships, even if that does not always translate into sympathy.

In *In A Winter City* (1876), gossip turns to the memoirs of Jenny Léa, "a young lady who had seduced the affections of an Emperor, three archdukes, and an untold number of the nobility of all nations; she was utterly uneducated, inconceivably coarse, and had first emerged from a small drinking shop in the dens of Whitechapel; she was the rage of the moment, having got a needy literary hack to write her autobiography" (Ouida, 1876 [1892]: 215). This fictional publication, however, does not curry sympathy as much as sensation and scandal: "the book had no decency, and as little wit, but it professed to show up the scandals of a great Court, and it made some great men ridiculous and worse, so eighty thousand copies of it had been sold over Europe, and great ladies leaned from their carriages eager to see Mdlle. Jenny Léa pass by them" (216). Whereas this reads like an allusion to Cora Pearl, whose greatly anticipated memoirs promised exactly such exposing anecdotes – and which, ostensibly, she leveraged to obtain payments in exchange for anonymising former lovers – Pearl's memoirs were not published until 1886. The "forced sale of her effects in Paris" (216) might allude to Pearl having to sell her rue Chaillot home in 1873, but the memoirs Ouida alludes to may be Mogador's, Lola Montez' (1848), Léonide Leblanc's *Les Petites Comédies de L'amour* (1865), or one of the fictionalised biographies published in 1864 about British courtesan Catherine 'Skittles' Walters. In any case, Ouida here configures the courtesan narrative as a sensational commercial endeavour that illustrates the *haute monde*'s fascination with the *demi-monde*, but in so doing also conceives of the *lionne* as autonomous (if ruthless) agent leveraging her unique social position for profit. While she adopts some dominant stereotypes, her depictions of courtesans sit somewhere between courtesan narratives and Zola's *Nana*.

Ouida adapts instances like the Affaire Duval and other duels fought about Pearl, echoing the dominant meta-narrative of *lionnes* as ruining men (Rounding, 2003: 207; Ouida, 1870: II, 200–1), a perspective Zola amplifies to make Nana the avatar of and scapegoat for the Second Empire decadence that he ultimately blames for the humiliation of the Franco-Prussian War (1870–71). However, she also imagines many of the *lionne*'s hardships and difficulties that Zola glosses over to portray Nana as an indomitable force. More importantly, Ouida also never participates in her *lionnes*' objectification, which Zola's narrator clearly enacts.

Indeed, whereas Ouida charts Avice's ascent to power and agency through strategic self-commodification, Nana, inspired by Blanche D'Antigny, Hortense Schneider, or Valtesse de la Bigne, whom Zola, unlike Dumas *fils*, never met, is presented as both a childish, vapid, avaricious ingénue and voluptuous temptress, a sexual fantasy whose agency Zola is at pains to deny. Her appearance on stage as Venus warrants a voyeuristic exploration of her nakedness, especially her "firm breasts with their hard, erect, pink nipples" and "broad hips rolling and swaying voluptuously", which, in the eyes of the narrator, turns "the good-natured girl" into a disturbing woman offering "frenzied sexuality" and a "man-eater" (Zola, 1880 [2009]: 25). Her lovers' obsessive intrusion and possessive gestures, even desperate self-harming (380), and financial ruin are all laid at the door of the "fiery red of her pubic hair" which "glowed triumphantly over its victims [...] like a rising sun shining in triumph over a bloody battlefield" while she remains "a superb, mindless animal, oblivious of what she'd done, never anything but 'a good sort of girl', a big, fat wench bursting with health and the joy of life" (409). While the novel occasionally acknowledges her subversive potential as "magnificent and untamed" (277), or as avenging the world of the under-privileged (409), it also configures "this tart whom all Paris was itching to have" as carrying "foul infection" (279, 398): "with the smell of her body fermenting in the stuffy air, Nana was turning this whole society putrid to the rhythm of her vulgar tune" (364). In the end, Nana is punished with a strikingly unsubtle death by putrescent decay just as the Prussian army appears on the horizon, while the narrative voice that initially objectified her sexualised body now glories in lurid descriptions of "festering sores", "discharging ulcers", and "thick yellowish fluid" (425) and gleefully lauds her demise.[4]

Ouida's *lionnes*, like her adventuresses, survive and even attain happy endings through successful marriages. Instead of punishing and reigning in the subversive courtesan figure, Ouida lets her wreak havoc and get away, even if largely to condemn a mindless commodity culture in which no morality prevails. While Ouida endorses her male characters, they also ultimately wield little power over the women and their bodies. As such, whereas she certainly mobilises the courtesan to satirise and indict commodity fetishism and economies of spectacle in which the artistic and moral ideals Ouida champions have no purchase, she also recognises *lionnes* as intelligent social agents who, self-aware as both objects and players in the social and sexual marketplace, self-fashioned into cultural icons and trend-setting celebrities. Attaining access to cosmopolitan glamour, luxury, and sexual liberty, her *lionnes* may therefore also constitute vicarious fantasies of female agency.

Octave Feuillet and the Femme Galante

The Second Empire *lionne*, emblematic both of a rising commodity culture and the gendered dynamics in it, lastingly inspired Ouida's explorations of female agency, even as the latter turned her sights back on the *haute monde*. Indeed, as Thérèse Bentzon comments on *In A Winter City* (1876):

> Nous ne doutons pas d'ailleurs que la peinture très crue qui nous en est donnée ne soit ressemblante; on rencontre cette même aristocratie nomade dans toutes les grandes auberges

---

[4] A similar analysis can be found in my *Victorian Popular Fictions* article (Esser, 2022: 120).

de l'Europe. Il y a ici des types *d'étrangères* plus vrais que ne l'est celui de la créature fatale et mystérieuse que M. Alexandre Dumas a choisie pour personnifier l'espèce; elles laissent fort à désirer sous le rapport du ton et des mœurs, cela va sans dire, et risquent d'être confondues souvent avec les demi-mondaines, méprise qui du reste ne leur déplairait pas. (Bentzon, 1877: 386)

[We do not doubt that the very raw paint that we are given is resemblant; we meet this same nomadic aristocracy in all the big inns of Europe. There are here types of strangers more true than that of the fatal and mysterious creature that Mr. Alexander Dumas chose to personify; they leave a lot to desire in terms of tone and morals, that goes without saying, and risk being confused often with *demi-mondaines,* a mistake which, moreover, would not displease them. (translation mine)]

Ouida's aristocratic Femme Galantes, equally self-aware objects within a cultural marketplace, self-fashion towards dominant gender ideals to maintain their status, while simultaneously exercising a *lionne*'s sexual liberty. *Moths'* Lady Dolly, for example, enjoys access to a cosmopolitan sphere of leisure and luxury, and recognises this mobility as dependent on her social performance: she "liked to go everywhere, and she knew that, if people once begin to talk, you may very soon go nowhere" (Ouida, 1880 [2005]: 236). "Lady Dolly", as Wendy Parkins notes, "is equally at home frequenting the gaming tables in Monte Carlo or attending morning services in London in order to maintain the social visibility crucial to her continued social acceptance" (2009: 50). Like the *lionne,* the Femme Galante entertains a string of lovers, with no intention of letting them jeopardise her status: Lady Dolly "had never been on the debatable land; [...] She had never let 'Jack', or anybody who preceded or succeeded 'Jack', get her into trouble" (Ouida, 1880 [2005]: 236). *In A Winter City*'s

Madame Mila likewise, "was always careful of appearances. Even if you called on her unexpectedly, [Maurice] Des Gommeux was always in an inner room, unseen, and you could declare with a clear conscience that you never found him alone with her, were the oath ever required in any drawing-room in defence of her character" (Ouida, 1876 [1892]: 79). Being "very chic and very rich, and very lofty in every way", she is also "very careful to make Maurice go to a different hôtel" than the one in which she stays (77).

Is this astonishing candour, then, the 'Frenchness' with which Ouida identified and was identified? How the Femme Galante sits within a 'French' literary imaginary may be illustrated by Octave Feuillet (1821–90), who, like Ouida, was considered a literary staple of his time, but has lapsed into obscurity now. A playwright and novelist who collaborated with Dumas *père* and Paul Bocage, and followed Alfred de Musset, Feuillet wrote for the *Review Des Deux Mondes*, where Ouida's works appeared in French translations, and was known as a writer of high society romances. Maxine Du Camp called him "the accredited painter of the Faubourg St Germain" (1905: vii), that is of Empress Eugénie's circles. Indeed, Feuillet was a regular guest at the imperial revelries of Compiègne, St. Cloud, and Fontainebleau (see Seward, 2013), where he premièred his plays and "on one occasion the empress Eugénie deigned to play the part of Mme de Pons in *Les Portraits de la Marquise*" (Gosse, 1911: 304). He was appointed to the French Academy in 1862 and imperial librarian in 1868. His novels and plays were translated and adapted for the English, German, Italian, and US market and stage (with Sarah Bernhardt starring in the 1874 production of *The Sphinx*), included in Henry Vizetelly's *Popular French Novels* series, and reviewed (like Ouida) in the *Athenaeum*, the *Saturday Review*, the *Examiner*, and the *Fortnightly Review*. Feuillet's works adorned Wilkie Collins' library (Atkinson, 2017: 252) and his *Dalila* (1857) was pirated in Mary Elizabeth Braddon's *Circe* (1867) (see Atkinson, 2017: 262–3,

276).⁵ In 1890s' essay collections on "French Novelists", Feuillet was featured canonically alongside Théophile Gauthier, Alexandre Dumas, Alphonse Daudet, Guy de Maupassant, Victor Hugo, and Émile Zola. He was, in short, a well-known French author closely associated with the Second Empire culture and spirit.

Considered "foremost among the dealers of forbidden fruit", namely the "Byzantine literature of the Second Empire" (Matthews, 1881: 203), Feuillet provided "a perfect panorama of Parisian life [...], with all its bright lights and sombre shadows" and "social rottenness concealed under that glittering pageant [of] French society" ("Translator's Preface", 1891: 11–2). Depicting dysfunctional marriages and adultery, deemed staples of French literature, he was seen to be influenced by Dumas *fils*' *Dame aux Camelias* and the demi-monde (Matthews, 1881: 215; see Mauris, 1880). He was especially notorious for his female characters, considered emblematic of the Second Empire and "known as 'Feuillet's women', [...] those fatal creatures, those enchantresses, of splendid beauty and strange perversity" (Doumic, 1899: 34). Indeed, Feuillet's novels (much like Ouida's) abound with cynical, worldly men and "listless, excited, nay, feverish" women, "moved by a secret and nameless unrest borne by idle luxury" (Matthews, 1881: 221). In *Julia de Trecœur* (1872) and *Le Roman d'un jeune homme pauvre (The Romance of a Poor Young Man)* (1858), we find mysterious and manipulative ingénues setting out to seduce respectable heroes. Haughty, wilful, disdainful, and ironic – or, to some, "mal équilibrée, excentrique, [...] abandonnée tout entière à ses instincts" ("unbalanced, eccentric, [...] entirely abandoned

---

⁵ Braddon's practise of liberally adapting plots and characters from contemporary French literature into what she termed "composition novels" engendered much debate among readers. Atkinson explores at length the correlations between sensation writers Braddon and Charles Reade and French writers Honoré de Balzac and Octave Feuillet. See Atkinson, 2017: 262–83.

to [their] instincts", Pélissier, 1893: 185, translation mine) – they exhibit the characteristics of high society ladies in the making. In *Un Roman parisien* (*A Parisian Romance*), also *Madame de Maurescamp* (1881) and *Un mariage dans le monde* (*Marriage in High Life*, 1882), virtuous wives, abandoned by callous husbands, turn towards pleasure and flirtation, become coldly seductive, and incite deadly duels between their lovers. As such, they are certainly reminiscent of Ouida's adventuresses, *lionnes*, and Femme Galantes, and the high society intrigues they move through.

For example, Feuillet's *Monsieur de Camors* (1867) chronicles the amorous entanglements of what American publishers espoused as "the typical Frenchman of the Second Empire" ("Translator's Preface", 1891: 12) with his best friend's young wife, an intelligent widow *and* her young daughter, and the enigmatic Marquise de Campvallon, wife to his mentor and father figure. Camors, the listless but gallant dandy with a fatalist streak, certainly echoes Granville deVigne, Strathmore, Chandos, and even Bertie Cecil, moving as he does between gentlemen's clubs, duels, and drawing rooms. It is the Marquise, however, whose languid beauty and cold serenity most recall the Ouidean Femme Galante:

> The immense fortune of her husband, and the adulation which it brought her, had placed her on a golden car. On this she seated herself with a gracious and native majesty, as if in her proper place. The luxury of her toilet, of her jewels, of her house and of her equipages, was of regal magnificence. She blended the taste of an artist with that of a patrician. Her person appeared really to be made divine by the rays of this splendour. Large, blonde, graceful, the eyes blue and unfathomable, the forehead grave, the mouth pure and proud. (Feuillet, 1867 [1905]: 183–4)

With her dazzling beauty and indifferent coquetry, the Marquise echoes Femme Galantes like *Under Two Flags*' Lady Guenevere, whose liaison with Bertie is described as follows: "[n]either of them believed very much in their attachment, but both of them wore the masquerade dress to perfection. He had fallen in love with her as much as he ever fell in love, which was just sufficient to amuse him, and never enough to disturb him" (Ouida, 1867 [1995]: 49). The Marquise also anticipates the flirtatious hauteur of Princess Napraxine (from the novel of the same name 1884) or *The Massarenes*' (1897) Mouse. Camors and the Marquise echo their tone: "'I love you, Madame; and as you wish to be loved. I love you devotedly and unto death – enough to kill myself, or you!' – 'That is well,' said the Marquise, softly'" (Feuillet, 1867 [1905]: 208).

However, whereas the Marquise dares Camors to behave increasingly brazenly, kissing him in front of her sleeping husband, Lady Guenevere, albeit "queen of one of the fastest sets", is also "very scrupulous never to violate conventionalities" (Ouida, 1867 [1995]: 91), Lady Dolly is "always careful of appearances" (Ouida, 1880 [2005]: 235), and Madame Mila "indeed, abhorred a scandal; it always made everything uncomfortable" (Ouida, 1876 [1892]: 79). For the Femme Galante, flirtations, like everything else in her life, are elaborate but ultimately insincere charades – Mila's "passion for Maurice was the fifty-sixth passion of her soul" (340) – and she has no intention of being ruined by it, knowing instead to safeguard herself through performances in which her husband and indeed her social set are often implicated: Madame Mila "had had twenty Maurices in her time indeed, but then [her husband] the Count de Caviare never complained, and was careful to drive with her in the Bois, and pass at least three months of each year under the same roof with her, so that nobody could say anything" (78). As such, the Femme Galante satirises and exposes a high society in which casual adultery is silently sanctioned:

> When the Prince of Cracow, with half Little Russia in his possession, entertains the beautiful Lady Lightwood at

a banquet at his villa at Frascati, Richmond, or Auteuil, a score of gilded lackeys shout "La voiture de Madame la Comtesse!" the assembled guests receive her sweet good night, the Prince of Cracow bows low, and thanks her for the honour she has done to him; she goes out at the hall door, and the carriage bowls away with loud crash and fiery steeds, and rolls on its way out of the park-gates. Society is quite satisfied. Society knows very well that a million roubles find their yearly way into the empty pockets of Lord Lightwood, and that a little later the carriage will sweep round again to a side-door hidden under the laurels wide open, and receive the beautiful Lady Lightwood: but what is that to Society? It has seen her drive away; that is quite sufficient, everybody is satisfied with that. If you give Society very good dinners, Society will never be so ill-bred as to see that side-door under your laurels. (78)

It is no coincidence that the Femme Galante is closely identified with the Second Empire, whose loss Mila mourns until discovering that "flying the Red Cross flag had saved her hotel, [...] [and] that MM. Worth and Offenbach were safe from all bullets" (43–4). In addition to the *lionne*, she calls up Feuillet's "choice and luxurious beings", those goddesses and sphinxes who (Doumic, 1899: 13, 35), as one reviewer comments, "demand in one way or other to fall, or at least to be fallen in love with" (Saintsbury, 1878 [1891]: 298). However, Feuillet's haughty seductresses do, indeed, fall and die whereas Ouida's survive happily. Feuillet's romances ultimately end conservatively with death-bed repentances, heroic suicides, or tragic demises, while the Femme Galante all but rides into the sunset. Nonetheless, some reviewers diagnosed his works as "unhealthy", "insidious", and "dangerous" (Matthews, 1881: 222) – a verdict also often levelled at Ouida. Like her, he "finds a lack of culture in women, a lack of sympathy in men, and a lack of principle in both" (Saintsbury, 1878 [1891]: 299).

More than that, Ouida and Feuillet, with their glamorous settings, aristocratic values, romantic style, and illicit excitements (such as duels and adultery), both inspired Henry James' cosmopolitanism (Tintner, 1991), itself "associated with modernity, mobility, and social privilege" (Evangelista, 2021: 15). However, that same romantic, proto-aesthetic style which Walter Pater appreciated in both (Coste, 2019: 13–4; Bristow, 2015: 43) rejected realism for romance grounded in a certain chivalrous idealism: "[t]o dream of an ideal", explains Doumic about Feuillet, "even the most chimerical one, demands a certain nobility. It is a quality unallied to egotism and opposed to baseness" (1899: 30). Ouida, citing *Moths*' Corrèze in her essay on "Romance and Realism", similarly laments: "[a]ll that is heroic, all that is sublime, impersonal, or glorious, is derided as unreal. It is a dreary creed. It will make a dreary world" (Ouida, 1882 [1895]: 309). "We are not perishing from enthusiasm", Doumic explains and it may be their shared motto, "but dying from the commonplace" (1899: 30). Both idealise the aristocracy in a time in which its power is giving way to a rising bourgeoisie and simultaneously, as Gustave Flaubert suggests, provide vicarious glamour for a middle-class readership: "la basse classe croit que la haute classe est comme ça, et la haute classe se voit là-dedans comme elle voudrait être" ("the lower class thinks that high society is like that, and the high society sees itself in it as it would like to be" (Flaubert, qtd. in Grewe, 1974: 286, translation mine)). This seems certainly plausible, given that Feuillet was championed by the Empress herself, and both authors also enjoyed a wide and popular readership.

However, whereas Feuillet was known and praised for his 'character studies', it is certainly Ouida who, against the backdrop of Second Empire aesthetics, fashions Femme Galantes like the insouciant and hedonistic Madame Mila or the frivolous and shrewd Lady Dolly into outstanding comedic heroines and sharp social satire. Devoted to – and dependent on – the endless pageantry of high society, in which youth and beauty translate into female social power, Dolly, who is thirty-four but looks seventeen (Ouida, 1880 [2005]: 48), continuously self-fashions herself with make-up, hair pieces, and dress (or undress), using commodities to enhance her body's capital for men's pleasurable consumption (see Schroeder and Holt, 2008: 186–8): "'[y]ou *should* want to please'", she instructs her daughter (Ouida, 1880 [2005]: 115, original emphasis). Indeed, to "women like Lady Dolly life is a comedy, no doubt, played on great stages and to brilliant audiences", even if that means "the bore of being 'done up', and the bore of being 'undone'" every day (125–6). Literally making and unmaking themselves each time, "they bear it heroically, knowing that without it they would be nowhere; would be yellow, pallid, wrinkled, even perhaps would be flirtationless, unenvied, unregarded, worse than dead!" (126). Artifice, spectacle, and play-acting, Dolly knows, are the entry fee to a high society in which sex, at least for women, is power – in their relationships with men as well as in competition with other women. After all, anticipating Oscar Wilde's *bon mot* that the only thing worse than being talked about is not being talked about, Dolly's worst nightmare is to be "unregarded". Attracting the gazes of others, much like Laura Pearl on stage, might mean being exposed, scrutinised, and objectified, but also, if done skilfully, draws power in the form of envy and flirtation, which in turn are social currency. This is why Dolly is so perturbed by the arrival of her adolescent daughter (who has been living with her grandmother), even though, as Ouida brilliantly comments, she

> ought to have been perfectly happy. She had everything that can constitute the joys of a woman of her epoch. She was at Trouville. She had won heaps of money at play. She had made a correct book on the races. She had seen her chief rival looking bilious in an unbecoming gown. She had had a letter from her husband to say he was going

away to Java or Jupiter or somewhere indefinitely. She wore a costume which had cost a great tailor twenty hours of anxious and continuous reflection. [...] She had her adorers and slaves grouped about her. She had found her dearest friend out in cheating at cards. [...] She had had a new comedy read to her in manuscript-form three months before it would be given in Paris, and had screamed at all its indecencies in the choice company of a Serene Princess and two ambassadresses as they all took their chocolate in their dressing-gowns. (47)

Consumption and commodities, from costumes to comedies and chocolates, are intrinsic to Dolly's life and self-understanding. In a cosmopolitan high society of spectacle, they translate into social leverage and are rewarded with attention and access to more consumption. Dolly, for all her vapid frivolity, instinctively understands that the presence of her sixteen-year-old daughter Vere (discussed further in the next chapter) undermines her carefully curated youthful and desirable persona and puts them in competition with one another for male attention: "'[i]t makes one look so old!' she had said to herself wretchedly" (48). In the end, however, Dolly remains "just as lovely, sexually voracious, and daringly dressed as ever, as unnatural as the toy her name invokes" (Schaffer, 2000: 130).

The Femme Galante, much like the *lionne*, is thoroughly immersed in a gendered economy of spectacle in which power dynamics are masked by a social pageantry of respectability and can be momentarily undermined and re-negotiated as long as she is willing and able to self-commodify and leverage her (young, beautiful, sexual) body. In exchange, she gains access to a cosmopolitan sphere of conspicuous consumption, travel, and entertainment, as well as sexual independence, agency, and even power.

Conclusion: Your Cursed French Novels![6]

As late as 1930, a character in W. Somerset Maugham's *Cakes and Ale* proclaims "'I can't believe that any lady would read a book by Ouida'", and her companion replies: "'I must say, it's more what you'd expect from a Frenchman than from an English gentlewoman'". Together with their final verdict, namely that "'she isn't really English'" (Maugham, 1930 [2000]: 71), this conversation illustrates Ouida's lasting reputation as an un-English, un-feminine writer. A 1936 edition of *Under Two Flags* by Chatto & Windus, released concurrently with the film starring Ronald Colman and Claudette Colbert, even marketed her as a "French novelist". If her works were perceived as morally infectious and dangerously French, she certainly welcomed that verdict, allying herself frequently to the French literary context.

In her fiction, "French novels" often appear as self-indulgent, leisurely, and decadent pastimes, usually enjoyed by her dandy heroes in recumbent posture and while idly smoking. "On De Vigne's pet sofa", we find, "with a French novel in his hand, and a meerschaum in his lips, [the] lazy, girlish-looking, lighthearted 'Little Curly'" (Ouida, 1863 [1891]: 59). Bertie Cecil, too, considers "[u]nlimited sodas, three pipes smoked silently over Delphine Demirep's last novel, a bath well dashed with eau de cologne, and some glasses of Anisette" the appropriate antidote to a day on guard duty and (Ouida, 1867 [1995]: 11), loath to be disturbed, only "lift[s] his eyes with plaintive resignation from the Demirep's yellow-papered romance" (62). The fictional 'Demirep's name points to the French novel's 'half-reputable' status, and Ouida certainly mobilises anxieties around their distinctly "unEnglish" influence to invest her dandies with insouciant self-indulgence (see Atkinson, 2017: 221, 226–7), aristocratic idleness, exotic consumption, and even, as 'Little Curly' exemplifies, languid effeminacy. After all, "Paris novels" are found in Cecil's bachelor

---

[6] Ouida, 1867 [1995]: 82.

apartment exactly between the masculine "box-spurs, hunting-stirrups, cartridge cases, curb-chains, muzzle-loaders, hunting flasks, and white gauntlets" and the "pink notes, point-lace ties, bracelets, and bouquets to be dispatched to various destinations" (Ouida, 1867 [1995]: 4). Conversely, 'fast' women and Femme Galantes may also read French novels, and enjoy them, like Lady Dolly, over an unfeminine cigarette (see Ouida, 1880 [2005]: 58, 93).

Indeed, Ouida suggests that Curly, in the passage above, is reading Feuillet (Ouida, 1863 [1891]: 59), and she frequently mentions the latter in connection with female reading pleasure, especially that of her Femme Galantes and their luxuriously cosmopolitan consumption. Whether by glancing, during their morning toilette, "alternately from Octave Feuillet's or Feydeau's last novel to her Dresden-framed mirror" (284), or enjoying "a new story of Octave Feuillet [...and] a new volume of charming verse by Sully Prudhomme, only sold on the Boulevards two days before" among "tea-roses and the heliotrope" (Ouida, 1876 [1892]: 35), they consider Feuillet's Second Empire romances part of their pleasures and even, somewhat meta-fictionally, their social repertoire: "'[g]ood gracious, Hilda!' said Madame Mila, with wide-open eyes of absolute amazement; 'you talk as if you were one of the angry husbands in a comedy of Feuillet or Dumas'" (128).

Here is, then, yet another way in which Ouida consciously allies her work to a collectively imagined 'Frenchness', particularly the Second Empire whose impact on Europe she considered crucial even in 1895. Feuillet's work and its reach especially, suggest that there existed a popular, pan-European literary imaginary of Second Empire glamour, epitomised and maintained by his novels and plays, against which Ouida's own, luridly luxurious and sexually promiscuous high society could be contextualised even after the Empire's end in 1871. Feuillet's spoiled and wanton heroines, like Ouida's, combine innocence with capricious worldliness or represent virtue corrupted by pleasure, but also retain intriguing agency. With their *demi-mondaines*, cosmopolitan glamour, and casual adultery, it is not surprising that Ouida's novels became linked to an identifiably 'French' habitus and even as French novels written in English. As a 'French' novelist, she enjoyed greater license to fashion sensation fiction's transgressive women into ambitious socialites, celebrity courtesans, and happy adulteresses, for all of whom marriage is little more than an elaborate social charade.

Ouida, of course, stretched that license as far as she could. Feuillet, writing for the Faubourg St Germain's *haute monde*, shies away from openly portraying *lionnes*. Similarly, whereas Braddon's eponymous sensation heroine Aurora Floyd (1863) takes some characteristics from London's own, but last, celebrity courtesan, Catherine 'Skittles' Walters (1839–1920), Braddon's is a very different portrait. Skittles, an accomplished equestrienne, could be seen, like Parisian courtesans in the Bois, on Hyde Park's Rotten Row, exhibiting high-bred horses which she accessed through a deal with a livery stable owner, while wearing notoriously tight-fitting riding habits. Skittles was allegedly the model for Edward Landseer's 1861 painting "The Shrew Tamed", which depicts a sensuously confident equestrienne and her horse, and is a frequent cover image on editions of *Aurora Floyd*. Skittles' horsemanship informs Braddon's wilfully independent heroine, as well as a series of anonymously penned popular novels in the 1860s – including one titled "Cora Pearl" (Buurma, 2008: 840; Conary, 2023). In Ouida's work, Skittles appears in *Puck* as Lillian Lee, "with her glistening chignon, and her velvet habit, and her jewelled whip, leaning down from her hundred-guinea hack" (Ouida, 1870: I, 202)[7]. While the *lionne* (who also travelled across Europe), was

---

[7] The poet and traveller Wilfred Scawen Blunt, whom Ouida befriended and to whom she dedicated an essay in 1900, based on their shared anti-imperialist views, had entertained an affair and later friendship with Walters.

thus not an exclusively French phenomenon, Ouida's Zu-Zu, with her "Mabille oaths" and "Fontainebleau hunting costume" (Ouida, 1867 [1995]: 52, 54), as well as Laura Pearl, who moves from the Paris-influenced London stage to Parisian celebrity as Cléopâtre, bring lurid Second Empire entertainment and high society glamour to London.

Notably, the evolution of Ouida's *demi-mondaine* into the Femme Galante may have been inspired by Ouida's high society friend Janet Ross, who, she learned in 1876, was entertaining an affair with Ouida's beloved Marchese della Stufa despite being married. Drawing on such inspirations as well as real Parisian celebrity courtesans and French aristocratic romances allowed Ouida to write sexually liberal and empowered women – although, if Feuillet's ultimately conservative novels serve as a benchmark, she also 'out-Frenched' the French novelists. At the same time, her cosmopolitan women become a prism through which she continuously examines and lays bare the explicitly gendered power dynamics of commodity culture, even a glamorous, cosmopolitan, and aristocratic one. Here, flirtation, sexual encounters, and purely superficial marriages are part of a larger social pageant which ambitious women, whether safeguarded by their aristocratic birth (the Femme Galante) or with no social capital at all (*lionnes*), may navigate and outwit as self-aware objects in the social marketplace. As such, they provide crucial insights not just into Ouida's ongoing social critique, but the deeply entrenched, gendered interrelations between celebrity, female agency, self-commodification, and economies of spectacle whose impact is still felt in today's mass culture.

CHAPTER 4

Aces and Aesthetes: Sex, Violence, Marriage

Introduction: The New Woman Question

If the Femme Galante's irreverence embodied Ouida's response to a gendered commodity culture in the form of ironic mockery, she also entailed her rejection of marriage as either a space for female self-fulfilment or a viable social institution: to be happily married at all, one must resort to casual adultery. Indeed, as Wilde's Lord Henry Wotton (whom Ouida no doubt inspired; Schaffer, 2002: 222) proclaims, "the one charm of marriage is that it makes a life of deception absolutely necessary for both parties" (Wilde, 1890 [2008]: 20). Towards the 1880s, however, Ouida also increasingly turned her sharp satirical gaze on the darker aspects of women's status within marriage, and so prefigured approaching feminist debates, catalysed in the collective symbol of the New Woman, a term she herself coined (Ouida, 1894 [1895]b). In light of her scepticism of the New Woman, which has so disproportionally affected her reception as to disqualify her from the larger literary canon, "in which she can be classified neither as canonical nor as a feminist foremother" (Gilbert, 1999: 170), no study of Ouida can omit her complicated relationship with late-Victorian emergent feminism. Whereas initial indictments of Ouida as anti-feminist in 1980s scholarship have been persuasively complicated (Gilbert, 1999; Schaffer, 2002; King, 2011b; Hager, 2014; Pykett, 2016), the New Woman catalogue also still remains the barometer against which 'feminism' is measured, and the framework in and through which an author is evaluated.

The New Woman's quest for female autonomy was, akin to the 1960s-1980s second-wave feminism which sought to excavate that kinship, ultimately directed towards participation in public life through work and voting rights. As a democratic, bourgeois movement, that endeavour clashed with Ouida's elitist views on aristocratic values and her rejection of state government, but, as previous chapters have demonstrated, she was nonetheless keenly interested in models of female autonomy, and in the social prism of marriage at least, her views converge with New Woman interests. After all, as Gilbert notes, "many New Women writers must have grown up reading Ouida", and her novels "allowed, in however carefully mediated a context, identification with female characters whose notions about female sexuality ran counter to middle-class norms at mid-century" (Gilbert, 1999: 173). Scholarship has acknowledged the influence of 1860s sensation fiction and its transgressive women on the New Woman, and no doubt Ouida's own life and work figure prominently into that genealogy (Gilbert, 1999: 170; Hager, 2014: 93). If Mona Caird's 1888 essay on "Marriage" in the *Westminster Review* catalysed and galvanised the Woman Question, and New Woman discourse subsequently re-negotiated its programme of deconstructing feminine ideals and Angel/Fallen binaries, as well as exploring female sexuality, agency, and education on the battlefield of the marriage plot, Ouida had been vocally critiquing marriage since her first novel, *Granville de Vigne*. Here, the heroine Violet asks her mother: "'Would you not put me up to auction, knock me down to the highest bidder? Marriage is the mart, mothers the auctioneers, and he who bids the highest wins. Women are like racers, brought up only to run for Cups, and win handicaps for their owners'" (Ouida, 1863 [1891]: 377–8).

Mother-daughter relationships – and, inevitably, betrayals – also lie at the heart of *Moths* (1880), in which Ouida, with perceived

Zola-esque frankness (Fiske, 1880), tackles the taboo topic of marital rape, then "denied a name under British law" (Jordan, 1995: 96), and which is, ostensibly, the first novel to portray a divorced woman attaining a happy ending (Mitchell, 1981: 140). Whereas *Moths* snidely parodies Gothic constellations (Schaffer, 2000: 128) to expose how marriage leaves women vulnerable to socially sanctioned abuse that can neither be articulated nor appealed, *Princess Napraxine* (1884), drawing on ideas from *In A Winter City* (1876), mobilises aestheticism and, I argue, queer sexuality, to explore bids for female autonomy that are only partially successful. *Guilderoy* (1889), then, concurrent with emergent New Woman fiction such as George Meredith's *Diana of the Crossways* (1885), Sarah Grand's *Ideala* (1888) and Caird's *The Wing of Azrael* (1889), debates the limited and stigmatised options of unhappily married women, and seeks forms of female agency and voice in the face of complacent male guardians. These novels, which form the basis for this chapter's analysis, illustrate multiple ways in which Ouida engages with marriage as the tangible and most immediate manifestation of patriarchal power. This chapter interrogates the strategies and literary models Ouida uses to examine female dependence and indict male violence, as well as explore avenues for autonomy and escape. In doing so, it demonstrates Ouida's grasp of women's entanglement in a patriarchal economy through love, sex, and desire, their bodies and social status, and how that entanglement evolves. It also shows how prominent late-Victorian social debates and literary currents are indebted to popular culture.

Gothic Marriage, Gothic Parody

Moths begins with Femme Galante Lady Dolly, discussed in the previous chapter, who is "a sweet-tempered woman by nature, and only made fretful occasionally by maids' contretemps, debts, husbands, and other disagreeable accompaniments of life" (Ouida, 1880 [2005]: 53). Dolly's frivolously hypocritical life in Trouville is troubled by her daughter's arrival. When Jack, one of her lovers, suggests marrying Vere away, Dolly is peeved: "'[o]f course! One always marries girls; how stupid you are'" (49). Ouida's heroines and adventuresses, whether virtuous or wicked, are often married at sixteen, younger even than the era's eighteen-year-old débutantes. Marriage then usually constitutes a symbolic and traumatic break with childish innocence. In Vere, too, married to the middle-aged Prince Sergius Zouroff through Dolly's scheming, "childhood perishe[s]" overnight: her eyes tell "of an innocence and a faith stabbed, and stricken, and buried for ever more" (178). Indeed, the novel's light, satirical beginning is increasingly – and jarringly – juxtaposed with Vere's nightmarish experience of marriage, and the consciousness that she has been bartered away to a stranger to clear her mother's (invented) debts: "[a] sense of unreality had come upon her, as it comes on people in the first approach of fever. She walked, sat, spoke, heard, all as in a dream. [...] Let them stare as they would, as they would stare at the sold slave-girl" (180). Vere is thus betrayed by her mother, whose benchmark for success is attention, and whose accomplice, social eminence Lady Stoat, likewise makes girls "feel that love and honour were silly things, and that all that really mattered was to have rank and to be rich, and to be envied by others" (110). Corrupted by the high society of spectacle, these women equate power and agency with money and status, which women may secure and wield through marriage. In this, they echo conceits already laid out in Ouida's first novel when Violet's mother counsels a marriage with a peer based on his diamonds and his Parisian taste, to which Violet responds: "'[o]h yes! I could not sell myself to better advantage!'" (Ouida, 1863 [1891]: 377).

Zouroff, too, considers marriage to be transactional, but unlike the women and like even the 'good' men of Ouida's 1880s novels, seeks to gratify his whim and commodifies Vere the more for her resistance: he is willing to "pay a high price for innocence, because it was a new toy that pleased him. But he never thought that it would last, any more than the bloom lasts on the peach. [...]

Since it would be agreeable to brush it off himself, he was ready to purchase it" (Ouida, 1880 [2005]: 176). Vere is reduced to an object in his eyes, the more so because he believes she sells herself to gain money and status, like the *lionnes* he keeps: he "only saw a lovely woman whom he had bought as he bought the others, only with a higher price" (390). Repeatedly, archaic imagery around slavery and rape is transposed into modern, fashionable society:

> Only a generation or two back his forefathers had bought beautiful Persian women by heaping up the scales of barter with strings of pearls and sequins, and had borne off Circassian slaves in forays with simple payment of a lance left in the lifeless breasts of the men who had owned them: [Zouroff's] wooing was of the same rude sort. Only being a man of the world, and his ravishing being legalised by society, he went to the great shops of Paris for his gems, and employed great notaries to write down the terms of barter. The shrinking coldness, the undisguised aversion of his betrothed only whetted his passion to quicker ardour, as the shrieks of the Circassian captives, or the quivering limbs of the Persian slaves, had done that of his forefathers in Ukraine; and besides, after all, he thought, she had chosen to give herself, hating him, for sake of what he was and of all he could give. (195)

Indeed, "Zouroff, in whose mind all women were alike," takes sadistic delight in tormenting his wife "because she had fallen in his sight by her abrupt submission; she seemed at heart no better than the rest. She abhorred him; yet she accepted him" (195). In his (enduringly misogynistic) view, women are commodities available for consumption, but because they (apparently) willingly participate in their objectification in exchange for rank and riches, they degrade themselves, and this in turn justifies his degradation of them, even his use of violence: "[t]o Sergius Zouroff innocence was nothing more than the virgin bloom of a slave had been to his father – a thing to be destroyed for an owner's diversion. It amused him to lower her, morally and physically, and he cast all the naked truths of human vices before her shrinking mind, as he made her body tremble at his touch" (225). Here, Ouida heavily implies that Vere is subjected to marital rape by her husband.

Yet his physical and mental abuse are not only permissible by law but safely hidden behind the façade of social pageantry: "[s]ometimes he liked to hurt her in any way he could. [...] Yet he always lavished on her so much money, and so many jewels, and kept her so perpetually in the front of the greatest of great worlds, that everybody who knew him said that he made a good husband after all" (206). Thus, even though "the rapacity of an ignoble passion let loose and called 'marriage' tore down all her childish ignorance and threw it to the winds, destroyed her self-respect, and laughed at her, trampled on all her modest shame, and ridiculed her innocence" (205), "[s]ociety had set its seal of approval upon this union and upon all such unions, and so deemed them sanctified" (199). Ouida vocally and repeatedly indicts marriage as a form of socially sanctioned prostitution in which sexual intercourse catalyses unequal power dynamics and violence or shame cannot be voiced. On the contrary, marriage is to be seen as duty and accomplishment: "Pollution? Prostitution? Society would have closed its ears to such words, knowing nothing of such things, not choosing to know anything. Shame? What shame could there be when he was her husband? Strange fanciful exaggeration! – society would have stared and smiled [...] To marry well; that was the first duty of a woman" (199).

Ouida therefore anticipates and even illustrates Mona Caird's argument that "modern 'Respectability' draws its life-blood from the degradation of womanhood in marriage and in prostitution" (Caird, 1888: 197). Vere's traumatic experience, in which Zouroff's rank and wealth, symbolised by a pearl necklace clasped around her neck, "seemed to her in no way different, save in their beauty, to the chains locked on slave-girls bought for the harem" (Ouida, 1880 [2005]:180), indirectly parallels Caird's argument that "there must be a full understanding and acknowledgement of the obvious right of the woman to possess herself body and soul, to give or withhold herself body and soul exactly as she wills" (Caird, 1888: 198). As such, Ouida rehearses, possibly even inspires, core arguments of New Woman discourse across multiple axes: not only does she denounce the invasion and destruction of female integrity within the patriarchal system which marriage institutionalises, but she also draws particular attention to the conspiracy of silence around sex and marriage in which women – especially mothers – become complicit: "[the] crime of her mother against her seemed the vilest the earth could hold. She herself had not known what she had done when she had consented to give herself in marriage, but her mother had known" (Ouida, 1880 [2005]: 198). Here, she anticipates George Egerton, who in her 1894 short story "Virgin Soil", lets a daughter confront her mother thus: "I simply did not know what I was signing my name to, or what I was vowing to do. [...] You sent me out to fight the biggest battle of a woman's life, the one in which she ought to know every turn of the game, with a white gauze [...] of maiden purity as a shield'" (Egerton, 1894 [2005]: 109, 111).

Moths is remarkably frank in its critique, but also delivers a psychologically insightful portrait of the effects of domestic abuse, especially Vere's isolation, disconnected-ness from society as well as herself, and internalised shame, in such passages as: "[a] great disgust filled her, and seemed to suffocate her with its loathing and its shame. Everything else in her seemed dead, except that one bitter sense of intolerable revulsion. All the revolted pride in her was like a living thing buried under a weight of sand, and speechless, but aghast and burning" (Ouida, 1880 [2005]: 198). Vere once proposes a separation, but Zouroff will not give her up: "[y]ou belong to me, and you must continue to belong to me, nilly-willy. [...] You forget you must pay now and then for your diamonds" (390). Still, she also refuses to "take [her] wrongs into the shame of public courts" and sue for divorce (474), declaring that a "'woman who divorces her husband is a prostitute legalized by a form, that is all'" (422–3). Whereas this is certainly a conservative indictment, Vere's refusal to bare her shame in a public forum acquires some nuance for modern audiences against the backdrop of the #MeToo movement and recent, polarising celebrity court cases centred on domestic abuse, of which the Depp v Heard case might be the most prominent example (Reidy et al, 2023; Nelson, 2024; Robinson and Hiltz, 2024). These cases demonstrate that to 'drag one's wrongs into public' can be a disastrous affair, especially for women, particularly when detailed claims about domestic violence depend on that forum's validation and often incur misogynistic backlash. Ouida's women explore other forms of resistance and agency instead.

Vere, renamed Princess Vera upon her marriage (another way in which her identity is subsumed and re-defined by her husband), reacts to both the shallow social pageantry she despises and her husband's abuse with passivity, silence, and withdrawal. Schaffer even diagnoses her to be "pathologically absent" (2000: 128), but as *Folle-Farine* demonstrates (as discussed in Chapter 2), withdrawal and withholding constitute at least partially viable strategies of resistance for Ouida. This withdrawal is not least symbolised by Vere's pale beauty and her habit of dressing mostly in white. Initially, she wears brown serge or "skirts of olive velvet" (Ouida, 1880 [2005]: 197) that underline her Gothically old-world disposition. Soon after her marriage, however, Vere is continuously encased in "white furs" (203), "a white morning dress with a white mantilla of old Spanish lace" (207), "white velvet [with] sapphires and diamonds in her bright hair" (217), "a cloak of white feathers" (218), in "ermine folds, which clothed her as in snow from head to foot" (273), or "a gown of white wool stuff and a silver girdle of old German work" (321). In addition to her medieval or sensationally Pre-Raphaelite aesthetics mirroring her character, this absence of gaudy colour, rouging, or artifice also denotes purity – but it likewise encodes a "marble-like coldness, and passive indifference" (205) often compared to snow and ice (220). At a costume ball, "[s]he, by a whim of his own, was called the Ice spirit, and diamonds and rock crystals shone all over her from head to foot" (266). Whereas Zouroff so displays her cold beauty as a symbol of his own wealth, to her the dress symbolises the "barrenness and loneliness of her life" (267): "[s]he felt as if all her youth were dying in her; as if she were growing hard, and cruel, and soulless" (265). Society (falsely) interprets her aloofness as a sign that "life spent by the side of that brute has not tainted her" (282), but Zouroff's comment that her pallor will arouse comments about his tyranny if she does not rouge (200) also implies that Vere might wear her whiteness as a silent accusation, refusing to mask her victimhood.

Indeed, in true Ouida fashion, Vere's moral integrity, grave beauty, and silent, scornful pride at times move Zouroff to awe: "[h]e knew the bitterness and the revolt that were in her, yet he saw her serene, cold, mistress of herself. It was not the childlike simplicity that he had once fancied that he loved her for, but it was a courage he respected, a quality he understood. 'One might send her to Siberia and she would change to ice; she would not bend', he thought" (181). This line in particular foreshadows Vere's eventual exile to a Gothic castle in Poland, where the snowy, white barrenness of her life becomes literal and all-encompassing, nearly killing her, but from which she ultimately breaks free when Zouroff shoots the man she loves, the tenor Raphael Corrèze, in a duel. However, even before Vere travels alone to Paris and obtains the annulment of her marriage and a happy ending in an alpine, Romantic idyll far from society, she weaponizes her silence and her absence.

For one, she encounters and buys a painting of a slave market by French Orientalist painter Jean-Leon Gérôme, with Vere remarking: "'did you have to go the East for *that*?'" (260, original emphasis), and hangs it, in silent but symbolic reproach, in her Paris bedroom. She refuses to occupy a charity bazaar booth near actress-*lionne* Croisette, Zouroff's mistress, and refuses to ride with him on the Promenade des Anglais after seeing him there with his other *lionne* mistress, Casse-une-Croûte. Finally, learning that Jeanne de Sonnaz, Femme Galante and also Zouroff's lover, has been sleeping with him in her home, Vere demands that either de Sonnaz or she leave, threatening to implode the unspoken rules of high society charade with a scandal. Not only is this episode an important instance in which Vere finds agency through her refusal to comply, but it also throws into relief the hidden but agreed-upon, gendered rules of female reputation. Zouroff, enraged that Vere defies him, strikes her, seeing in Vere's resistance a double threat to his power and his pleasure. De Sonnaz however, versed in gendered social dynamics like Dolly or Madame Mila, prioritises her reputation and even says: "'[s]he was right enough to insult me; she is more right still when she insults you'" (475). Here emerges some semblance of, if not sympathy, then solidarity in the way women read and leverage social cues because it is the basis of their potential agency. Whereas Vere ultimately learns to navigate at least some of these cues, Yseulte, in *Princess Napraxine*, fails to do so and succumbs to her passivity.

Yseulte de Valogne, like Vere, is an ingénue and a young saint identified with the proud but impoverished old-world aristocracy and is likewise entrapped in what Schaffer calls "Ouidean Gothic": novels in which unspoiled girls are whisked away into doomed marriages by idle aristocrats and consigned to isolation because they reject the world of aristocratic spectacle in which their husbands move (2000: 131). Notably, Pre-Raphaelite aesthetics and a "nightmarish inversion of the domestic ideal" (130) are also staples of sensation fiction, as exemplified by Wilkie Collins's *The Woman in White* (1860), a genre in which Ouida's fiction was formatively embedded. In *Princess Napraxine*, she develops her repertoire of popular genre tropes with irony, and transplants them into the sphere of cosmopolitan high society glamour in what amounts to a dark parody. Otho Othmar, rejected by the object of his adoration, Princess Nadine Napraxine (discussed below), marries Yseulte in an act of both spite and charity. When told that Yseulte will enter a convent for lack of prospects, he laments that her beauty will be shut up there, and so preserves it for the public gaze, "thinking of that supple slender form disguised under the nun's heavy garb, of that abundant hair shorn and falling to the stone floor" (Ouida, 1884 [1886]: 74). Othmar here imagines Yseulte's physical beauty markedly through a male gaze, considering the girl, even unconsciously, to be a public object whose body should be on display. He thinks similarly about the marriage: "'[w]hy could I not meet her and find my heaven in possessing her […]?'" (123). Alain de Vannes, her cousin Aurore's husband, embodies this more clearly. Endeavouring to seduce Yseulte for sport, he muses: "What was the use of occupying a high position if one could not successfully conduct and cover a little intrigue like that?" (125). Knowing his wealth and status will protect him, de Vannes is ready to compromise on a whim a young woman in his care, and "whose position ought in its sheer defencelessness to have been her best safeguard with any man of honour" (125). This episode resonates powerfully after #MeToo, a movement that has demonstrated how such gendered power dynamics prevail in all areas and industries.

Othmar merely marries Yseulte, proving Dolly's adage that "one always marries girls" as a matter of course, and although he is never discourteous, let alone abusive towards Yseulte, whom he exclusively considers and addresses as "my child" (111, 116, 190, 247, 293, 300, 312), his utter indifference to her nonetheless designates her, in Schaffer's analysis, as Gothic victim, and makes him an unwitting Gothic villain (Schaffer, 2000: 140–1). As his young, materially spoiled but emotionally neglected wife wastes away, Othmar is too consumed by his desire for Princess Napraxine to fulfil his meta-narrative duty: "[t]he tragic Gothic ending involves the woman's transformation into a murdered martyr.

Alas, Yseulte discovers that Othmar is just as uninterested in his role as household villain as his role as contented patriarch. Yseulte finds she has to engineer her own death, committing suicide when her insufficiently tyrannous tyrant fails to kill her" (147).

Although Vere and Yseulte share their old-world pride, young saintly demeanour, physical beauty, and unhappy marriages, they also differ in their reactions to the latter. Whereas Vere seems at times frustratingly passive, she also finds ways to rebel through that passivity. She can do so, perhaps because she does not love Zouroff, but Corrèze. Yseulte, on the other hand, adores Othmar, welcomes his caresses, and dies broken-hearted when she learns he loves Princess Napraxine.

Female Aesthetes, Self-Fashioning, and Asexuality

Nadine Napraxine is exceptional even among Ouida heroines as a woman who is at once integrated fully into fashionable society, yet aloof from it, and who wields both independence and power precisely through her strategic withholding. In addition to being considered an aesthete or female dandy (Schaffer, 2000: 141), she may be productively read, I argue, as asexual, and as an evolution from the Femme Galante as well as from *In A Winter City*'s Lady Hilda, who I consider first.

Hilda combines a Pre-Raphaelite fashion sense with curated aesthetic taste: she "was dressed in the height of fashion, i.e., like a mediaeval saint out of a picture; her velvet robe clung close to her, and her gold belt, with its chains and pouch and fittings, would not have disgraced Cellini's own working" (Ouida, 1876 [1892]: 22-3). At other times, she wears "feuille morte velvet slashed with the palest of ambers; a high fraise; sleeves of the renaissance; pointed shoes, and a great many jewels", looking as though "she might have stepped down out of a Giorgione canvas" (23), or dazzles with "the silver fox-furs fringing her dress, [...] the repoussé gold and silver work of her loose girdle, [...] the ends of the old Spanish lace about her throat" (183). Whereas she so prefigures Vere's and Yseulte's mediaevalism, Hilda's is luxurious, meticulously envisioned, and intrinsically entwined with her aesthetic taste and purposeful self-fashioning: "[s]he could theorise about making herself into Greuze or Gainsboro' pictures in serge or dimity; but, in fact, she could not imagine herself without all the black sables and silver fox, the velvets and silks, the diamonds and emeralds, the embroideries and laces that made her a thing which Titian would have worshipped" (18). Like the dandy guardsman who cannot abide sleeping under a false Fragonard (Beerbohm, 1899: 113), Hilda "had so educated her eyes and her taste that a *criant* bit of furniture hurt her as the grating of a false quantity hurts a scholar. She knew the value of greys and creams and lavenders and olive greens and pale sea blues and dead gold and oriental blendings" (Ouida, 1876 [1892]: 9). She is physically repelled by what she deems bad taste.

As such, Hilda embodies not only the advent of the female dandy, but also the conscious engagement with aestheticist ideas. Ouida's status as a female aesthete and even originator of the aesthetic novel has by now been established, and Bristow indeed identifies "the genesis of aesthetic fiction in Ouida's ostentatious romances" of the 1860s (Bristow, 2015: 38; see also Schaffer, 2000; King, 2013a; Hallum, 2015). With her lavishly described interiors and exuberant prose, he argues, Ouida seeks to "transform the Victorian romance into a remarkably innovative – because aesthetically excessive – literary object" in ways that inspired Walter Pater (43, 46–7), whose seminal *Studies in the History of the Renaissance* (1873)[1] in turn influenced Ouida's novels of the

---

[1] In what quickly came to be regarded as a manifesto of Aestheticism, Pater lays out his approach to art as centring on the intense, sensory experiences produced by artworks as the true expression of their essential beauty. The much-quoted line from the study's conclusion formulates the core tenet of aestheticism as follows:

"To burn always with this hard, gem-like flame, to maintain this ecstasy, is success in life" (Pater, 1893 [2020]: 189).

1870s. Indeed, not only did Arthur Symons later remark, "Who of us has not, to a certain extent, admired the bizarre genius of Ouida? Walter Pater did, at one time" (1922: 124), but the *Saturday Review* suggested in its review of *Ariadnê* (1877, the novel that followed *In a Winter City*), that "Ouida can burn, with a hard gem-like flame, with the best of them" ("*Ariadnê*", 1877: 710). As King notes, *Ariadnê* enters into dialogue with Pater's *Renaissance* and its key influences (2013a: 218), so it is not unreasonable to surmise Ouida rehearses some of these ideas in *Winter City*. Not least the Duc de St. Louis' declaration that "Principles – ouf! – they go on and off like a slipper; but good taste is indestructible; it is a compass that never errs" (Ouida, 1876 [1892]: 29) signals a semi-ironic, proto-Wildean de-coupling of morals and art.

Hilda's evolving relationship with art and taste is crucially bound up with her identity and agency, and how they conflict with her budding romantic desire. Married to cover her father's gambling debts and widowed at sixteen, Hilda commands an immense fortune which she will lose by decree upon a second marriage. A woman of intellect and integrity, of fashion and society, if not a Femme Galante like her cousin Mila, Hilda participates in but also wearies of the glamorous cosmopolitan life of Floralia (a thinly disguised Florence). Female independence and agency are here again bound up with mobility and world citizenship: "[i]ndeed your true élégante is raised high above all such small things as nationalities; she floats serenely in an atmosphere far too elevated to be coloured by country; a neutral ground on which the leaders of every civilized land meet far away from all ordinary mortality" (122). Unlike Vere, who is passively whisked away by the currents of fashionable society, Hilda finds it "very pleasant to be mistress of herself – to do absolutely as she chose – to have no earthly creature to consult – to go to bed in Paris and wake up in St. Petersburg if the fancy took her" (144). Her physical mobility also translates into an emotional one, as the "passionless and cold" Hilda remains "altogether indifferent and insensible to all forms of love" (14). Indeed, Hilda is perhaps Ouida's first fully independent woman, unencumbered by dependences on male guardians or fortunes: "I can do exactly as I like; I have everything I want; I can follow all my own whims; I am perfectly happy; why ever should I alter all this? What could any man ever offer me that would be better?" (14–5). Her independence comes under threat from the Duca Della Rocca, who pursues her, first for money, then for love. Hilda, too, falls in love with him, a transformation externalised through her changing relationship with art.

Initially, art "had remained with her rather an intellectual dissipation than a tenderness of sentiment" (59), although, in true aestheticist fashion, she also never feels "sensations and emotions [...] except before a bit of Kronenthal china or a triptych of some old fogey of a painter" (128). In exploring local medieval paintings and frescoes with Della Rocca, however, she begins "to unlearn many of her theories, and to learn very much in emotion and vision, [...]. Her love of Art had after all been a cold, she began to think a poor, passion. [...] Her theories melted away into pure reverence, her philosophies faded into tenderness; new revelations of human life came to her" (153–5). As she falls in love, "[a]rt ceased to be science, and became emotion in her" (155–6). Hilda's new, more personal and intimate relationship with art and beauty rehearses what Dustin Friedman has identified in the context of queer aestheticism, namely that, drawing on Kant and Hegel's aesthetic theory in which "artworks are the sensual expression of humanity's capacity to develop freedom, and that our responses to art cultivate our individuality", art for aesthetes provided a space in and through which identity could be realised independently from social norms (Friedman, 2019: 5). Whereas for the heterosexual Hilda, that non-conformity extends foremost to a fashionable society of spectacle instead of tabooed sexualities, she nonetheless puts into play "the individual's ability to reflect critically on his or her historical moment and test whether it is possible to envision new modes of seeing, forms of thinking, and ways of living" (6). Paradoxically, while such new ways of living here mean a disenchantment with and disentanglement from high society pageantry, Hilda is simultaneously drawn into the conventional marriage plot by her new romantic attachment – a sentiment with which, like most Ouida heroines, she struggles.

At first "impatient of these new weaknesses which haunted her" and "contemptuous, ill at ease, and out of temper with herself and all the world; half ignorant of what moved her, and half unwilling to probe her own emotions further" (Ouida, 1876 [1892]: 203, 206), Hilda resists the emotion and the marriage it heralds: "[t]he freedom and the self-indulgence she had so long enjoyed had become necessary to her as the air she breathed" (302). Indeed, it takes Della Rocca's heartbroken departure and heroic near-death fighting Sicilian bandits before she renounces "the base things of a worldly greatness" in exchange for a simple but happy Florentine idyll (376).

In *Princess Napraxine,* Ouida's ideas about aestheticism and female independence are more fully – and more cynically – developed, particularly in her depiction of Nadine, the titular character. For one, the novel is intensely visual, the descriptions of lavish interiors which Bristow identifies as intrinsically aesthetic in *Under Two Flags* (2015: 41) here translate to an "aesthetic dreamscape" (Schaffer, 2000: 141) and extend to the luscious Riviera settings, where light and colour become especially significant. Settings such as these exerted no little influence on aesthete extraordinaire, Oscar Wilde. Indeed, contemporary reviews of *The Picture of Dorian Gray* (1891) noted that "Mr. Wilde's writing has what is called 'colour', – the quality that forms the main-stay of many of Ouida's works – and it appears in the sensuous descriptions of nature and of the decorations and environments of the artistic life" (Hawthorne, 1890: 413, qtd. in Fitzsimons, 2015: 198–9), and that, while "the style [of *Dorian Gray*] was better than Ouida's popular aesthetic romances the erudition remained nonetheless equal" ("A Study in Puppydom",

1890 [1908]: 9), or called it a "Ouida mixture most grotesque" ("At the Same Game", 1890: 41). Ouida in turn, writing before meeting Wilde in 1886, pays homage to his aestheticism through a character's remark that Nadine's Riviera villa is "a nightmare [that …] would give Oscar Wilde a sick headache" (Ouida, 1884 [1886]: 5). Indeed, Nadine, perpetually surrounding herself with "satin hangings, the Saxe mirrors, […] the little tray of silver and china, the bouquet of narcissus and violets" certainly lives up to her blue china (340).[2] The dressing room in her Paris Hôtel also exemplifies this: "[i]ts furniture was of ivory, like that of the adjoining library, bed-room, and bathroom, and its hangings were of silvery satin embroidered with pale roses and apple-blossoms; Baudry had painted the ceiling with the story of Ædon and Procris: the glass in the windows was milk white, and the floor was covered with white bearskins: the atmosphere was like that of a hothouse, and as odorous" (320). With its curated aesthetic programme, the novel also parallels Joris-Karl Huysmans' *À Rebours* (1884), published the same year.

Notably, *Princess Napraxine* also participates in Aestheticism's and Decadence's Orientalism through Mahmoud, "a little negro who, gorgeous in his dress and immovable as a statue, was often taken by new comers for an enamelled bronze cast by Barbédienne" when attending her boudoir, which is "painted with little doves and flowers; the carpet […] of lambskins; the corners […] filled with azaleas, rose and white, like her gown" (140). He is casually assembled as aesthetic object, yet also retains crucial and volatile

---

[2] In his Oxford days in the 1870s, when he was developing his aesthetic lifestyle against the backdrop of Walter Pater's theories, Oscar Wilde famously quipped that he found it "harder and harder every day to live up to [his] blue china". Costly Chinese porcelain had become a staple of the aesthetic 'House Beautiful', as possibly most notably exemplified by the still-surviving Peacock Room designed by Thomas Jeckyll and James McNeill Whistler in an Anglo-Orientalist style.

agency later in the novel (see Schaffer, 2000: 149). Nadine, who comments that "the East has very much to avenge, and I am not sure that [Western] civilisation would be any great loss" (Ouida, 1884 [1886]: 140), feels a paradoxical kinship.

Nadine, often lounging and smoking, "looking as indolent as a Turkish woman, and as delicate and useless as a painted butterfly" (52), or "dream-like and ethereal" (54), and with her "delicate and acute perception of what was beautiful" (131), has perfected the dandy's pose, but also consciously fashions herself onto an aesthetic object. Introduced as a "hothouse flower" of twenty-three whose dark eyes have "great inquisitiveness, penetration, and sarcasm in them, but were usually only lustrous and languid", Nadine's "delicate appearance [...] sheathed nerves of steel" (4). As with the Femme Galante, her dainty femininity is a carefully constructed front mobilised to navigate social convention, and as with Lady Hilda, her fashion sense expresses her discerning aesthetic taste. Nadine has evolved to a dainty feminine register of pastel colours, fine materials, and aesthetic markers such as "a large peacock fan" (30). She is sumptuously clothed in "skirts of India muslin, Flemish lace, and primrose satin" (10), "a loose gown of embroidered china silk" (339–40), or in "long trailing folds of the primrose-coloured satin [...] falling from her throat to her feet in the long lines that painters love" (166). Indeed, she is "one of those women who naturally make pictures of themselves for every act and in every attitude" (166), and this self-fashioning encapsulates her seductive power: "[t]o exist and to be seen was enough to secure her more victories than she chose to count" (139). Nadine therefore enacts and mobilises the difference between, as Kirby-Jane Hallum notes, "being a beauty and being beautiful" (2015: 81). Like Ice Maiden Vere, who lacks the social beauty's sex appeal, Nadine, who is herself called a Snowflake, consciously cultivates an aloof and untouchable persona, but unlike Vere instrumentalises her status as a beautiful object to her advantage.

Nonetheless, Nadine draws the male gaze and ignites men's desire to possess her: "[s]he drew the ermine over her pretty chin, the diamonds sparkled in her hair; the bouquet of gardenias swung in her hand. The eyes of [one of her suitors,] Geraldine grew very sombre and covetous" (Ouida, 1884 [1886]: 135). Despite being married, Nadine is besieged by suitors, but unlike the Femme Galante does not accept lovers, only admirers. As an object of adoration that encourages attention but prohibits actual engagement with, let alone penetration of, her boundaries, Nadine both frustrates and throws into relief the gendered dynamics which construct women as sexual objects and status symbols to be 'won' through competition with other men.

She can therefore be read as asexual, and her asexuality is productively encoded through, and intrinsic to, her aesthetic self-fashioning. Asexuality, though theorised briefly by nineteenth-century sexologists Richard Krafft-Ebing, Havelock Ellis, and Magnus Hirschfeld, as well as in works such as Lisa Orlando's *Asexual Manifesto* (1972), has occupied a complicated, marginalised position in feminist and queer activism and theory, which have increasingly centred on assertive and positive relationships with sex. Identifying sex as political, queer activism directly responded to the Victorian criminalisation of same-sex desire, while sex-positive feminism sought to counter the historically rooted erasure or repression of female sexuality, seminally identified with the Victorian era by Steven Marcus (*The Other Victorians*, 1964) and Michel Foucault (*The History of Sexuality*, 1978), and challenged by New Woman writers such as Mona Caird, George Egerton, or Kate Chopin. Asexuality, however, which has garnered more attention in recent years, is identified as a lack of sexual attraction to any gender, or a low or absent desire for sexual activity. Asexual, or "ace", in contemporary communities, describes "the individual who, regardless of physical or emotional condition, actual sexual history, and marital status or ideological orientation, seems to *prefer* not to engage in sexual activity" (Johnson, 1977: 97, original emphasis). As such, it fundamentally destabilises and challenges assumptions about gender and sexuality (Cerankowski and Milks, 2010: 655; Przybylo, 2006 [2016]) and necessitates "new intimacy, desire, and kinship structures" (Cerankowski and Milks, 2014: 3), giving rise to new ideas and categories, like 'aromantic' (the lack of romantic desire) or 'demisexual' (sexual attraction preconditioned by an intense emotional bond). To identify asexuality, an orientation primarily defined by absence or abstention, in an era where female sexuality is so often concomitant with silence at best or notions of 'hysteria' at worst, is a complicated endeavour, and present-day notions of asexuality naturally do not map seamlessly onto a nineteenth-century context. Nonetheless, reading Nadine Napraxine through an asexual lens makes visible Ouida's effort to radically disentangle her character from the sexual marketplace by disidentifying with sexuality itself. Whereas radical sexualities have long been associated with flamboyance, indiscretion, and the codex of pride (see Love, 2007) – and may be located in the Femme Galante – Nadine's asexuality also "breaks with normative narratives of identity" and prompts a re-investigation of ideas around identity and sexuality: "[t]he mere process of explaining what asexuality is radically alters the vocabulary necessary for talking about eroticism, sexuality, or sexual orientations" (Chu, 2014: 84, 89). Not least, her asexuality implements Ouida's strategy of withholding oneself from hetero-patriarchal power structures, highlighting how Nadine is constantly pursued by unwanted male sexual energy.

Nadine's wedding night at sixteen "filled her with an inexpressible disgust and melancholy" (Ouida, 1884 [1886]: 20). She declares "that all the caresses and obligations of love [are] odious to her" (20), and that "[l]ove is gross and absurd in its intimacies" (220). Even years later, she remembers with "disgust, [...] the early hours of her own marriage, when all the delicacy and purity of her own girlhood had revolted against the brutality of obligations which she had in her ignorance submitted to accept" and considers herself, like Vere, "as much violated as any slave bought in the market" (243): "[h]er marriage night still remained to her a memory of ineffaceable loathing" (261). Nadine is repulsed by sexual intimacy and considers it a violation of her body and her integrity. For most of the novel she is also aromantic, stating that the existence of love and sorrow "chiefly depends upon the imagination" (39): "'I do not think I shall ever care', she had said, with much accurate knowledge of herself. [...] 'melodramatic passions [...] are absurd. They are out of date. They are tiresome'" (37). Nadine considers love to be either non-existent or of little importance: "'[w]hy will men always talk of love? [...] After all, how little place it takes up in real life!'" (42). She develops a disdain for men and their passions, declaring that "'[a]ll men are tiresome when you have known them a month or so'" or that "'[m]en are certainly unlovely creatures'" (136). Her disinvestment in romance and sex constitutes a power reversal and inversion of contemporary gender notions, re-positioning her as the rational observer and her suitors as victims of their passions:

> "Men are such poor creatures", she thought with scorn. "They are all the slaves of their senses; they have no character; they are only animals. They talk of their souls, but they have got none; and of their constancy, but they are only constant to their own self-indulgence". The contempt of a woman, in whom the senses have never awakened, and for whom all the grosser appetites have no attraction, for those easy consolations which men can find in the mere gratification of those appetites, is very real and very unforgiving. [...] When men spoke of their devotion, they only meant their own passions; if these were denied, they sought refuge in mere physical pleasures, which at all events partially consoled them. She thought of [Othmar] with increasing intolerance. (219–20)

Nadine has no interest in participating in normative, hetero-patriarchal pageantry. She holds prospective lovers at bay (her husband included) and engages in coquetry purely as an exercise in power play. This involves a delicate balancing act in which she primarily deploys her attention, but never actively flirts: "'[n]o man lives, I can assure you, who could say he ever had a word of encouragement from me'" (133). Indeed, disappointed suitors find that they "ha[ve] no right to interrogate her, that no faintest breath of promise from her had ever given [them] title to upbraid her" (168), or that they "could not recall any sign or word or glance which could have justified [them] in the right to call himself her lover" (240). Others believe themselves entitled to her affection and her body because she has been friendly or indulgent (225). This importantly makes visible certain gendered dynamics and assumptions around participation and consent. Men pursue flirtation with and conquest of Nadine as a matter of course, and are frustrated (and baffled) by her passivity, forced to reconsider the boundaries she reinforces: "[i]f the remembrance of her embittered any man's existence it was not her fault; it was the fault of those who would not be content with adoring her as the poor people of this sea-shore adored their Madonna shut away behind a glass case" (42). Nadine constructs herself as an impassive aesthetic object. Anticipating Wilde's aesthetic manifesto, in which "[a]ll art is quite useless" (Wilde, 1890 [2008]: 17), she even states: "'I dare say I am quite useless" (Ouida, 1884 [1886]: 315). Her aromantic asexuality supports her self-fashioning into an aesthetic object, allowing her to protect her physical and emotional integrity.

Still, Nadine's withholding does not foreclose her status as an object of desire and competition: "[n]ow and then some one killed himself because she had laughed. Now and then two people were silly enough to fight a duel about a glove she had dropped, or the right to take her down the stairs at the opera" (23). Whereas Nadine gratifies her sense of power through "the jealousies, feuds, and quarrels which it amused her to excite and foment" (27), the novel also suggests she is desired precisely because she is not available. Othmar, the wealthy financier who has never been denied a whim, covets her because she resists, and is all the more humiliated and enraged because he takes that resistance personally: "[i]f she had rejected him from honour, duty, or love for any other, he would have borne what men have borne a thousand times in silence" (172). Because Nadine has not pledged herself to another man, he feels she should be available to him. That she remains loyal only to herself, especially when he asks her to become his mistress, for him amounts to a cruel betrayal (176).

However, women who 'belong' to a rival are by no means considered to be unattainable by all, but become newly attractive. Yseulte, Othmar's prospective wife, is thus objectified:

> [Now] that she had become the betrothed wife of Othmar, the charm of the forbidden fruit had come to her; she had suddenly become an object of interest in his sight; he was never tired of finding out her beauties, he was absorbed in studying the shape of her throat, the colour of her hair, the whiteness of her shoulders, [...]. To know that she was about to belong to another man, gave her all at once importance, enchantment, and desirability in his sight. (191)

The novel here highlights male homosocial rivalry and how it shapes women's perception in the sexual marketplace, but women, as the discussion of Dolly's vexed relationship with her daughter has shown, are no less in competition with one another. For example, when Yseulte is pursued by de Vannes and receives gifts from Othmar, that is receives attention from both men, Aurore de Vannes believes her ward is actively and deliberately leading them on: "'[you] begin well! Othmar and my husband! [...] I would never have believed you such a cunning little cat!" (160).

In the face of such skewered sexual politics, Nadine cultivates her enigmatic aloofness through epigrams that deflect the male gaze (Schaffer, 2003: 221). Indeed, Alice Meynell in 1895 recalled that the then-fashionable epigram originated in Ouida's "decorated pages" (4). Epigrams first appear in Ouida's play *Afternoon* (1883) (which features an aesthetic collector named Aldred Dorian), where she deploys epigrams as "women's way of expressing aestheticism that defends them against objectification" (Schaffer, 2000: 135): "[t]he eyes of Othmar dwelt on her now yearningly, sombrely, wistfully. 'It is of no use. [...] If you wish for men who can, whilst they adore you, sit and drink chocolate and talk epigrams, seek elsewhere; I am not one of them'" (Ouida, 1884 [1886]: 141). Like Lord Henry Wotton in *The Picture of Dorian Gray*, Nadine "would sacrifice [her] own life to an epigram" (Ouida, 1885 [1893]: 26), and, like the imperiously witty dames of Wilde's works she inspired (Schaffer, 2003: 222–4), Ouida's heroines use aesthetic banter to retain (verbal) power. In both Ouida's and Wilde's novel, this trait irritates men: "'[s]he is the only woman who makes me irritable,' the courtly Gervase Melville had once said of [Ouida's Nadine], and he might have said also, 'the only woman who reduces me to silence'" (Ouida, 1884 [1886]: 259), while Wilde's Lord Henry complains of Gladys, Duchess of Monmouth: "her clever tongue gets on one's nerves" (Wilde, 1890 [2008]: 164).

Wit and intelligence also inform Nadine's asexuality: "'[t]hat bloodless *mondaine*, that ethereal coquette", remarks Othmar's uncle, "will never give birth to anything save an epigram'" (Ouida, 1885 [1893]: 29). Echoing today's 'aces' theoretical approach to passion, Nadine may "dissect and weigh [her lovers'] emotions with perfect accuracy and philosophise upon them with a clearness of understanding" (Ouida, 1884 [1886]: 136). Nadine therefore contemplates social drama with the "vague expectation and gratification of a spectator at a theatre" (37), believing that "[l]ove is like all other fine arts – it should be treated scientifically" (215). Male passion and frustration, especially, become the subject of aesthetic study to her, enacting the hedonistic quest for new sensations of a Des Esseintes or Dorian Gray through a female aesthete's lens: "[a]gain and again she had recalled the accents of his voice, the sombre fire and pathetic entreaty of his eyes; they had not moved her at the time to anything more than the vague artistic pleasure which she would have taken in any emotion admirably rendered in art or on the stage" (183). Emotionally divested, she contemplates men's desires as artistic tableaux: "'[h]ow well he looks like that!' she thought. 'Most men grow red when they are so angry, but he grows like marble, and his eyes burn – there are great tears in them – he looks like Mounet-Sully as Hippolytus'" (168–9). She becomes an aesthete in her own right, objectifying men aesthetically, not sexually. Her ability to do so hinges on her non-conforming, queer identity, that is her divestment from sexuality, because 'the aesthetic' to her extends to social, gendered dynamics. In a way, she enacts Friedman's claim that, by "extending and transforming Hegel's belief that art serves as the sensual reflection of transcendent human freedom, queer aestheticism defined the aesthetic itself as the realm where one's autonomy could be realized in an oppressive social world", and "that queerness can be an advantage intellectually, creatively, and ethically, not in spite of but because of social opposition toward nonnormative desires, eliciting a sense of freedom perhaps unattainable by those who are never forced to confront their own social abjection" (2019: 6–7). Her asexuality allows Nadine to observe and exploit gender dynamics and maintain her independence and social power, at least for a while.

Ultimately, however, like Hilda, she is implicated in those dynamics, falling at least partially in love with Othmar "with a restless and unwilling tenderness" (Ouida, 1884 [1886]: 390). Eventually unable to escape the marriage plot, she nonetheless muses on her wedding day to Othmar (after her first husband has died in a duel), "with her old sceptical wonder at the ardour and the follies of men", that "'[if] one could only feel all that rapture which he feels, how charming life would be!'" (422), and in *Othmar* (1885), the sequel to *Princess Napraxine*, she muses:

"[w]hat a pity to have married him! It had been commonplace, banal, stupid – anybody would have done it. There had been a complete absence of originality in such a conclusion to their story" (Ouida, 1885 [1893]: 40). Marriage remains paradoxically unavoidable because there is no (sanctioned) alternative. It both entraps and empowers women, and whether they attain agency or not depends on their willingness to play the system. Indeed, in *Princess Napraxine*, marriage is not the Gothic trauma of *Moths*, not least because Nadine finds that "[n]othing is so easy to manage as a man, if you only begin in the right way with him […] it is just like a horse" (Ouida, 1884 [1886]: 334). Ouida here most clearly voices her view of the institution as a "legal transaction" and "social duty" decoupled from personal pleasure or sentiment, a "means to continue a race, so that it legally can continue to transmit property" (98). Her stance somewhat anticipates Caird's comment about spouses being "expected to go about perpetually together, as if they were a pair of carriage-horses; […] generally getting in one another's way" (1888: 196–7) when she writes: "[b]ut it is an altogether illogical idea, binding down two strangers side by side for ever, and it cannot be said to work well. It keeps property together, that is all; so I suppose it is good for the world; but certainly individuals suffer for it more than perhaps property is worth" (Ouida, 1884 [1886]: 21). Yet, marriage is inescapable, especially for young women as the rite of passage which marks the transition to womanhood, with the social access that entails:

> "Oh, my friend, why do girls always marry?" [Nadine] said, indifferently. "Because the marriage is there; because the families have arranged it; because one does not know; because one wishes for freedom, for jewels, for the world; because one does not care to be a *fillette*, chaperoned at every step. There are many reasons that make one marry: it is the thing to do – everyone does it; when a girl sees the young married women, she sees them flirted with, sought,

monopolising everything; it is like standing behind a shut door and hearing people laughing and singing on the other side, while you cannot get to them". (142)

Once again, marriage constitutes the only sustainable way of accessing the Ouidean cosmopolitan world of spectacle and pleasure, even if it is only a charade. Indeed, even though Nadine despises her husband, she declines to run away with Othmar not because she values her marriage, but because it safeguards the social power she prizes above everything.

Ultimately, Nadine is an ambiguous figure. Like the Femme Galante, she exploits the sexual marketplace to her advantage, but unlike Laura Pearl, does not seek power and riches because she already wields them. At once desirably feminine and stoically intelligent, she leverages her sexual capital as a beautiful object while also meticulously reinforcing her aloof integrity. As a noble, proud, and principled female dandy and aesthete "of supreme generosity, and a capacity [...] for heroic courage" (25), she echoes Bertie Cecil, and yet lacks all empathy in her aesthetic observation of social drama. She manipulates men in ways that both challenge and reverse the usual power dynamics and carefully maintains her passivity, but nonetheless both men and women lay the disastrous outcomes of male passion at her door, which Nadine both regrets and resents. Her friend Lady Brancepeth, for example, repeatedly condemns her particular kind of coquetry as especially "subtle, arrogant, cold, and cruel" (134), unforgivable because it "is the exercise of a merciless power which is as chill as a vivisector's attitude before his victim" (133). Whereas this certainly parallels Nadine's divested manipulation, Lady Brancepeth's accusations also reveal enduring gendered dynamics when she blames Nadine for essentially, in today's register, 'leading men on': "[y]ou had admitted him into the honour of a certain intimacy, which, in his blundering English way, he fancied meant all kinds of eventualities that it did not mean. No doubt his delusion was of his own creating, and of course he ought to have been prepared for his dismissal" (342). Despite the male suitor's over-interpreting their relationship with Nadine, it is her responsibility to decisively say no, because otherwise the assumption is that she remains 'in play'. Nadine's suitors interpret her friendly or indifferent attention as an invitation or consent to more, even though she has never voiced it. This balancing act encodes her power but also illustrates that her suitors believe themselves in some fundamental way entitled to her and that her aesthetic self-fashioning provides a defence through which she may channel and deflect their objectification of her. Curiously Ouida, never shy to condemn a female character through misogynist commentary, lets Nadine remain ambivalent.

Double Standards

Of Ouida's 1889 novel *Guilderoy*, Wilde remarked: "we must admit that we have a faint suspicion that Ouida has told it to us before" (Wilde, 1889: 3), but it also implements new, important variations on the marriage theme. While echoing previously explored configurations, including *Wanda* (1883; see Jordan, 1995: 98; Schroeder and Holt, 2008: 196–205), the story indicates that, for Ouida, the matter of marriage and female autonomy demanded continuous working through. She chronicles with psychological insight the failure of a marriage and the heroine Gladys' vocal resistance against her relegation to neglected wife in the face of male patronisation. With its large proportion of dialogue, *Guilderoy* is heavily argumentative.

Guilderoy, temporarily disenchanted with his Femme Galante lover, the Duchess of Soria, resolves to marry ingénue Gladys – and besieges her father John Vernon until the latter gives in – in an attempt to satisfy a constructed ideal of purity, composed of "a thousand qualities from women which he had never found in them; he had wanted at once passion and purity, high spirit and submission, romance and ignorance of all the emotions which make up romance" (Ouida, 1889: I, 84). No young woman can live up to such a composite and contradictory feminine ideal, and when the timid, unworldly Gladys fails to shed her ignorance of the world or grow into her sensuality, Guilderoy becomes bored, proving right Vernon's objections about marriage. "'[you] cannot'", he argues, 'prevent the divergence of character, the satiety of habit, the destruction of illusions, the growth of new passions – all which is inevitable in human nature, and in utter defiance of which marriage, the supreme idiocy of social laws, has made eternal'" (I, 103). From the outset, marriage is considered a failed institution, and both Guilderoy and Gladys illustrate at every turn why. Indeed, Guilderoy repeats Ouida's credo from *Princess Napraxine*, saying that marriage is merely "'a community of interests; a union of externals: a method of continuing the race and of consolidating property; it is not a life-long worship of Eros'" (II: 58). Notably, love is the pretext under which he woos Gladys, yet when he fails to fulfil his promise, he blames her for misunderstanding what marriage is.

Indeed, the marriage is markedly unequally disastrous for both parties: Guilderoy leaves to travel across Europe and reunite with Soria, while Gladys (who loves him) is stuck in his house, one more forgotten commodity among many. Gladys remarks: "'[he] had paid a great price for me and he regretted the price – just as he does again and again when he bids for a picture at Christie's, or the Hôtel Drouot'" (Ouida, 1889: II, 22). The novel therefore echoes Zouroff's transactional understanding of erotics as well as Nadine's comment that "'men [...] marry just as they buy a cane; they put the cane in the stand; it is bought and it cannot move; they are sure it will always be there'" (Ouida, 1884 [1886]: 164). Guilderoy has no interest in Gladys' intellect or her voice: "[h]e had no patience to discuss her opinions; he could not see why she should have any. This disdainful relegation of her to an utterly inferior place in intelligence, [...] gave her a passionate sense of offence, which was too deep to be easily expressed" (I, 205). Her husband, it is suggested, might have softened had she been "more facile, more pliant, more easily moulded to what he required" (II, 59). Gladys however refuses to be immobile, silent, and pliable, instead voicing her dissatisfaction. She reminds him that he pursued her, disdains his extramarital affairs, and actively searches for ways to regain her autonomy and her injured pride. Her exploration of the extremely limited and stigmatised possibilities open to her elicits a barrage of protest from her male guardians: her father and Guilderoy's cousin, Lord Aubrey.

Early on, when Gladys asks, "'shall I ever know if he really loves me?'", Vernon is "startled and dismayed" to see the marriage so soon imperilled, but nonetheless responds: "'[c]an you doubt it, dear? [...] I think you do Lord Guilderoy injustice and dishonour by your doubt'" (I, 174). Here emerges the novel's frustrating pattern: anxious to protect Gladys from the inevitable unhappiness she already experiences, Vernon lies to her, endeavours to (using a modern term) gaslight or brainwash her into (deluded) contentment, and berates her for being unhappy in the first place, when she has in fact accurately judged the relationship in which she is trapped. Like the mothers whose silence about sex becomes betrayal, Vernon implicates himself in a conspiracy against his daughter. Marriage, Ouida suggests, depends on women's ignorance and self-denial. When Gladys believes herself justified in wanting to leave, stating that, since Guilderoy violated his marriage vows, she should not be beholden to hers, Vernon claims that "'the cases are not parallel'", and that "'true womanhood [is] lacking in you, my dear'". To her question, "'[i]s true womanhood abject slavishness?'", he responds: "'[i]t is infinite abnegation of self'" (I, 254). So emerges a concurrent motif, namely that of men explaining womanhood to Gladys, exercising their *Deutungshoheit* (the power to define) to discursively re-inscribe the credo that "'the infidelities of the passions and the waywardness of the instincts are not sins so dark as to be unpardonable; they are, indeed, faults almost inseparable from manhood [...] which I think every woman should force herself to overlook'" (II, 182) – or, in short, that 'boys will be boys'. Implied here is also the recurrent idea that women make themselves unhappy because they expect from men what men cannot give: loyalty, attention, compassion. Remarkably, even contemporary reviews such as the *Athenaeum*'s commented that "Guilderoy and his relatives –including, we regret to say his father-in-law, [...] should have known better" ("Novels of the Week", 1889: 694). Notably, Ouida's narrator abstains from taking sides, leaving the debate open and ambiguous.

It pays to recount Glady's arguments and their counter. She considers it her right to refuse Guilderoy his conjugal rights: "[t]he moment that he has ceased to love me, he has set me free from all such obligations" (Ouida, 1889: II, 25). Vernon considers this rash and dishonourable, and counsels her to win her husband back. When, after her father's death, Gladys seeks separation and moves out, Lord Aubrey, despite agreeing that Guilderoy is "'beyond all defence'", declares: "'[y]ou have done most unwisely'" and "'I regret and blame your actions'" (II, 161, 163). Gladys defends herself:

> I cannot help it if his passions are so made that they do not last a year [...]. It is not my fault if he married me as he would buy a *cocotte*, and tired of me as he would tire of her. I have released him as far as I can possibly release him until death takes me. I will not eat of his bread, or live under his roof. I will not wear a gown he paid for, nor a ring he purchased. (II, 164)

Aubrey explains that society will believe she lives with another man and blame her for neither seeking divorce nor going "on her usual routine as if she saw nothing, which is what women who are gentlewomen do all their lives long" (II, 190). Like most Ouida heroines, however, Gladys refuses to acquiesce to high society's pageantry, becoming stubbornly unruly through her withdrawal, and like them, she lives by her own codex of pride and integrity:

"'[m]y own conscience is enough for me. And surely you forget; the world knows – it cannot choose but know – that Lord Guilderoy finds his happiness elsewhere'" (II, 166). Of course, such knowledge does not alter whom society blames. Nonetheless, Gladys vocally exposes gendered double standards, and so "effectively expresses the paradox of the female dilemma in marriage – the conflict between traditional expectations of devotion and personal desires for independence and self-expression" (Schroeder and Holt, 2008: 224).

In the end, Guilderoy returns, seeking restoration of his male power which Gladys' return would signify: "even the faithless husband finds himself the baffled dupe of cultural forces he has not fully understood" (226). Whereas Gladys eventually submits to conventions, she no longer loves him, and her pride shames Guilderoy, who finally understands what he has carelessly forfeited: "'[m]y poor child, believe me at least in this, – from my heart I beseech you to pardon me the mad caprice in which I bound your fate to mine'" (Ouida, 1889: II, 302). By keeping her marriage vows but withholding her affection, Gladys maintains her integrity, but even Guilderoy's acceptance of his guilt is only a pyrrhic victory: both are now condemned to their failed marriage. Once again, Ouida's characters fail to escape the marriage plot in which women must either suffer in silence and continue to "indulge" men's aberrant passions (II; 301), or become corrupted socialites gratifying only their own pleasure. They have no honourable or socially sanctioned way to re-attain independence, and when seeking alternatives to their failed marriages, must struggle against what amounts to a vocal and incessant brainwashing by the (male) guardians who shore up patriarchal behaviours, social norms and institutions.

Conclusion: Life Imitates Art

A decade after Ouida's Nadine Napraxine, Thomas Hardy's Sue Bridehead configured the New Woman as an independent, intellectual woman whose potential and self-fulfilment are hampered by male desires. Sue, while at first fiercely celibate in potentially asexual ways and unwilling to compromise her integrity, is ultimately undone by marriage, sex, and children (see Linde, 2012). As authors such as Hardy, or the previously discussed Egerton, exemplify, sexual intimacy, especially when legally demanded under marriage law, became a battleground of New Woman discourse in which female characters (often unsuccessfully) stake out new borderlands to protect the integrity of their selves and bodies in attempts to reclaim their desires without yielding to male power. They recognised sex as encapsulating the invasion of female integrity in body, mind, legal status, and economic power. In addition, they identified in the conspiratorial silence around sex, the ways in which parents become complicit, and how women's lack of articulation of their desires upholds male dominance.

Ouida, however, in the fifteen years before Hardy's *Jude the Obscure* (1895), and indeed her rejection of the New Woman as a viable political figure in 1894, engaged continually and in complex ways with exactly such key issues and ideas. Between *In A Winter City* and *Guilderoy*, her novels repeatedly play through different variations of similar conundrums – like later New Woman novelists, she struggled to resolve the problems she identified (Beller, 2020: 38). Finally allowing male characters to be unfavourably implicated, she identified marriage as a microcosm of patriarchal power structures, and in it sex simultaneously as a traumatic initiation into womanhood, a signifier of dependency and humiliation, a silence in which men and women fail to connect, and something that, if wholly rejected, may temporarily constitute a unique kind of liberty. Putting into play what today may be identified as aromantic asexuality to decouple her heroine from the sexual marketplace, Ouida capitalises on the notion that such a divestment forces us to "take new approaches not only to the study of sex, sexuality, and desire, but also to romanticism, intimacy, and monogamy" (Chu, 2014: 93). This is also exemplified by her long-standing and characteristic erosion of marriage as a viable institution: all marriages, Schaffer notes, "are necessarily broken marriages, all houses the sites of distaste and distrust. [...] [F]ailure of the domestic idyll becomes material for witticisms. [...] Not only did [Ouida's novels] not believe in Victorian domesticity, but they did not even believe the loss of domesticity was tragic" (2000: 146). Still, as her novels repeatedly illustrate, marriage is also ultimately inescapable, whether through ambitious mothers, male desire, or romantic love. Nonetheless, Ouida explored various strategies through which her female characters seek to resist, challenge, or escape their commodification through the marriage market, and attain degrees of independence, many of which take the form of withholding or withdrawal.

Other strategies are purposeful self-fashioning and speaking back through epigram, a trope Ouida cultivated before other aesthetes: "Ouida and Wilde both used epigrams to puncture bourgeois preferences for duty, work, morality, and earnestness, and to offer a new gospel of pleasure, passions, and unconventional modes of self-fulfillment" (Schaffer, 2002: 222–3). Moreover, aesthetic mindsets and behaviours fundamentally inform Nadine's ability to maintain integrity and power, indeed to divest herself from patriarchal sexual power, and are thus entwined with notions about female self-hood, especially one imperilled by or externalised through marriage. For Hilda and Nadine, and even Vere, relationships with art and fashion articulate female relationships with the self, desire, and dominant social norms.

That Ouida considered such aesthetic perspectives essential in asserting an individual identity is also illustrated by the aesthetic lifestyle she cultivated for herself. She let her long blonde hair fall openly across her back, wore Worth gowns made to her specifications in white satin or black velvet, preferred bejewelled slippers, prized sables and laces, and reportedly adopted the costume of the heroine she was currently writing about (see Yates, 1879: 246; Robinson, 1894: 5; Lee, 1914: 82–3; Ffrench, 1938: 73–4). She surrounded herself with expensive flowers, wrote her novels in purple ink on blue paper either in her candle-filled Langham suite with the black velvet curtains drawn, or in her Florentine villa (which, Yates claimed, would have delighted Ruskin), filled with Louis XV furniture and a Venetian writing desk (Yates, 1879: 241–2; Ffrench, 1938: 67, 106; Bigland, 1951: 64–5). One correspondent described Villa Farinola as "truly picturesque": much like Della Rocca's villa in *Winter City*, its "walls are painted with exquisite old Italian frescoes, and inlaid tables laden with pots of flowers (lilies and hyacinths abounding) line the walls" (Robinson, 1894: 5). Ouida also collected Italian art and priceless Capo di Monte china (Schaffer, 2003: 213), and, like many of her heroines, drove around in an extravagant carriage: hers was lined with gold brocade, the horses harnessed with black-and-silver trappings (Robinson, 1894: 5). As such, she lived out many of her heroines' strategic self-fashionings which she explored through her fiction: "Ouida lived", observed W. H. Mallock, "largely in a world of her own creation" (1920: 124).

Her fiction, however, was more than escapism: it also rehearsed important ideas and issues later identified not only with aesthetic literary works but also New Woman discourse. Ouida's aesthetic register evolves and changes from Hilda's Pre-Raphaelite mediaevalism associated with sensation fiction and later relegated to Gothic heroines like Vere and Yseulte, towards the fashionable dandy-aestheticism of Pater, Huysmans, and Wilde. Her heroines, meanwhile, seem at first to occupy a spectrum between independent socialite and traumatised victim, but also a recombination of the two: dandy *femme fatale* Nadine is haunted by her marriage night, whereas Vere and Gladys explore avenues of silent or vocal resistance; silent Vere is granted escape while the outspoken Gladys bows to convention. Ultimately, Ouida's popular fiction constituted not only a space in and through which such conundrums could be explored in variations without alienating a loyal readership but also a rich tapestry of ideas and tropes in which later, dominant *fin-de-siècle* discourses such as aestheticism and the New Woman were strongly rooted.

CHAPTER 5

The Artist as Critic: Italy, Decadence, and the Politics of Beauty

Introduction: With Great Genius Comes Great Responsibility

"The two qualities, I think, which underlie the best of Ouida's work", to recall Street's verdict, are "a genuine and passionate love of beauty, as she conceives it, and a genuine and passionate hatred of injustice and oppression" (1895: 175). Beauty and aesthetics were central to Ouida's libertarian ethos: they could encode or transform relationships between self and world, or be wielded purposefully in defiant female self-fashioning, but, as Street's conclusion suggests, and this chapter interrogates, they were also fundamentally and increasingly political as antitheses to the capitalist, industrialist, imperialist modernity Ouida despised.

Never shy to express her opinions, she nonetheless cultivated her privacy behind her deliberately mysterious and genderless pseudonym, despite her growing celebrity: "[t]he public has no business with what my name is or is not", she wrote to Tauchnitz in 1882, "Ouida is all they have a right to know" (Lee, 1914: 18). Her art, she felt, should speak for itself, and was as such inseparable from her self-understanding, especially as a woman "claiming the typically masculine role of public intellectual and artist" (Moore, 2011: 484). Indeed, as King argues, her novels of the 1870s centre on artist figures and interrogate art's relationship to the market, its place and function in society, and its gendered dimensions (2013a; 212). *Pascarèl* (1874), her first novel set and written in Italy, re-frames art as socially purposeful in the context of the Risorgimento, but as a novel narrated by the clever and outspoken donzellina[1], also challenges the notion of men as public faces for art (see King, 2009). In *Friendship* (1878), the thinly disguised *roman à clef* satirising the semi-public affair between Ouida's beloved Marchese della Stufa and the married Janet Ross, which understandably caused no little scandals in her Florentine circles, Ouida appears as venerated artist Étoile. Like Ouida, one surmises, Étoile grapples with celebrity and society's sexual hypocrisy (Dubuisson, 2021), which she refuses to condone, instead defying conventions by following her own moral standards. Like Ouida, she also produces "art that is inspired by her ability to see the world as others cannot" (Moore, 2011: 492). *Ariadnê* (1877), a "proper Künstlerroman" that won her admiration as the serious artist which she already saw herself to be (King, 2013a: 212), enters into a long discussion with Paterian aesthetics and negotiates the position of the female artist. Here, Ouida's conception of feminine genius is most clearly asserted and realised as an exception to gendered and social taxonomies. Indeed, as Pykett points out, Ouida conceived of "men and women of genius" as a "third sex which is above the laws of the multitude" (Ouida, 1894 [1895]b: 220; Pykett, 2013: 162). In her fiction, such men and women are serenely disconnected from the pervasive society of spectacle, or configured as anomalies in their time, no doubt reflecting Ouida's own self-perception (Moore, 2011: 484).

The Ouidean genius, so positioned outside the normative world, is endowed with unique capacities for independent thought, insight, and understanding, which in turn obliges them to exercise

---

[1] The novel's first-person narrator is addressed as 'donzellina', a diminutive of 'donzella', meaning 'maiden'.

it without fear of judgement: such independence, she postulates, "should be the attitude of all royalty, whether that of the king, the hero, or the genius" (Ouida, 1887 [1895]: 346). Similarly asserting in *Ariadnê* that "genius is nobility, and, like nobility, is obligation" (Ouida, 1877 [1891]: 103), she crafts for herself the female genius persona as an artist-aristocrat and social activist (King 2013a: 222). As a result, as King asserts, she configures "art as ethical utility", a "political, altruistic, view and practice where the artwork's impact upon society was more important than personal financial gain" (209) and a "political intervention beyond economic exchange" (King, 2009: 78). This view naturally extended to the publishing industry which, she felt, increasingly commodified literature for the mass market without "regard for the dignity and delicacy of art", indeed treating "authors precisely as the Chicago killing and salting establishments treat the pig; the author, like the pigs, is purchased, shot through a tube, and delivered in the shape of a wet sheet" (Ouida, 1891: 3). However, the "older, more artisanal and humane relations" (King, 2013c: 28–9) between authors and publishers she desired existed only between her and Tauchnitz (see Esser, forthcoming [2024]; Law, 2013). Indeed, in 1892, Heinemann & Balestier acquired her novel *The Tower of Taddeo* for the American market and misrepresented the fact they sought to establish an 'English Library' in competition with Tauchnitz – a ploy to whose "unfair, secretive, and perfidious means" she publicly objected (qtd. in St. John, 1990: 23). Internally, Heinemann indicted her behaviour as unladylike with the following, sexist comment: "[i]t's a sweet sight to see a woman doing business as a man and *then* claiming all the advantages of the sex" (qtd. in St. John, 1990: 24, original emphasis). Ouida's altruistic ideals, centred on "passion, sympathy, and moral imperative" (King, 2013a: 219), not only fell prey to the same commercial interests she condemned but remained entangled in gendered perceptions.

In accordance with her genius persona, Ouida was undeterred by criticism. Italy, her adopted home, became not only the canvas for art-commerce relationships but also the catalyst for her politics. From *Pascarèl,* commissioned for a Florentine magazine and espousing the Risorgimento's cause (see King, 2009), to *A Village Commune* (1881), the tale of a village slowly ruined by a corrupt government official that incurred outrage and even an assassination attempt on her (Lee, 1914: 111), to her last novel *Helianthus* (1908), Ouida deployed Italy as the prism through which the failures of modernity could be diagnosed. It became, as Richard Ambrosini remarks, "a model of imperilled beauty [... in which she] found the required terms for critiquing a modernity that she read as a process of cultural homogenization which exported all that she despised in an imperial Britain that she had come to believe had lost its soul" (165). Taking up the position of expert ex-pat in Italy to comment, through the many non-fiction essays she published from 1882 onwards (to supplement her ailing finances) on politics and cultural developments in Britain, France, Germany, Italy, and the US, Ouida also configures the artist-aristocrat genius (much like the jet-setting Femme Galante) as decidedly cosmopolitan. Her hybrid position exemplifies how "the cosmopolitan identity defamiliarizes and ultimately invalidates traditional categories of perception rooted in the idea of belonging" (Evangelista, 2021: 15). Indeed, in her essay on her friend Wilfred Scawen Blunt, a fellow "standard-bearer of all lost causes", she declares: "'[c]ountry' is but a restricted boundary for whoever has the vision which sees beyond the ordinary range of men. To the true poet his native land lies wherever what is beautiful can be beloved, or that which is sorrowful needs solace" (Ouida, 1900c: 144, 147). As W. H. Mallock, to whom she dedicated her first essay collection, *Views and Opinions* (1895), remarks, she "depicted herself to herself as a personage of European influence" (1920: 124).

Indeed, in her non-fiction, Ouida rallied against the Boer War (1899), Italy's move into Africa (1895–96), the German Kaiser, Joseph Chamberlain, and the Italian Prime Minister,

Francesco Crispi, as well as science, vivisection, urbanisation, state intervention, and many other symptoms of what she considered a corrupting modernity. As Schroeder and Holt note, in Ouida's novels of the 1890s, the programmatic issues identified across her work become "symptoms of a comprehensive, irresolvable cultural malaise that Ouida envisions as ultimately smothering all capacity for change" and so affiliate her with *fin-de-siècle* decadence in attitude if not in style (2008: 229–30). In discussing how Ouida's self-perception as cosmopolitan artist-genius shapes her later fiction, this chapter examines how she conceptualises the female artist in *Ariadnê*, especially in the context of aesthetic and decadent gendered frameworks, before investigating Ouida's vocally anti-modern, anti-imperialist, anti-capitalist, last three novels *The Massarenes* (1897), *The Waters of Edera* (1900) and the unfinished *Helianthus* (1908). These novels enact the political views laid out in her non-fiction, and *Helianthus*, hitherto virtually untouched by scholarship, translates, I argue, an increasingly nationalistic Europe into a semi-Ruritanian satire, in which the major cultural forces historians have identified as contributing to the First World War, as well as the spectre of Italian fascism, may be identified. Encapsulating what amounts to Ouida's political manifesto against "the tyranny of narrow minds" (Ouida, 1881: 863), the novel not only chronicles the death of beauty under oppressive forces but also illustrates how Ouida's artistic positioning (re-)frames the role of (popular) fiction as a powerful political agent in its own right.

Pygmalion Redux

Ariadnê not only marks a shift in Ouida's artistic self-conception (King, 2011b), but also most closely and deliberately engages with Paterian aestheticism, the nature of art, the role of the artist, and a female artist identity. It was lauded as Ouida's most artistic novel, described by reviewers as "on an altogether loftier level than anything previously attempted by the author": "[i]t is as a work of art that *Ariadnê* must be judged" (qtd. in Jordan, 2011a:

42). Indeed, as King discusses at length, the novel enters into dialogue with the aesthetic theories of Heine and Winkelmann, cornerstones of Pater's *Renaissance* (2013a), and plays out their rediscovery of antiquity through the narrator Crispin (an alias, we learn, of Rufo Quintilio, exiled from Rome in his youth by the Church for republican rebellion). Crispin continuously conjures ancient Rome, which comes to manifest as a constant co-presence in the present city, and so enacts the decadent practise of collecting and archiving: Rome is viscerally presented as a living archive and artistic dreamscape. The narrator's incessant myth-making also applies to Giojà, the novel's hybrid, half-Jewish heroine, whom Crispin perceives as emerging from a vision of Ariadne he experiences at the Villa Borghese. She not only manifests from a sculpture, evoking the Pygmalion myth, but is consistently framed through the Ariadne myth by Crispin that it becomes a self-fulfilling prophecy: Giojà, a promising artist genius, is abandoned and undone by the man she loves. Alongside this exploration of women as artists in their own right, Ouida juxtaposes Maryx and Hilarion, Giojà's suitors, as opposing incarnations of both masculinity and artistic nature.

The vigorous, dashing, insouciant, womanising, and selfish Hilarion is a celebrated poet and an echo of *Folle-Farine*'s Arslan (see chapter 2). Crispin first meets him during a plague in Paris, disposing without sympathy of his companion, a dying *lionne*, whom he describes as "a pretty animal, with a sleek skin and an insatiable appetite" (Ouida, 1877 [1891]: 73), and whose demise seems somewhat to anticipate that of Zola's Nana. Hilarion embodies, not the disappointed idealism or frustrated romanticism with which Ouida identifies, but instead the ennui of over-indulgence:

> Life had been always smooth for Hilarion, and though the sadness in him was real and not assumed, it was that more selfish sadness which takes its rise from fatigue at the

insufficiency of any pleasure or passion to long enchant or reign. [...] Half his sadness was discontent, and the other satiety; but this kind of sadness is widely different from the noble and passionate grief which protests against the illimitable torture of all creation and the terrible silence of the Creator. It is a melancholy that is morbid rather than majestic, – the morbidness that has eaten into the whole tenor of modern life. (77–8)

As the "chosen prophet" of the modern age, "restless and dissatisfied" despite being courted, celebrated, loved, and overall privileged, Hilarion seems to satirise certain aesthetic and decadent characteristics, such as the constant search for new pleasures, which Ouida posits as superficial and self-indulgent, and also an affected morbidity that might call up the air of melancholy and malaise of Baudelaire's poetry: "[a]nd their passionate protest of pain would be grand in its very hopelessness, only that it is spoiled by being too often rather querulousness than despair" (78).

It is not entirely clear whether Ouida's snide commentary is indeed aimed at the French decadence of Charles Baudelaire, whose influence she would not least have encountered through her salon guest and his avid follower, Charles Algernon Swinburne. But Hilarion's framing of Lilas, the dead *lionne*, as "a pretty cat, a little sleek beast of prey [...] but not a woman", and a bloodsucker (73) certainly calls up Baudelaire's (in)famous misogyny, expressed towards his muses (Haitian-born actress and dancer Jeane Duval and *lionne* and salon-hostess Apollonie Sabatier) in the vampire-women of *Les Fleurs du Mal* (1857), and through the conception of woman as "graceful animal" or "a kind of idol, stupid perhaps, but dazzling and bewitching" in *The Painter of Modern Life* (Baudelaire, 1863 [1964]: 30). Indeed, Hilarion seduces (and then abandons) Giojà, as he freely admits, out of childlike defiance of Crispin's guardianship, Maryx's feelings, and Giojà's own, independent genius. Hilarion explains that when he "'saw that Maryx loved her: that was a temptation the more", and that "I never had met a woman with a pure soul; hers was quite pure; I wrote my name across it out of sport'" (Ouida, 1877 [1891]: 323, 329). Finding that "[a]ll beauty is unlovely, once possessed" (78), Hilarion tires of Giojà and writes a celebrated and tangibly decadent poem called "Fauriel", to which readers react with visceral emotion while Giojà, alone, suffers a mental breakdown:

> Fauriel loved and wearied of love; there was little else for a theme; but the passion of it was like a pomegranate-blossom freshly burst open to the kiss of noon; the weariness of it was like the ashes of a charnel-house [...] As I read, the scorching passion, like a sand-wind that burns and passes, – the hollow love, that even in its first fresh vows was not sincere, – the cruel analysis, the weary contempt of human nature, – the slow voluptuous and yet indifferent analysis of the woman's loveliness and of the amorous charm that could no more last than lasts the hectic flash of the sky at evening-time, – they all seemed to cut into my very flesh like stripes. (283–4)

Hilarion's indifferent consumption of Giojà also evokes Baudelaire's notion of women as muses and mere conduits for art, as beings "for who, but above all, *through whom*, artists and poets create their most exquisite jewels" (1863 [1964]: 30, original emphasis). In Ouida's critical framing, Hilarion is not a true genius, but only mistaken for one.

Against him, Maryx is positioned as the true artist, for whom art is joy, "an imperious necessity", "adored for its own sake and purely" (Ouida, 1877 [1891]: 99), and never commercial. Uplifting naturalism and beauty, his art lacks vanity and scorn (133), does not curry fame, and challenges rather than embodies modernity: "[t]o go against all the temper of your age, that is the true greatness" (95). It is the momentary and elusive communication of higher truths and other worlds (103), and hinges on "its expressions of sympathy" (106), as Giojà also learns. Indeed, as King identifies, sympathy and altruism were cornerstones of Ouida's individualist politics (2011b). Only through "the infinitude of sympathy [one] attains to the infinitude of comprehension" (Ouida, 1869: 313). Through sympathy and (even disappointed) idealism, art is imbued with emotive force and transformative potential, contrary to art that expresses only derision: "Hilarion, who had written much to emasculate it, spent all the brilliancy of his brain in heaping endless contumely upon his own generation; Maryx, who had done much to enrich it, regarded it with affection and regret, as a man may do his country when its ways are uneven and its future is dark" (Ouida, 1877 [1891]: 133). This, then, is Ouida's earnest reflection on the role of art and aesthetics, when not deployed for social satire.

Giojà embodies the aloof woman of genius that would become a type in Ouida's repertoire. She is indeed a temporal anomaly in that the myths and fictions of ancient Rome are so real and alive to her that she suffers acutely whenever confronted with the real world. Crispin devises various schemes to sustain her (ultimately untenable) delusions, for example in lying about the money she earns to shelter her pride and sense of liberty. Conversely, when Giojà leaves for Paris with Hilarion and 'falls' in the eyes of the world (although, as Hilarion asserts, she remains untouched (323)), she never understands her ruin, perceiving her pure love for Hilarion as "her one chief glory upon earth" (313), and Crispin, following likewise his own moral codes that challenge society's, never explains. As a genius, she is apart from sexual politics (and so retains, like Princess Napraxine – discussed in the previous chapter – some aspects of strategic asexuality). As such, Giojà stands out from much of Victorian fiction as a woman who has 'fallen' but also retains her purity.

It is her art and her artistic identity that are transformed instead. Crispin and Maryx repeatedly claim women cannot be artists, let alone geniuses: "[s]culpture is always an epic; and what woman ever has written one?" (92). Giojà's talent defies them, and in the end, her genius surpasses Maryx's, but her greatest creation is also a testament to her lost love, and so the female artist remains, like many Ouidean heroines, caught between agency and romantic undoing. Notably, she first encounters Hilarion as a sculpture, and the novel implies she falls in love with him then as an ideal of beauty; he, too, emerges from marble. Giojà, likewise born from marble, also takes charge of the stone as a sculptor, and in the end, her art manages to touch Hilarion's emotions where her mere body and self have failed to arouse sympathy: "this message sent to him in the marble, this parable in stone, moved him as no words and as no woe would have done" (355) (naturally, his repentance comes too late: he confesses his love on her deathbed). Her art suffers from her passion, but also gives her agency and voice, indeed asserting her humanity to the world. Nonetheless, when her sculpture is exhibited at the Paris salon (and even enters the canon "between a group of Clesinger's and a figure by Paul Dubois" (353)), she remains framed by her relationship with men as she is framed by them through the narrative. Perceived either as Maryx's pupil or "one of the loves of Hilarion" (359), the latter has, as Maryx claims, ruined not only her name, but her artistic legacy.

Between 'Fauriel' and Giojà's sculpture, Ouida mobilises Paterian and (French) decadent notions of art and aesthetics to make visible the gendered dimensions of artistry: who may wield art, and who falls victim to it? Whose voice is heard, whose silenced? Who elicits compassion, who shame? No doubt this novel, which also ponders "that mystical power of artistic creation", sometimes "spontaneous, electric, full of sudden and eager joys, like the birth of love itself; sometimes […] accomplished only with sore travail, and many pangs, and sleepless nights, like the birth of children" (340), has an autobiographical dimension (King, 2013a), especially considering that 1877 marked the high point of her (doomed) love for della Stufa (Lee, 1914: 91). In the end, art and genius are fraught but wonderful obligations: "genius is only a power to suffer more and to remember longer" (Ouida, 1877 [1891]: 363), but "Art is, after Nature, the only consolation that one has at all for living" (45).

Liberty, Genius, and Capitalism

Twenty years after *Ariadnê*, not only had the decadent fatalism she satirised come to inform Ouida's own writing, but she now deployed her art for a more focused social and political critique than ever. The artist's "affection and regret" (Ouida, 1877 [1891]: 133) gave way to a sharper, more cynical commentary, palpable in *The Massarenes* (1897), her last novel concerned with Britain. In it, she indicts unfettered capitalism, embodied by the self-made William Massarene, an unethical, misogynist bully who "owned [American] railway plants and cattle ranches and steam-boats and grain-depots, and docks and tramways and manufactories, and men and women and children laboured for him day and night by thousands harder than the Israelites toiled for the Pharaohs" (Ouida, 1897 [1904]: 388). His ambition to join – and buy – high society and politics shows up the latter's moral corruption and hypocrisy, positioning Massarene as the canker of modernity. In its greed, Ouida posits, society cares only for appearances and spectacle, but not that "rotten ships and starved crews, and poisonous trades and famished families had helped to make the splendours of Harrenden House" (202). In courting Massarene's money, despite despising his class and character, both the impoverished aristocracy and its politicians are soon subjugated by his ruthlessness – even the Femme Galante Mouse cannot escape his "sheer brutal savage force" (324).

Ouida here remains particularly alert to women's legal precariousness. Massarene is a callous misogynist who thinks of women as either brood mares or high-bred fillies, exploits his wife's labour, but leaves her nothing of his millions: "[a]ll the use she had been to him, all her industry, patience, affection, and self-denial had all counted for nothing with him; she was a blot on his greatness, [...] and her existence had stood in the way of his marrying some fair young virgin of noble race who might have given him an heir, and let him cut off his daughter with a shilling" (388). At least Margaret, whose labour is repeatedly acknowledged, also speaks back to her husband (387). Lady Kenilworth or Mouse, Ouida's last Femme Galante, is similarly disadvantaged by her husband's will. 'Cocky', who marries her to gain money from his father, the Duke of Otterborne – and whose effeminacy, gambling, alcohol abuse, and ill health echo *fin-de-siècle* discourse on degeneration[2] – resents Mouse's sexual liberty (and the fact that her four children's father is clearly her lover, Harry Brancepeth), and although their marriage has long been treated by both as a convenient arrangement, resolves to divorce her when he inherits the title. Soon falling deadly ill, his will instead denies her all rights to the family's possessions and properties, which fall to her eldest son Jack, as well as rights over her children, for whom he appoints guardians. Mouse is left with the title of Duchess, and nothing else. In a novel concerned with wealth, power, and possession, Ouida foregrounds women's economic precarity, but also their resilience.

Mouse is a clever manipulator who channels Dolly's frivolity and Nadine Napraxine's cunning, and who, in the heyday of Liane de Pougy and Èmilienne d'Alencon, is likened to "any courtezan [sic] of ancient Rome or modern Paris" (416), and once

---

[2] Pervasive late-Victorian anxieties around degeneration as a collective counter-evolutionary decline of 'the British race' in which social flaws such as crime, poverty, homosexuality, hysteria/ neurasthenia, or certain genres of art acted as pathologized symptoms of de-evolution were outlined in treatises from across medical and biological disciplines and perhaps most notoriously enshrined in Max Nordau's *Degeneration* (1893, translated to English in 1895). See Greenslade, 2010.

imitates "the dancing of Nini-Patte-en-l'air" (83), the cancan dancer immortalised by Arthur Symons (1892 [2012]: 139). Like the Femme Galantes before her, she "was not in the least afraid of doing wrong, but she was keenly afraid of being found out" (Ouida, 1897 [1904]: 271). However, when the Otterborne jewels, which she has secretly pawned, fall to her son instead of her, she borrows money from Massarene, who then blackmails, abuses, and rapes her, indulging in a "love of hurting her, of mortifying her, of ordering her about as though she were a factory wench in one of his cotton-mills in North Dakota" (333): "[o]nce he wiped his dusty boots on the hem of her gown" (334). Mouse then exhibits the same markers of trauma as Vere: "[s]he grew thin, she looked harassed and hectic, she contracted a nervous way of glancing back over her shoulder" (835), "she was nervous, pale, had lost her spirits, and shut herself up a great deal" (825), and "[s]he let things drift in apathy and disgust and fear" (326). Ouida here renders the traumatised Femme Galante sympathetic, and in letting her withstand and defy her brother Hurstmanceaux's obsessive shaming – he not only blames Massarene's abuse on her but contemplates an honour-killing (423) – also undercuts his patriarchal force. Indeed, like Napraxine, Mouse ultimately finds that "[m]en were like horses. Ride them with a firm hand and you could put them at any timber you chose" (550). Like Dolly, she understands marriage as a social tool that cannot be sidestepped: "[s]he wanted to have two things in one: liberty and money. Of marriage she was afraid. […] Still in her moments of sober reflection she knew that she must marry, or risk drifting into an insecure, shifty, and discreditable position" (466). When she ultimately manipulates the millionaire Vanderlin to finance her marriage to a minor German prince, she declares: "'one doesn't marry for good looks […]. One marries for bread and butter'" (562). As such, Mouse, although not the heroine, is certainly the novel's most interesting character and is given much more space than Katherine Massarene, the story's moral centre.

Katherine, who abhors her father's wealth as "blood-money" (390), "amassed by wickedness, and cruelty, and fraud" (400), "crimes which in the successful man society has agreed to let pass as virtues" (395), struggles with her fraught inheritance and her own independence and embodies Ouida's individualist politics. As several critics have outlined at length, Ouida espoused the post-liberal belief "that the happiness of humanity can only be secured by the liberty of the individual" (Ouida, 1894 [1895]a: 382; Maltz, 2009; King, 2011a and 2011b; Ambrosini, 2013; Pykett, 2013). Influenced by Wilde's "The Soul of Man under Socialism" (1891), Herbert Spencer's *The Man Versus the State* (1884), and the politics of W. H. Mallock and Auberon Herbert – who appears in the novel as applauding Katherine's actions (Ouida, 1897 [1904]: 502) – individualists shared "a belief in the value of each person's liberty to think and to act for themselves" (King, 2011b: 567), and so staunchly opposed "that tyranny of mediocrity which is called the authority of the state" (Ouida, 1891 [1895]b: 366). Indeed, Ouida's commitment to individual liberty required the absence of intervention and control by collectives, be they State, Church, education, science, socialists, or even feminists: genius, to be "a guiding light to society" (King 2011b: 568), must be free from constraints or censure. Accordingly, her objection to socialism as a conformist collectivism that quenched "the sublime in humanity" and vested authority in "those most undeserving of it", that is the mediocre masses (Maltz, 2009: 100), echoes her philosophy about aesthetics and the artist-genius, especially as allied to Kant's subjective autonomy and Hegel's belief in art as expressing an innate human freedom, discussed in the previous chapter.

Enacting this credo through her fiction, Ouida lets Katherine attempt reparations by using her father's money to build asylums, human and animal charities, and return it to his American labourers after he is killed by a man he once swindled out of his land. However, illustrating that "it is easier to move the mountains or to arrest the tides than it is to do any real good to the mass of mankind" (Ouida, 1897 [1904]: 36, 442), Katherine's endeavours are widely critiqued as shocking examples of attempting what amounts to a welfare state: "[o]ught big bankers, instead of going to court and marrying dukes' daughters, to live on bread and cheese, and give their millions in pensions and bonuses?" (501). Although claimed by various parties, which the novel portrays as equally corrupt (King, 2011b: 569), Katherine, in line with individualism, "resolutely refuses any alliance, collective action or even to define her own stance in public: to do so would be to compromise her individuality and personal freedom" (King 2011a: xii). However, opposing the Spencerian notions of the "survival of the strongest [as] the law of nature" which inform Massarene's capitalism (Ouida, 1897 [1904]: 349), Katherine's actions also prioritise sympathy and altruism. Through her, who like Hurstmanceaux, is repeatedly positioned as "out of harmony with her destiny and her generation" (509), and like him appreciates art over spectacle, thus embodying the man and woman of genius, Ouida renders sympathy political, "constantly linking it to everyday acts, evoking a sympathy for helpless living beings, both animal and human, with the explicit intention of making them as free as possible" (King, 2011b: 569). In this approach, which also reverberates through her non-fiction of the 1890s, Ouida differs from other individualists. Indeed, by positing that "[m]ental liberty and genius are important, but without sympathy and selfless action they are worthless" (King, 2011b: 570), Katherine's story enacts Ouida's belief that the genius in particular has the right to exert their individualism independent from the majority in connection with her credo that this position obliges the genius to do just that.

Accordingly, the novel also enacts colonial critique through commentary on India ("[o]ne wishes for a second and successful mutiny", [Ouida, 1897 [1904]: 142]), but primarily through Harry Brancepeth's heroic death, which anticipates Ouida's fierce opposition to the Boer War, although she clarifies it is not inspired by the Jameson Raid (1895–96) (Ouida, 1897 [1904]:

3). Somewhat echoing Bertie Cecil, Harry, impelled by the "generosity of a manly temper [...] to take part with the weak, the oppressed, the natural owners of the vast plains", "disgusted by the cruelty of the white men, touched by the helplessness of the natives, alienated by the avarice and violence of the former", and opposing the Boer's "excesses of barbarous brutality which invariably characterize the introduction of civilization anywhere" (449), sides with the native Loomalis against the Boers allied to England and, to the embarrassment of politicians at home, fights and dies at side of chief Mehembele.

Altogether, *The Massarenes* enacts a visceral critique of late-Victorian industrial capitalism, not far afield from the decadents. Like Arthur Symons, who attributed decadence to "a civilization grown over-luxurious, over-inquiring, too languid for the relief of action, too uncertain for any emphasis in opinion or in conduct" (1893 [2012]: 252), Ouida, after all, linked the modern era's "apathy, despondency and cynical indifference" (Ouida, 1896 [1900]: 212) to the "ever-increasing luxury [...] and the ever increasing materialism of all kinds of life into which mechanical labour enters" (Ouida, 1891 [1895]a: 129). However, believing that neither capitalism or socialism could produce the sympathetic altruism required to enact lasting change, Ouida also has no alternative to offer. In the end, Katherine not only doubts her decisions and beliefs ("'[l]ead me, guide me, take me if you will', she said brokenly. 'I have trusted to my own wisdom, and perhaps I have always done wrong'", [Ouida, 1897 [1904]: 566]), but, once again unable to escape the marriage plot, forsakes her dreams of supporting herself as a teacher and, enacting Auberon's principles (King, 2011a: x), withdraws from society to private estates with Hurstmanceaux, like Idalia and Erceldoune before them.

Rivers Change Like Nations

The Waters of Edera is the story of the idyllic Italian village, Ruscino, whose life-sustaining river is annexed and harnessed "in the name of collectivism and equal access" by a corrupt government seeking to build a chemical factory and a railway without ever consulting the villagers (Maltz, 2009: 100). It echoes *A Village Commune* (1881) in its vocal condemnation of industrial capitalism and the associated destruction of nature, which Ouida also argued in numerous essays. With its focus on the destruction of natural resources, it is also "perhaps the first Victorian novel to take environmental action as its central theme" (Carroll, 2019: 146), and has been claimed as "the first ecofeminist novel" in English (Poster, 1997: 3). Enacting the premise that "[r]ivers change like nations" (Ouida, 1900 [1902]: 74), it chronicles, through Ruscino as a case study, Italy's "transition from a golden past to an iron modernity" as Ouida perceives it (Carroll, 2019: 151). Pastoral Italy, whose "unspoiled country life [...] [is] the best that remains to humanity on the face of the earth" (Ouida, 1881: 367), is as yet untouched by, but under threat from, the industrialist-capitalist forces that had, in her estimation, already ruined Britain.

While certainly romanticised or imagined as "block-headed, feudal" people (Maltz 2009: 100), however, her characters also emerge in turns as psychologically complex, crude, stubborn, violent, passionate, or apathetic. Don Silverio, the aesthetically inclined scholar and country priest, advocates for them, like Ouida herself, "not on the grounds of reason and progress, but only on the grounds of their preservation as an aesthetically valuable, vibrant, rustic people close to 'nature' like the river" (Carroll, 2019: 160). He unsuccessfully attempts to save Ruscino from ruin, but also knows "that in this age there is only one law, to gain; only one duty, to prosper: that nature is of no account, nor beauty either, nor repose, nor ancient rights, nor any of the simple claims of normal justice. [...] He knew that, in the age he lived in, all things were estimated only by their value to commerce or to speculation" (Ouida, 1900 [1902]: 100). During his meetings with local government, the Syndic indeed claims that "[p]rivate interest must cede to public" (234), but Don Silverio's direct, sensible questions expose the Syndic's attempts to swindle the villagers through misinformation and bureaucratic obfuscation that amount to Kafka-esque absurdity, or reveal corrupt favouritism between government officials and capitalist investors. Concurrently with Ouida's politics, the State's laws are so exposed as "'[t]he law of pirates, of cut-throats!'" (181). As she states elsewhere: "the Italian people are perpetually tormented by [political and bureaucratic] interference: by exaction, by eviction, by both Imperial and local spoliation, by the tyrannies and insolence of a brutal police, by the multitudinous irritations of a torturing administration, which apes in infinitesimal things the tyrannies and oppressions of the greater government" (Ouida, 1898: 246). Indeed, Don Silverio's meeting also reveals that the government is spying on Ruscino and its budding rebellion, led by the fierce and stubborn Alba Adone.

Adone loves the river, and his almost symbiotic, trans-human bond challenges the notion that this "most precious, vibrant, living thing has no economic value and hence no legal protection" (Carroll 2019: 156): "[i]t was a living thing, a free thing, a precious thing, more precious than jewel or gold. Both jewels and gold the law protected. Could it not protect the Edera?" (Ouida, 1900 [1902]: 126). Ouida in this way indicts a turn-of-the-century European culture in which "[t]wo gigantic dominions now rule the human race; they are the armies and the moneymakers" (183).

Though romanticised with Ouida's typical affinity for rebels, Adone's resistance movement is doomed from the beginning. Moreover, in a short but vital commentary on gender, he carelessly ruins the young Nerina's name by letting her run errands at night. Nerina, a fierce, wild child of the mountains, is described as a "bird" and "lioness" (317, 318) and thus echoing Cigarette and Folle-Farine, makes the river her ally when she leads a group of dastardly soldiers to their deaths in the swamp (even if they kill her before dying). Adone is injured and captured, but at the last finds freedom and radical escape by drowning himself in his beloved river: "'[t]ake me! – save me! – comrade, brother, friend!'" (340).

The novel echoes Ouida's own activism through letters, memberships, and advocacy. As Alicia Carroll notes, Ouida championed environmental and animal rights, for example as a member of the British Guild of Gentleness or co-founder of the Italian Society for the Prevention of Cruelty to Animals and the British Humanitarian League (Lee, 1914: 304–5), and so "ecological protection was a key activity for her and should be considered part of her legacy" (Carroll, 2019: 150). Lastly, the novel puts into play not only Ouida's anti-industrial anti-capitalism, but also embodies the altruistic force of observing, listening, and bearing witness (King 2011b: 573), which she puts into practice through her fiction.

War Games

Contracted to Macmillan in March 1903, the genesis of Ouida's last and only twentieth-century novel encapsulates her later misfortune: the manuscript was lost to her landlady's sons, who burgled and forcefully evicted her from her lodgings in Viareggio. Although her lawsuit was successful, Ouida had to reconstruct the story from memory while grappling with financial difficulties and ill health. When she died in 1908 in Bagni di Lucca, the unfinished novel was published with twenty-nine chapters.

Although her palatial aesthetic is "defiled by the shrieking tramway engines, the stinking automobiles, [...] the electric wire and the petrol car" (Ouida, 1908: 3), Ouida deploys her trademark mixture of romance and satire: "[h]ad the manuscript of 'Helianthus' been found buried beneath a snow drift in Alaska", one reviewer writes, "there would be no one to dispute the fact that it was Ouida's" ("The Latest and Last of Ouida's", 1908: viii). This is especially interesting as this explicitly political and indeed prophetic caricature of pre-war Europe also departs from her usual repertoire. The transposition of Europe into hyperbolic counterparts such as Gallia, Guthonia, Septentriones, Candor, or indeed, Ouida's beloved Italy into Helianthus, somewhat recalls Ruritanian heterotopias – so-named for Anthony Hope's 1894 *The Prisoner of Zenda* – that confront readers with their own, picturesquely distorted reflection, especially due to Ouida's prevalence for romantic stylisation. But *Helianthus* really constitutes the antithesis to Ruritania's safely contained, unindustrialised "fairy-tale and daydream" settings in which "real heroes and heroines can still flourish" (Daly, 2020: 4). Here, pomp and ceremony are mobilised to indict modernity and militarism as Ouida spins into narrative her political beliefs as something approaching a manifesto that strips "the tinsel from regal pomp and platitudes from royal character with a bitter determination" ("Helianthus. By Ouida": vi).

In Helianthus, the industrial modernity that threatened Ruscino has "sullied or silenced its falling or rushing waters, had befouled with smoke its white marble colonnades, its towering palm plumes, its odorous gardens. Modernity had driven his steam-roller over the narcissus, the hyacinth, the cheiranthus; and steam pistons throbbed where the doves of Aphrodite had nested" (Ouida, 1908: 2–3). Italy, Ouida's aesthetic ideal, now disastrously aping the industrialist-capitalist modernity that has already ruined Britain (as laid out in *The Massarenes*), provides the stage and catalyst for her anti-modern stance (Pykett, 2013: 153). As such, it echoes other late-Victorian assessments, in which Italy's ancient beauty is destroyed by becoming "like any other European city, big, noisy, vulgar, overgrown" (Harrison, 1894: 254; see also Kukavica, 2023):

> The land is sadly changed in its physical and architectural features; the destruction of its forests, the drying up of its rivers, the appropriation by speculators of its torrents and lakes, the demolition of its castles and palaces, have in many parts made it featureless, shadeless, arid, the few green things which still keep life in them being ruthlessly gnawed, as they sprout, by the famished flocks of goats and sheep. But in

many other portions of its legend-haunted soil it is beautiful still; in its limpid atmosphere, in the lovely colour of its mountains, in its ancient gardens, in its gorgeous sunsets, in its moonlit nights, in its roseate dawns, in its immemorial woods, melodious with the voice of the nightingale, something of the youth of the world still lingers, still awakes with the blossoms of spring. In harsh incongruity with it, incongruous as the scream of steam on its waters, as the buzz of machines in its plough-furrows, as the rush of electric cars down its ancient streets, is the House of Gunderöde, which has ruled over it for three generations. (Ouida, 1908: 52)

This House of Gunderöde, which rules Guthonia, usurped power after a revolution led by forgotten national hero Platon Illyris, who is modelled on Garibaldi. Ouida therefore indicts the Risorgimento and its efforts "to create a fair Utopia of free action and untroubled peace" as a failure, as she had already done in *A Village Commune*: "[e]very noble-hearted theorist of a future of freedom has died in heart-broken disillusion. [... All] that, in the end, is born of their sacrifice is a horde of weazels and of leeches, who suck the body of the nations dry" (Ouida, 1881: 363–4).

Foremost among these are industrial capitalists, opportunistic politicians, and militaristic autocrats, whom she here casts as what reviewers identified as easily recognisable portraits of contemporary figures of state, although they wisely refrained from elaborating ("Ave-Atque Vale", 1908: 368; "Helianthus. By Ouida", 1908: 6; "The Latest and Last of Ouida's", 1908: 8). These are now more difficult to reconstruct. For example, Gallia, "a republic [...] indistinguishable from a monarchy", may be easily identified as France (Ouida, 1908: 277), but Emperor Gregory of Septentriones, whose domain is "at once Oriental and barbaric, stretching from the ice of frozen seas to the hot sands of parching plains" (130), and who is grand-sire of virtually all European rulers, at once resembles Tsar Nicholas II and Queen Victoria.

No doubt the novel contains attacks on Ouida's chosen enemies: Joseph Chamberlain, whom she blamed for the "hysterical creed of Imperialism" and the orchestration of the Boer War in collusion with the profit-hungry yellow press (Ouida, 1899: 171), or Italian ex-Prime Minister Francesco Crispi (Ambrosini, 2013: 174). The latter, Garibaldi's former compatriot turned reactionary, against whom Ouida rallied in "L'Uomo Fatale" and "The Italy of To-day" (Ouida, 1894 [1895]c; Ouida, 1895a), is here immortalised as Domitian Corvus, "Judas to his country's Christ" who, with "a craft so cunning, a force so pitiless, a brain so utterly unscrupulous" has "plunged [Helianthus] into disastrous wars, seduced her with injurious ambitions, led her blindfold to the brink of bankruptcy, filled her prisons with her young men, and cultivated corruption upon her soil (Ouida, 1908: 254, 251). For him she reserves one of her sharpest – and interestingly gendered – indictments: "[t]he world thinks the woman's prostitution of beauty a greater sin than the man's prostitution of intellect, but it is not so. Of the two, the prostitution of the mind is more far-reaching, more profound, and more evil in its effects on others, than the sale of mere physical charms: the woman sells herself alone, the man often sells his generation, his country, and his disciples, with himself" (255). It was Crispi who oversaw Italy's ill-fated colonial campaign into Abyssinia, which Ouida attributed to the influence of British jingoism, and which marked her increasing "concern for the changes wrought by imperialism on the psyche of Europeans" (Ambrosini, 2013: 175), palpably evident in this novel.

Another easily recognised portrait is Emperor Julius of Guthone, wanting "worlds to conquer" (Ouida, 1908: 47) and continually threatening to invade Helianthus (which his uncle John of Gunderöde rules) "by the one law of which he would be unable to dispute the justice: the law of superior strength" (93), as Kaiser Wilhelm II, Ouida's avatar of "military despotism" (Ouida, 1897 [1900]: 83). Although Helianthus' vassalage to Guthone also resembles Italy's position under Austria before 1871, Guthone recalls Imperial Germany under the leadership of Bismarck as a state "in which militarism was the law of national life, and mere babes were drilled in the infant schools": "[n]o dominions in the world were so exclusively dedicated to the possibilities of war as those of Julius" (93, 94). Ouida here continues her antagonism towards Germany, unsubtly articulated in her 1872 short story, "A Leaf in the Storm", where the Prussians invade, occupy, and ransack the French countryside, settling "on the village as vultures on a dead lamb's body" (Ouida, 1872: 291), and which prompted the only serious point of contention between her and Tauchnitz (Lee, 1914: 69–70). A second, if much smaller, conflict was caused when the latter censured her essay on Georges Darien in which she called William of Germany a "war-lord" (Ouida, 1897 [1900]: 83; Lee, 1914: 188): unsurprisingly, Ouida opposed all forms of censure (King 2011b: 568). In her 1894 essay, "The Legislation of Fear", she declared it "a violation of intellectual and personal liberty which [...] should rouse alarm, the indignation and the sympathy of every thinker in every clime who from his study endeavours to enlighten and liberate the world" (Ouida, 1894 [1895]a: 394) – a position with which she certainly identified. In the same essay, one of the many anecdotes she collages, in which "eight young lads were flung into prison for singing the Hymn of Labour" (Ouida, 1883 [1895]: 387) no doubt inspired a similar event in *Helianthus* surrounding the (outlawed) Hymn of Eos, anthem of the War of Independence (Ouida, 1908: 287).

Indeed, cornerstones of Helianthus' alarming regression into authoritarianism are press censorship, domestic surveillance through spies ("[h]ere statues have ears, and trees have tongues" (25)), the imprisonment of dissenters, and cannons trained on its own populace. Ouida thus fictionalises her thesis that "in Italy [...] civil liberty is wanting, and free speech and free acts are forbidden" (Ouida, 1900b: 274–5). Whereas the many incidents from which she draws were often amalgamated from newspaper reports which were not always credible, her fictionalisation presciently identifies ultimately dangerous cultural currents and political mechanisms that undermine Italy's/Helianthus' claims to modern liberalism through such sardonic epigrams as "the wounded were carried into hospital; the festivities were over" (Ouida, 1908: 9), or "this kind of conversation is dangerous in Helianthus, which is a free country" (12). On the contrary, King John's "future of absolutism which he had built up under the cover of constitutionalism" (437) is the antithesis of the "advice of Herbert Spencer, 'Govern me as little as you can'" (114), and not only exposes all Ouida opposes, but a country braced with the scaffolding of oncoming totalitarianism, if not the fascism that would rise to power not twenty years later in 1925.

Such dangerous political tendencies are not least rooted in the semi-religious observance of militarism, and leaders "who place machinery before men, who value appearances and are blind to facts, who think a button awry or a tape untied more terrible than any catastrophe to the populace" (20), a turn of the century phenomenon Ouida had already criticised at length in her essay on French writer Georges Darien (Ouida, 1897). In *Helianthus*, militarism is the "tyranny of narrow minds" incarnate as an oppressive, soul-crushing pageantry that not only offends Ouida's sense of natural beauty and liberty but also violently glorifies state power and prepares to kill its people: "Europe has swept her youth into the dragon's maw of militarism and is not inclined to let them escape. War is the plaything of governments. They are not likely to give it up merely because the playthings get broken" (Ouida, 1908: 78). Indeed, sooner or later, this "perpetual game of *kriegspiel* without protest" ('war game' (42)) must erupt into real conflict, based on "the pleasure of Julius or of the financiers, or the fear of internal troubles" (19). In positing Julius/William of Guthone/Germany as the most likely aggressor looking for "the excuse, the opportunity, the pretext which he craved" (43), Ouida alludes once again to the German unification wars (1864, 1866,

1870–71). Meanwhile, her stylised Europe is not so much at peace as in a ceasefire: "[w]hat the world calls peace is but a suspension of hostilities, a jealous watching of wild beasts" (43). She satirises contemporary pre-war alliances, ententes, and surreptitious armament when she writes: "Europe was at peace – that is, was armed to the teeth, but afraid to move" (178).

Until a pretext arises, Helianthus's metaphoric sword "was essentially a domestic instrument, and was generally only used on black, brown, and yellow bodies, which of course are not counted as true war-game" (179). Here, Ouida's anti-imperial stance finds its full, scathingly satirical expression: hankering for war as for a sporting contest, the European nations not only wager the lives of their citizens but also completely erase the ongoing colonial violence against non-white peoples that is normalised as a pastime. When Candor proposes a financial alliance to "colonise, to civilise, to open new markets, to change sandy wastes into rich cornfields" (180), Helianthus is "as a whole flattered by the idea that she could go a-colonising with her flag flying" (180), but the endeavour fails when Candor's administration changes, to the "grateful barbarian's relief at having escaped invasion and education" (185–6). With such biting satire, Ouida exposes a New Imperialist rhetoric in which colonies act as status symbols of 'civilisation' – whose merits the novel continually challenges – and which becomes a keystone of propaganda. Her sharp, cynical diagnosis illustrates her virulent anti-imperialism, which, as Ambrosini notes, was rooted not in "a political-economic analysis", but instead in her ethical and aesthetic rejection of consumerism (2013: 176): colonialism, she posits, is an extension of capitalism. More than that, as she warns in her 1900 essay "Imperialismo Inglese" (English Imperialism), British jingoism is an infectious mass hysteria, a "moral and psychological degeneration" (Ouida, 1900a, qtd. in Ambrosini, 2013: 178): "I abhor the greedy and shameless parcelling out of Africa by a mob of European speculators", she wrote to *The Times* (qtd. in Lee, 1914: 173–4). As Pykett rightfully points out, this anti-imperialism is already evident in *Under Two Flags* (2013: 156), when a Bedouin chief declares:

> To rifle a caravan is a crime, though to steal a continent is glory. [...] But the locust-swarms that devour the land are the money-eaters, the petty despots, the bribetakers, the men who wring gold out of infamy, who traffic in tyrannies, who plunder under official seals, who curse Algiers with avarice, with fraud, with routine, with the hell-spawn of civilization. It is the "Bureaucratie", as your tongue phrases it, that is the spoiler and oppressor of the soil. (Ouida, 1867 [1995]: 214–5)

His sentiments on governments and capitalists are echoed in *Helianthus*:

> No one should say that rich men stole; they accumulate. Even so, Governments do not ever steal; they annex. Everything is excused when it is *en gros,* or *en bloc:* you kill one man, you go to the scaffold or the hulks; you kill fifty thousand men, you are decorated, pensioned, honoured, deified. Certainly you do; what could be more right and proper? The whole question lies in your quantities. The whole matter is one of degree. (Ouida, 1908: 170–1)

In a similarly sardonic tone, Ouida lampoons politics, in which the "ideal public servant [...] [is] intelligent, supple, pliant in form, tenacious in fact, adroit in speech, unburdened by prejudice or principle [... and] absolutely devoted to the royal House; without any initiative, or opinions, except such as were suggested from above, i.e. by Providence, by Princes, or by the Conservative Press – a triad which is always working in common for the general good of nations and humanity" (85).

Indeed, with its emphasis on political commentary, the novel is highly episodic, accumulating a string of vignettes that add up to a psychological portrait of a whole nation, and the idiosyncratic temperaments that uphold an inane system. In addition to King John, the ambitious, paranoid autocrat who would, "with fierce pleasure in his slow veins [...] have arrested his son, have called out the troops, have raked the streets with musketry fire, and blocked the squares with cannon" (370), there is the brutally ignorant Crown Prince Theo, "a redfaced, bullet-headed, angry, alarmed person, twisting bristling moustaches and breathing fiercely like a chained-up bull-dog" (362), with the makings of a superstitious despot. His wife Gertrude, gentle and sympathetic, "a religious woman, half a saint", has nonetheless been so "trained and so saturated with prejudice" that she obstinately defends the status quo, prompting Prince Elim to exclaim: "'[w]hat you call duty is a mere fetish to which you sacrifice and slay all your best instincts, all your most humane impulses, all your upright honesty of purpose, all the sensitive feelers of your conscience'" (205–6). Elim, Duke of Othyris, a would-be democrat, is so caught between his familial duty and his beliefs, his privilege and compassion, that he is routinely compared to Hamlet (342). He once gives a speech "worthy of a Liebknecht or a Karl Marx" (167), but also refuses to champion a more liberal movement. His younger brother Tyras, a louche and happily amoral *bon vivant*, "a ruin, wholly in body and partly in mind" (302) embodies the era's self-inflicted degeneracy as Cocky had in *The Massarenes*. Shoring up this both complacently and unwillingly compliant cast are politicians like Soranis, the Prime Minister who, as the "son of a provincial apothecary", "loved the familiar intercourse with sovereigns, the smiles of royal women, the luxury of special trains", desires only "that the nation should be quiet and orderly, reasonable and pliable" and, as "always the advocate of middle courses, of safe concessions [...] was not brave, either morally or physically" (341–2, 343, 347, 352). Thoroughly without backbone, his downfall is "the inability of a feeble politician to cope with an unexpected situation" (365).

His successor, Kantakuzene, equally centric but disillusioned, "cared principally for his own interests; but after his own – a long way after – he did care for the interests of his country" (366).

Ouida thus weaves a narrative study of ignorance and ineptitude, in which politicians are given "some Department of which [they know] absolutely nothing, this condition being an essential rule in the formation of all modern governments" (85), and politics are dictated by self-aggrandisement, favouritism, and petty squabbles, "neither party wasting either time or trouble in looking into the question as it stood on its own merits" (109). Not only does Ouida illustrate what she had laid out in essays on militarism and imperialism, namely that complacency perpetuates "received doctrines" and that "cowardice and egotism" foster a fundamentally corrupt system as a symptom of a larger social malaise (Ouida, 1897: 55, 78), but she also outlines, as Ambrosini argues, the underlying structures of what Hannah Arendt later identifies as a bureaucratised, racist totalitarianism (Arendt, 1950 [2004]: 221; Ambrosini, 2013: 179). However, Ouida's fictional tapestry contains another paradigmatic diagnosis of Arendt's, namely that of the banality of evil. Evil, Arendt argues through her case study of a German fascist, is perpetrated by people who unquestioningly follow received doctrines, obey orders and the law (1963: 135). They acquiesce to the system without exercising the Kantian imperative or, as Elim states, "the supreme obligation of acting according to one's convictions whatever construction may be put on those" (Ouida, 1908: 205). Accordingly, Theo, Tyras, Gertrude, and Soranis, however different in character, are all equally complicit in Helianthus' proto-totalitarian, colonial-capitalist, eco-catastrophic destruction of beauty and liberty.

This poses interesting conundrums for the novel's men and women of genius, Platon Illyris, his recluse daughter Ilia, and Elim, who – somewhat frustratingly – have no alternatives to offer. Illyris is a cantankerous, obstinate, and sexist pessimist, who condemns all choices of action alike. Ilia, an independent recluse and woman of genius, that is "of a finer mould, a firmer texture, than her sex in general" and "aloof from all mortal weakness", refuses to engage with the world (238, 391), and even though she once wishes she could lead a rebellion (402), retreats into feminine passivity. Elim, the idealist, remains a theorist without conviction to act, and "when contradicted he was apt to remember that he was a prince" (210), that is, he can never entirely shed what today's discourse would call his privilege. Even though he involuntarily rises to becoming his father's challenger, he remains thoroughly defeatist. He fears succeeding to power, knowing that one man cannot dismantle the socio-political system: "[t]he great engines of torture, the great grindstones of pressure, militarism, commerce, taxation, cheap labour, the dropsy of capital, the exploitation of misery; all these, and all the ills which they engender, he would be no more able to touch than if he were a stevedore labouring in the hold of a steamship in the harbour" (76). In line with Ouida's biases (see Maltz, 2009), neither socialism nor anarchism, while sensational in their imagined potential, provide valid options. Indeed, the novel seems to articulate Ouida's own doubts about the artist-genius' reach and impact when Elim ponders, "[i]t is I who am wrong, perhaps, since everything which pleases others displeases me" (Ouida, 1908: 135), or when Illyris declares that "'[i]ndecision is an intellectual defect; it accompanies acute perception, it belongs to philosophic doubt, but it paralyses action'" (244).

Although Ouida, as King suggests, might simply refuse to do the thinking for us (2011b: 575), these may be the limits of the artist-genius' insight and sympathy: she can discern and diagnose, arouse indignation and compassion through her art, but action and solution lie without her scope. This is not least illustrated by Ouida's challenge to royal deification through passages such as: "[a]n atom of flesh is born into the world, different in no way from all other flesh except in the superstitions and imaginations of men" (Ouida, 1908: 192), while she paradoxically also clings to the conceit that people of genius have "in [their] veins the blood of an ancient and heroic race" (234). In the end, it is unclear how the novel would have resolved. It ends with King John's plan to assassinate Elim – no doubt a dramatic high point – but it is difficult to envision either a cataclysmic revolution or the radical escapes of former works.

Ultimately, this brazenly outspoken, sharply satirical novel which, as one reviewer recognises, re-asserts Ouida as a critic in her own right and would "have proved to be the cornerstone of its writer's fame" ("Ave-Atque Vale" 1908: 368–9) was overshadowed by the sensational reporting on Ouida's poverty and her death. It puts into play Ouida's radical belief that "[n]o government (as no war) could be conducted on humane principles" (Ouida, 1908: 36), but also reads as astoundingly prophetic and (ironically) modern. While certainly a commercial endeavour, it also demonstrates popular fiction's potential as a wide-reaching political medium that dramatizes and so makes accessible a host of aesthetic and political arguments.

Conclusion: The Personal is Political

Stefan Zweig, who had been forced to flee Vienna from the Nazis, eulogised the nineteenth century as

> honestly convinced that it was on the direct and infallible road to the best of all possible worlds. [... It] was a mere matter of decades before they finally saw an end to evil and violence, and in those days this faith in uninterrupted, inexorable 'progress' truly had the force of a religion. [...] In fact a general upward development became more and more evident, and at the end of that peaceful century it was swift and multifarious. (1943 [1947]: 14)

Zweig's nostalgia for a lost golden age and his meta-narrative of progress and an oncoming modernity echo popular post-war receptions of the nineteenth century, which to him encodes an idealism, optimism, and humanism lost to fascism in 1938. However, although Zweig and Ouida certainly share a belief in glamorous bohemianism and the romance of art, their respective conceptions of Europe at the turn of the century could not differ more. Ouida's twentieth century is by no means the culmination of a progressive teleology, but instead an increasingly corrupted, decadent modernity built on destruction, exploitation, anti-libertarianism, and greed, laced with the foundations of war and totalitarianism.

In this apocalyptic, but prophetic perception, Italy acted as a central catalyst, as Ouida understood herself to witness the gradual loss of the stereotypically pastoral country as yet untainted by industrialist-capitalist modernity: "[a]ll [Italy's] peace and its joy", she writes, "lie amidst its smiling fields" (Ouida, 1881: 367). Indeed, Ouida's work in part echoed common English perceptions of the European South "as a counter-geography of modernity", an internal Other to British liberalism and progress (Kukavica, 2023: 126; Ambrosini, 2013: 171), but she increasingly mobilised that imaginary for her anti-modern critique (see Jordan, 2009c; Maltz, 2009: 99; Ambrosini, 2013: 175), leveraging her artist-genius identity to speak "on behalf of the world of culture and speaking out against the degeneration of Italian taste" (Pykett, 2013: 150). Indeed, Italian journalists remembered her as endowed with that "special English characteristic that makes every Albion's son firmly believe he is an envoy both of God the Father and of Apollo sent to watch over the fate of Italy, entrusted with the special mission of coming to rule in our country, giving us lessons of humanity, public decency and [...] aesthetics", but also credited her with a "tender and good heart" (Guidi, 1908: 649, 654–5). Whereas her Italian novels were initially conceptualised as part travelogues to show readers a hitherto unknown Italy (Jordan, 2009c: 65), they became increasingly political towards the turn of the century, dramatizing the views she voices across numerous newspapers and letters.

Her ex-pat position, cosmopolitan outlook, and artist-aristocrat identity obliged her, she believed, to comment on Italy's ill-fated modernisation as symptomatic of dangerous phenomena that affected or would affect all European nations in the future. Although her eco-critical, anti-imperialist, anti-capitalist critique could not offer viable alternatives, quite a few of her warnings proved to be prescient, given that not only would World War One break out six years after *Helianthus*' publication, but her beloved Italy would become the first European nation to adopt fascism in 1925. Although often perceived still as a lady novelist of flamboyant sensationalism, Ouida clearly considered herself an intensely political person, as her animal rights activism alone shows: she campaigned against horse racing as cruel and publicly denounced the hunting of foxes, hares, and birds as a pastime – in *Helianthus*, she comments on "that insane impulse of the sportsman to kill everything that flies, [… as] a form of dementia" (Ouida, 1908: 66). She publicly commented on the Russo-Japanese War, and when Olive Schreiner, a fellow protester against the Boer War, was interned by authorities, Ouida published a long letter in the *Daily News*. Some, like Street, appreciated her as a champion of beauty and fierce critic of injustice in her own time, others validated her later. American anarchists and feminists Emma Goldman and Clara Dixon Davidson, as Ambrosini notes, drew inspiration from her and quoted her by name (2013: 173). Norman Douglas, a fellow ex-pat in Italy, in his 1921 memoir *Alone* advised aspiring authors to read her novels "for their tone, their temper; for that pervasive good breeding, that shining honesty, that capacity of scorn. These are qualities which our present age lacks, and needs" (1921 [1922]: 113). He also proclaims she was right about "the Japanese, about Feminism and Conscription and German brutalitarianism […,] Marion Crawford and D'Annunzio" and asks: "[d]o we not all now agree with what she wrote at the time of Queen Victoria and Joseph Chamberlain? […] When she says that the world is ruled by two enemies of all beauty, commerce and militarism – out of date?" (114). Remarkably, he saw her views validated from his post-war perspective.

Italy, then, provided not only a space in which to cultivate her aesthetic taste and live out the adventure, romance, and splendour of her heroines but also in which to implement her personal politics. Visitors to Villa Farinola infamously noted that Ouida, the dog lover and collector, was so committed to her animal rights philosophy and libertarian ideals that she refused to house-train her dogs (King, 2011b: 570). She also kept notes on her horses (Lee, 1914: 311–2). Whereas Pykett rightly notes that Ouida privileged "the personal and the aesthetic over the political" (2013: 161), I would qualify that the personal was itself, to mobilise the 1960s battle cry, intensely political to her. Fiction played a central role in this understanding as the space in which the two intertwine – that is, where the individual and the world collide symbolically, as behaviour in rehearsal – be it through the kaleidoscopic satire of *The Massarenes* and *Helianthus*, or the personal and sympathetic struggles of small casts in *Ariadnê* and *The Waters of Edera*. Good fiction, in Ouida's estimation, "touched social and political problems [...] in a manner which induced thought in the thoughtless; and it brought some knowledge of culture, some sympathy with pain, some insight into higher natures, to large classes of persons who could have been reached by no other means" (Ouida, 1885: 213). It was, therefore, her duty to dramatize her insights "to a wider public through journalism and fiction, evoking a sympathetic response from her readers which would in turn incite them to political action" (King 2011b: 574). Identified primarily with her larger-than-life imagination, her world of dandies and duchesses or picturesque peasants, in hindsight, at the very least, Ouida proves that the popular novel's proclivity to excite and entertain did not foreclose its potential for scathing social critique, idealist philosophies, or political diagnosis.

CONCLUSION

High Priestess of the Impossible

In 1892, Robert Louis Stevenson and friends amused themselves by writing "A Ouida romance" together (*An Object of Pity, or: The Man Haggard*), imagining that, in witnessing visits and journeys during the first Samoan Civil War (1886–1894), they had found themselves "walking in broad day in the halls of one of [her] romances" (Stevenson, 1892 [1900]: 5, 15). Whereas there is a certain, Orientalist gaze at work in casting Samoa as a space of Ouida's "tropical imagination" (15), Stevenson, a fellow defender of romance over realism, in this way also demonstrates Street's claim that "[o]ne may write directly of 'Ouida' as of a familiar institution" (Street, 1895: 168) identified with a larger-than-life vision and a "gorgeous but peculiar point of view": "[m]any have made it their goal and object to Exceed; and who else has been so Excessive? Many have desired to see the world otherwise (and, if possible, Larger) than God made it; and in this ambition none has been prospered to succeed like the author of *Strathmore*" (Stevenson, 1892 [1900]: 15, 16). As each group member pays homage by describing the events and themselves "in the Ouida glamour" (6), her received, distinct register emerges as a catalogue of atmospheric, stylised settings, visual descriptions, and operatic narrative twists, of French expressions and invocations of the Classical world, of dashing adventurers, intrepid, coquettish ladies, sinister schemers, and noble animals, of high society habits, fierce tempers, and fiery gazes, and of, lastly, a disdain for fame and luxury in favour of love, adventure, and art.

"Ouida", then, was a recognisable institution, for her stylistic repertoire as much as for her capacity to render life as more intense, romantic, and adventurous. This, indeed, was the one thing readers and reviewers, critics and admirers alike unanimously agreed on: that Ouida's exuberant style, even if overwrought for some, was nevertheless seductively evocative and never failed to conjure visionary worlds. In addition to those already cited – like Beerbohm, who extolled the "sheer vitality" of "that unique, flamboyant lady, one of the miracles of modern literature" (1899: 107, 115) – Norman Douglas lauded the "picturesque and vigorous independence" of her language (1921 [1922]: 114), Van Vechten praised the "congenital frenzied glamour" of the worlds she created, which were always "a little wickeder, a little gayer, a little richer than the real thing" (1926: 55, 61), and Anton Chekhov, reading her novels in translation, wished he knew English "so he could do them justice" (Schmidt, 2014: 447). Henry James, who described Ouida first as an "uppish, or dauntless, little spirit of arrogance and independence" and parodied her in his short story, "Greville Fane" (1892), also admired her "original genuine perception of the beauty [...] of Italy", drew inspiration from her for his cosmopolitan fiction, and kept a painting she had done for him (qtd. in Tintner, 1991: 11). George Bernard Shaw, who, writing in the *Pall Mall Gazette* in 1886, called her writing diffuse and perverse, also admitted it was "yet imaginative, full of vivid and glowing pictures" (1886 [1991]: 107), Ambrose Bierce, likewise no fan, nonetheless conceded that "[h]er prodigality was seen in the expenditure of intellectual force" (qtd. in Van Vechten, 1926: 55), and G. K. Chesterton, who called *The Waters of Edera* "picturesque, animated, poetic, eloquent and supremely nonsensical" (qtd. in Stokes, 1983: 246), also later wrote: "[s]he had a real power of expressing the senses through her style; of conveying the very heat of blue skies or the bursting of palpable pomegranates. [...] Ouida, with infinite fury and infinite confusion of thought, did fill her books with Byron and the remains of the French Revolution" (1913: 117–8).

Ouida's romantic exuberance, her "taste for the extraordinary [...and] impatience in supporting the yoke of reality, [... her] belief that happiness exists only outside the established rules" to recall Doumic (1899: 26), her commitment to "[a]ll that is heroic, all that is sublime, impersonal, or glorious" (Ouida, 1882 [1895]: 309) or, as she phrased it, her credo that "the passion flower is as real as the potato" (303) was clearly central to her works' appeal, which frequently impressed readers and critics despite what they strove to present as their better judgement. Her craft — and it deserves to be acknowledged as such — was such that her fiction bypassed other, rationalised criteria for assessing literature, and — then as now — simply captured the imagination. Indeed, Ouida is a master storyteller, always staging the narrative to maximum effect. Whether it is the dramatic skill and vivid intensity with which she narrates battle scenes and revolutions, the way she mines characters' unspoken desires or the intense picturesqueness of her settings, she always taps into some inherent and universal sense of romance: Erceldoune is beset by dastardly brigands, not in any forest, but in lonely mountain ravines sizzling with Ruritanian glamour. Vere finally unites with Corrèze, not only because he lies dying in Paris after a duel defending her honour, but after she speeds alone and undaunted, through snowy, wolf-ridden wildernesses. Cigarette not only saves the French Army at the last possible minute, while Cecil, uniform torn and bloody, hands powder-black, is at last surrounded by enemy Arabs after a desperate last stand, but she also pries him from under a pile of dead soldiers and chargers, and nurses him in a lonely tent, surrounded by empty dishes and fallen comrades. In Ouida's world, which is either opulent or unforgiving, and often both at once, both revolutionary plotting and doomed love declarations take place in opera boxes, and valorised rebels and doomed idealists of all genders choose death over surrender.

As such, her fiction exemplifies Stevenson's claim that romance must be "picture-making" and "satisfy the nameless longings of the reader, and to obey the ideal laws of the day-dream [...], to embody character, thought, or emotion in some act or attitude that shall be remarkably striking to the mind's eye" (1882 [1887]: 246, 241–3). The author, states Stevenson, must become a "showman" who "changes the atmosphere and tenor of his [reader's] life" (249, 253). This Ouida certainly accomplishes, not only through her evocative descriptions, but also the expert movement of her narrative lens: when she composes scenes like paintings, or moves from a panoramic setting description to an individual, more intimate place, she makes her worlds feel theatrical, even, if anachronistically, cinematic to the modern reader (Erickson, 2020: 48). No wonder, then, that *Under Two Flags* was so often adapted by golden age Hollywood.

And yet, whereas her dramatic skill supplied loyal readerships with vicarious, potentially incendiary fantasies – after all, Richardson's protagonist seeks out the "strange currents" of Ouida's novels, as well as "the feeling of being strongly confronted" (1917: I, 286), and indeed experiences a formative sensual and aesthetic awakening (Rainwater, 2021) – contemporaries and scholars alike have refused to acknowledge her talents as literary ones or those of an artist. It is here, in the derisive or self-defensive reception of her work and life, that the entwined categories of gender and the popular become especially visible, as well as the multiple ways in which Ouida challenges the paradigms of Victorian fiction.

For one, Ouida's deliberate rejection of realism increasingly manoeuvred her into a defensive position with contemporary critics and later incurred the dismissal of both the modernists (King, 2011a: viii) and F. R. Leavis acolytes. The rise of aestheticism provided new frameworks through which her work could be understood and potentially elevated, had not her publisher's marketing undermined that endeavour, as Van Vechten noted as early as 1926 (1926: 64). Indeed, Ouida palpably influenced not only late Victorian decadents like Wilde, Street, and Beerbohm, but also camp modernists Van Vechten and Ronald Firbank (Bigland, 1951: 179; Brooks, 1951; Poster, 1996: 287; Severi, 2009: 138–9; Bristow, 2015; Marucci, 2020: 94–5).

Nonetheless, "[b]elittling Ouida became a reflex in the early twentieth century" (King, 2013b: 3). Throughout the 1980s and 1990s, "Ouida's stylistic lapses and exaggerated plots and characters preclude[d] her from being ranked among the major writers of the century" (Poster, 1996: 301), and to this day studies adopt an apologetic or derisive stance towards her "long, pulpy, over-rich" fiction (Marucci, 2009: 593). Such responses reveal crucial and persistent biases in scholarship that replicate expressly gendered responses to women's (popular) fiction. After all, ongoing biases in favour of the Leavisite realism paradigm not only skewer our mental map of Victorian literature but, considering that realism invests in naturalising hetero-patriarchy as invisible but ontological, also disregards queer and non-white/non-Western storytelling modes. Whereas Ouida neither qualifies as non-white or queer (unless we speculate about her potential asexuality), her life and work illustrate how re-interrogating our prioritisation of realism is therefore intrinsic to the endeavour to undiscipline Victorians studies (Chatterjee, Christoff, and Wong, 2020). Male canonical Victorian writers after all rejected realism: Stevenson proclaimed that the "question of realism, [...] regards not in the least degree the fundamental truth, but only the technical method, of a work of art" (1883 [1905]: 97–8), and Wilde famously claimed that "truth is entirely and absolutely a matter of style" (1891a [2008]: 981). Why, then, should Ouida have a lesser claim to truth and artistry, especially considering that style was the main element she had mastered to the majority's satisfaction? Why have Stevenson and Wilde's non-realist styles earned them places in the Victorian canon of adventure and aestheticism, respectively, when Ouida's non-realism is also an innate expression of being in "conflict with the implacable order of things", of the "imagination in revolt against reason escap[ing] towards the rare, the exceptional, the difficult, the impossible" (Doumic, 1899: 26)? Indeed, reducing Ouida to a stylistically exuberant but ultimately sloppy sentimentalist ignores the snide irony, verve, and sharp indictments of her satire, which is so often fuelled by genuine, righteous idealism and anti-modern critique, and no less observant for being embedded in the sumptuous decadence of consumerist glamour.

Some, at least, acknowledged this. Douglas called her "intelligent, fearless, [...] courageous not only in matters of literature" (1921 [1922]; 113), and Van Vechten wrote: "Ouida was an excellent critic, clear-sighted, unshackled, fearless. She formed independent judgements and said what she thought" (1926: 61). Whereas her work certainly merits such recognition, these instances were few and far between. From the moment "Ouida" was revealed to be a woman, critics who had hitherto taken her for a gentlemanly scholar with military experience, now subjected her work to new, incessant scrutiny, pointing out her errors in French, Italian, Latin, and Greek, and questioning her ability to portray men, male relationships, and life in general (Molloy, 2008: 163, 165; Jordan, 2013: 56–8). As a woman writer of popular fiction, Ouida's expansive adventures incurred the ongoing and clearly gendered policing of literary boundaries, especially because she did not conform to acceptably feminine subjects of realism (Pykett, 1992: 26). As Gilbert notes about Margaret Oliphant's infamous diatribe against sensation fiction, "what is sensational and reprehensible about a novel written by a woman becomes realism in the case of a man" (2005: 74). "That a woman should write with such vigorous power", acknowledged a friend of Ouida's, "and display such a keen knowledge of human nature, and soar above the namby-pamby twaddle of the day, is to them perfectly outrageous" (Hume, 1867: 7). Marie Corelli, too, who recognised Ouida's case as prismatic and exemplary of women writers' treatment, remarked: "we find most professional men-critics somewhat contemptuous and intolerant of women's literary attainments, [...] more willing to give the helping word of praise to any member of their own sex who makes the mildest and most random 'hit' of one season" (Corelli, 1890: 363; see Moody, 2013). As this study shows, following Nancy Armstrong's call to read popular and sensation fiction "in their own terms, rather than as failures of realism" (2011: 139), yields a multitude of insights, not only into popular culture as an important site of cultural negotiation (Hall, 1981 [2019]), but also into how, both in and after the nineteenth century, sensation, popular, and women's fiction have been policed, scrutinised, and dismissed.

The same gendered bias was extended to Ouida as a professional writer and celebrity. How her various publishers, including the Tinsley Brothers, Chapman & Hall, Chatto & Windus, and Heinemann & Balestier, who all profited profusely from her work, nonetheless tried to dismiss, exploit, or dupe her, has been well documented, here and elsewhere (Phillips, 1978; Jordan, 2011a; King, 2013c; Vrachnas, 2013). Whereas some, among them William Tinsley and Bernhardt Tauchnitz, saw her literary merit, others cultivated her reputation as quarrelsome and eccentric (Vrachnas, 2013: 122). This does not mean Ouida was not a demanding author – reputedly, she did not edit her first drafts but later demanded numerous edits, and was at times almost paranoid about having her work stolen (Molloy, 2008: 130; Vrachnas, 2013: 122). However, as Carla Molloy also points out, other authors like Henry James or Balzac were no less demanding, and Ouida's desire to control her literary output was by no means without justification, given how often her work was stolen and pirated. Such efforts to control her image extended to the public sphere: in the 1880s, Ouida wrote several letters to *The Times*, the *Contemporary Review*, and the *Athenaeum* responding to reviews of her novels and defending her fiction against the realism paradigm (Molloy, 2008: 11). Despite her rejection of the latter, she clearly considered herself a serious artist in the footsteps of George Eliot (Lee, 1914: 104) and had to invest considerable energy into the fraught endeavour of convincing everyone else.

Indeed, as a female writer, her refusal to adopt the customary false humility or amateur persona of the woman writer, and her pride in her work, which she often expressed in her letters to Tauchnitz, earned her a reputation as arrogant. For all her self-fashioning, on the page and in life, which she modelled after her heroines, her failure to perform conventional femininity, that is, to be sufficiently beautiful, socially adept, and gracious, translated into a lasting reputation as eccentric, grotesque, and unmannered (Jordan, 1995: 83; Jordan, 2009a), a reputation potently enshrined in the unflattering 1881 *Punch* cartoon that has become a dominant representation, and the description of her voice as "like a carving knife" (Lee, 1914: 49). Her biographies increasingly exaggerated that reputation with gleeful misogyny into portraits of a ridiculous, self-important, deluded spinster with ambitions and amorous desires beyond her merits, as she, like Cigarette, fell out of the category of her own sex. Thus, while there is no telling how accurate at least contemporary reports by friends and visitors were, Ouida's personality has been on trial often enough. Her voice, whether literal or literary, was no doubt challenging, polarising, abrasive, distinctive, and demanding, and then as now drew out the gendered and artistic biases encoded in responses to it.

As a popular author who freely synthesised a variety of trans-cultural styles and genres, went against the grain at every opportunity, and with her cosmopolitan outlook challenges stereotypical ideas about Victorian literature as insular or centred on realism or domesticity, Ouida's place in nineteenth-century culture is complex, but undeniable, especially because she remained a household name for so long. Her influence on aestheticism, decadence, camp modernism and twentieth-century desert adventure have by now been noted (Sutherland, 1995: x-xiii). There is also a case to be made for the afterlives of Ouida's cosmopolitan dandies, those "Lanky guardsmen with their wasp-waists" whom Van Vechten recognised across 1920s films (1926:

61), and whom Evelyn Waugh, as late as 1948, called up as debonair adventurers in *The Loved One* (1948: 83), as lastingly shaping the gentleman spy heroes of William Le Queux's Edwardian fiction – and gentleman spies after that. Le Queux wrote very much in the paranoid, nationalistic vein of invasion fiction and spy hysteria which Ouida strongly criticised. Nonetheless, Duckworth Drew, who recovers stolen jewels, U-boat plans, and princesses, and cavorts with diplomats and aristocrats in Paris, Rome, Berlin, and at the French Riviera, Jack Jardine, "[a] book-collecting gentleman, and bachelor with rooms in Great Russell Street, an ancestral home in Cheshire, and a commission in the cavalry" (Stafford, 1981: 490), or Hugh Morris, "an accomplished linguist, a brilliant raconteur, a good all-around sportsman, a polished diplomat, a born adventurer, a cosmopolitan of cosmopolitans, still under forty, and a personal friend of half a dozen sovereigns" (Le Queux, 1911: title page), certainly sound familiar to the Ouida reader. They not least recall Beerbohm's portrait of her guardsmen.

Whereas some, like Maugham, remembered Ouida as a French writer well into the 1930s when *Under Two Flags* was adapted as a spectacular Hollywood production, others, from Ruskin to the Archers in Edith Wharton's *Age of Innocence* "read Ouida's novels for the sake of the Italian atmosphere" (Wharton, 1920 [1996]: 28). French author Colette, though certainly inspired by her acquaintance with Liane de Pougy and Natalie Barney's Left Bank salon, might nonetheless, in imagining the sexually independent and defiantly happy courtesan Léa de Lonval and her younger, androgynous lover Chéri in the so-titled novel (1920), have drawn on Ouida, especially considering she adopted a blasé attitude towards the demi-monde and gave her courtesans happy endings (Sullivan, 2016: 92–3). And while, by the 1960s, Ernest Hemingway – arguably the least likely to appreciate Ouida – vaguely remembered her fiction as symbolic of old-world quaintness and antiquated social codes (1964 [2010]: 77–8). To the 1920s' American Black Women's club movement, reading Ouida for pleasure could encode self-indulgence as a defiant reclaiming of social, intellectual, and gendered spaces formerly denied to them (Erickson, 2020: 38–9). Today, her fiction's cosmopolitan hybridity and resistance to the social status quo can also become a cathartic reading experience for Black readers like Ouida collector and aficionado Jesse Ryan Erickson, while her hyperreal, stylised form inspires a reparative Black dandyism (51).

Ouida thus offers so many diverse points of connection, yet whether or not she provides a fruitful subject of study has for so long hinged on the question of whether or not she can be considered a feminist. Why, it is pertinent to ask, does that matter so much, and what do we mean by "feminist"? After all, evolving iterations of feminism have hardly ever been coherent, monolithic, or singular beacons of progress, and were instead multiple, fraught, and even entangled in problematic racist or classist biases and dangerous radical movements, such as eugenics then or transphobia now. Gender is undeniably central to every aspect of Ouida's life, work, legacy, and reception, to her life choices and how they were received, her self-curation as romantic heroine, her ability to write both men and women and how that ability was judged, her rapport with publishers, her reception as both artist and critic and, above all, her fiction. So why does her claim to legitimacy hinge on whether or not she endorsed the – discursive, de-centred, and heterogeneous – New Woman movement?

As an individualist, Ouida was suspicious of ideologies that made universal claims about groups of people or politics that could not account for the exceptional. She was also suspicious of the hubris of "progress" and, if she opposed women's suffrage, she did so because, by the 1890s, she opposed all participation in the state as detrimental to individual liberty (King, 2011a: 567, 572). However, Ouida, as a single, self-supporting woman and professional writer who had always been able to make every non-conforming decision she desired, also refused to see women as victims and urged them to become active from their current social position (Pykett, 2013: 162). In her very first novel, she declares:

> Women have, if they acknowledge them, passions, ambitions, impatience at their own monotonous rôle, longings for the living life denied to them; but everything tends to crush these down in them, has thus tended through so many generations, that now it has come to be an accepted thing that they must be calm, fair, pulseless, passionless statues, and when here and there a woman dares to acknowledge that her heart beats, and that nature is not wholly dead within her, the world stares at her, and rails at her, for there is no bête noire so terrible to the world as Truth!" (Ouida, 1863 [1891]: 195)

If women wanted to resist against or re-negotiate how the category "woman" defined them – as indeed so many of her characters did – all that was needed was courage and resolve. This view she expresses in the infamous 1894 essay, "The New Woman", but demonstrates in detail in one of two essays written in the early 1880s for Lippincott, but which she (curiously) stipulated should be published only after her death. "We can", she wrote, "thoroughly sympathize with the impatience of a clever woman at seeing herself excluded from an arena of public life in which some masculine fools and many masculine mediocrities succeed. We are fully prepared to admit that here and there may rise a woman of such brilliant abilities that she would fully be capable of governing an empire or manoeuvring an army" (1909: 587). This stance conformed with her self-perception as genius-artist as well as the belief that genius levelled sex altogether: true genius, she also explains, will always make its mark on the world. She also postulates that, if women at large were capable of it, they would already have "conquered for themselves some sort of supremacy": "[w]e cannot see what there is to prevent women attaining to the highest mental elevation if they are personally capable of doing so […] and we cannot think that if women genuinely desire high culture and fine attainment they would find any difficulty in attaining both" (588, 592). She welcomes women's "desire for greater intellectual light" as "of the utmost promise" and believes that "their lives would be infinitely happier" in the pursuit of study (588, 591), but because she herself had undertaken extensive self-education from early on – "I must study," she wrote in a diary aged fourteen, "or I shall know nothing when I am a woman" (Lee, 1914: 20) – she did not understand the call for larger systemic changes. In the autobiographical *Friendship*, Étoile, "free to think and dream and study", models herself on exceptional historical women like Sappho and Heloise, finding "a cloudless and all-absorbing happiness in the meditations of great minds, in the myths of heroic ages, in the delicate intricacies of language, and in the immeasurable majesties of thought" open to the "girl-scholar" alone (Ouida, 1878: I, 40). If she had so created her self-fulfilment, why should not others? If women wanted to lead extraordinary lives, why did they not simply do it, like her, or the heroines of her novels?

That her heroines' exceptional individualism often remains temporary and unsustainable (as it proved to be at the end of her own life), that moral victories demand radical escapes and triumphs demand ruthlessness, is a curious blind spot in this reasoning, but as King suggests, this withholding of solutions might also be Ouida's call to action (2011a: 574). Her fiction repeatedly identifies and analyses the systemic inequalities of a gendered commodity culture, and imagines individualist solutions to them, usually centred on altruism, sympathy, and resistance, that readers might be able to replicate, or at least internalise. In consistency with her romantic idealism, Ouida envisions a chivalrous, aristocratic paternalism inherited from Walter Scott or Alexandre Dumas as a counter-balance to an increasingly apathetic, cynical, and catastrophic modernity, although that belief seems to falter in her last few novels. Altogether, Ouida was fundamentally invested in matters of agency and liberty, and highly alert to how these were shaped by gender. Subjective and evolving debates about whether that qualifies as feminism should not obscure the fact that she provides an intensely worthwhile object of study, due to her own, exceptional life and views, the multiple ways in which her work challenges expectations about Victorian fiction, and, not least, the compelling case she makes for popular fiction as a volatile but insightful area of study. Ultimately, Ouida was perhaps only one thing for certain: namely, as Wilde recognised, "the high priestess of the impossible" (1889: 3).

Bibliography

Ackroyd, Peter, 2017. *Queer City: Gay London from the Romans to the Present Day*. London: Chatto & Windus.
Acland, Thornton. "*Two Little Wooden Shoes*", 1874. *Examiner* (1 August), pp. 827–8.
Addcox, Stephen, 2009. "Inoculation and Empire: Cigarette's Healing Power in Ouida's *Under Two Flags*", *Victorian Network*, 1.1 (Summer), pp. 22–38.
Ambrosini, Richard, 2013. "Politicizing the Aesthetic: Ouida's Transnational Critique of Modernity", in Jane Jordan and Andrew King (eds.), *Ouida and Victorian Popular Culture*. Abingdon: Routledge, pp. 165–82.
Anderson, Amanda, 1993. *Tainted Souls and Painted Faces: The Rhetoric of Fallenness in Victorian Culture*. New York: Cornell University Press.
Apraxine, Pierre, 2000. "The Model and the Photographer", in Pierre Apraxine and Xavier Demange (eds.), *La Divine Comtesse: Photographs of the Countess Castiglione*. New Haven: Yale University Press, pp. 22–51.
Arendt, Hannah, 1950 [2004]. *The Origins of Totalitarianism*. New York: Schocken Book.
———, 1963. *Eichmann in Jerusalem: A Report on the Banality of Evil*. New York: Viking Press.
"*Ariadnê*", 1877. *Saturday Review*, 43 (9 June), pp. 709–10.
Armstrong, Nancy, 2011. "The Sensation Novel", in John Kucich and Jenny Bourne-Taylor (Eds.), *The Oxford English History of the Novel*, Vol. 3: The Nineteenth-Century Novel 1820–1880. Oxford: Oxford University Press, pp. 137–53.
Atkinson, Juliette, 2017. *French Novels and the Victorians*. Oxford: Oxford University Press.
"At the Same Game", 1890. *Judy: The London Serio-Comic Journal* (23 July), p. 41.
Authier, Catherine, 2015. *Femmes d'exception, femmes d'influence: Une histoire des courtisanes ai XIXe siècle*. Paris: Armand Colin.
"Ave-Atque Vale", 1908. *The Academy* (17 October), pp. 368–9.
Baudelaire, Charles, 1857 [1998]. *The Flowers of Evil*. Oxford: Oxford World's Classics.
———, 1863 [1964]. *The Painter of Modern Life*. New York: Da Capo Press.

Baumgardner, Jennifer, 2011. "Is There a Fourth Wave? Does It Matter?", *Feminist*, https://www.feminist.com/resources/artspeech/genwom/baumgardner2011.html. Accessed: 26 April 2022.

Beerbohm, Max, 1899. "Ouida", in *More*. London and New York: John Lane the Bodley Head, pp. 101–51.

Bell, Shannon, 1999. *Reading, Writing, and Rewriting the Prostitute Body*. Bloomington: Indiana University Press.

Beller, Anne-Marie. 2020. "Collapsing the Courtship Plot: The Challenge to Mid-Victorian Romance in New Woman Short Stories of the 1890s", *Victorian Popular Fictions*, 2.2, pp. 28–40.

Bentzon, Thérèse, 1877. "Les Romans italiens d'un auteur anglais", *Revue des Deux Mondes*, 22.2, pp. 367–88.

Berlanstein, Lenard R., 2001. *Daughters of Eve: A Cultural History of French Theater Women from the Old Regime to the Fin de Siècle*. Cambridge MA: Harvard University Press.

Bernheimer, Charles, 1998. *Figures of Ill Repute: Representing Prostitution in Nineteenth-Century France*. Cambridge: Harvard University Press.

Bigland, Eileen, 1951. *Ouida: The Passionate Victorian*. New York: Duell, Sloan, and Pearce.

Black, Barbara J., 2014. *A Room of His Own: A Literary-Cultural Study of Victorian Clubland*. Athens: Ohio University Press.

Bloom, Clive, 1900. "The Spy Thriller: A Genre Under Cover?", in Clive Bloom (ed.), *Spy Thrillers: From Buchan to Le Carré*. London: Macmillan, pp. 1–11.

Bristow, Joseph, 1991. *Empire Boys: Adventures in a Man's World*. London: Harper Collins.

———, 2015. "The Aesthetic Novel, from Ouida to Firbank", in Gregory Castle (ed.), *A History of the Modernist Novel*. Cambridge: Cambridge University Press, pp. 37–65.

Brooks, Jocelyn, 1951. *Ronald Firbank*. London: Arthur Barker.

Brown, Michael, 2010. "'Like a Devoted Army': Medicine, Heroic Masculinity, and the Military Paradigm in Victorian Britain", *Journal of British Studies*, 49.7, pp. 592-622.

Budd, Michael Anton, 2009. "C. G. Gordon: Hybrid Heroic Technologist and Anti-Modern Other", in Heather Ellis and Jessica Meyer (eds.), *Masculinity and the Other: Historical Perspectives*. Cambridge: Cambridge Scholar Publishing, pp. 190–218.

Buurma, Rachel Sagner, 2008. "Anonyma's Authors", *Studies in English Literature, 1500–1900*, 48.4 (Autumn), pp. 839–48.

Caird, Mona, 1888. "Marriage", *Westminster Review*, 130 (August), pp. 186–201.

Capon, Gaston, and Robert Yve-Plessis, 1906. *Fille de L'Opéra, vendeuse d'amour: Histoire de Mademoiselle Deschamps*. Paris: Plessis.

Carroll, Alicia, 2019. "'Rivers Change Like Nations': Reading Eco-Apocalypse in *The Waters of Edera*", in Laurence W. Mazzeno and Ronald D. Morrison (eds.),

Victorian Environmental Nightmares. London: Palgrave Macmillan, pp. 145–66.

Cather, Willa, 1895. "The Passing Show", *Courier* (23 November), p. 7.

Cerankowski, Karli June, and Megan Milks, 2010. "New Orientations: Asexuality and Its Implications for Theory and Practice", *Feminist Studies*, 36.3 (Fall), pp. 650–64.

———, 2014. "Introduction: Why Asexuality? Why Now?", in Karli June Cerankowski and Megan Milks (eds.), *Asexualities: Feminist and Queer Perspectives*. London, Routledge, pp. 1–17.

Chatterjee, Ronjaunee, Alicia Mireles Christoff, and Amy R. Wong, 2020. "Introduction: Undisciplining Victorian Studies", *Victorian Studies*, 62.3, pp. 369–91.

Chesterton, G. K., 1913. *The Victorian Age in Literature*. London: Williams and Norgate.

Chu, Erica, 2014. "Radical Identity Politics: Asexuality and Contemporary Articulations of Identity", in Karli June Cerankowski and Megan Milks (eds.), *Asexualities. Feminist and Queer Perspectives*. London, Routledge, pp. 79–99.

Clarke, Laura H., 2022. "The Legend of the Legion: Nihilism and the Restoration of the Aristocracy in Ouida's *Under Two Flags*", *Victoriographies*, 12.2, pp. 153–67. DOI: https://doi.org/10.3366/vic.2022.0455.

Clark-Parsons, Rosemary, 2022. *Networked Feminism: How Digital Media Makers Transformed Gender Justice Movements*. Oakland: University of California Press.

Conary, Jennifer, 2023. "Heroines of the Demi-monde: Recovering the Courtesan in Popular Novels of the 1860s". (Unpublished conference paper). *Victorian Popular Fiction Association's 15th Annual Conference: Hidden Histories/Recovered Stories*. Bishop Grosseteste University, 12 July 2023.

"Contemporary Literature", 1879. *Blackwood's Edinburgh Magazine*, 125.761, pp. 322–44.

Cook, Matt, 2003. *London and the Culture of Homosexuality 1885–1914*. Cambridge: Cambridge University Press.

Cooke, Jennifer, 2020. "Introduction", in Jennifer Cooke (ed.), *The New Feminist Literary Studies*. Cambridge: Cambridge University Press, pp. 1–10.

Corelli, Marie, 1890. "A Word about 'Ouida'", *Belgravia*, 71, pp. 362–71.

Coste, Bénédicte, 2019. "French Beliefs: Walter Pater and Contemporary French Fiction", *Cahiers victoriens et édouardiens*, 90 (Autumn). DOI: https://doi.org/10.4000/cve.6722.

Coward, David, 1991. "Introduction", in Alexandre Dumas, *The Three Musketeers*. Oxford: Oxford University Press, pp. ix-xxiii.

Daly, Nicholas, 2020. *Ruritania: A Cultural History from The Prisoner of Zenda to The Princess Diaries*. Oxford, Oxford University Press.

Dawson, Graham, 1994. *Soldier Heroes: British Adventure, Empire and the Imagining of Masculinities*. London: Routledge.

De Pougy, Liane, 1901 [2021] *Idylle Sapphique: A Woman's Affair*. Trans. Graham Anderson. Sawtry: Dedalus Books.

Deane, Bradley, 2014. *Masculinity and the New Imperialism: Rewriting Manhood in British Popular Literature, 1870–1914*. Cambridge: Cambridge University Press.

Denisoff, Dennis, 2022. *Decadent Ecology in British Literature and Art, 1860–1910: Decay, Desire, and the Pagan Revival*. Cambridge: Cambridge University Press.

Douglas, Norman, 1921 [1922]. *Alone*. New York: Robert M. McBride & Co.

Doumic, René, 1899. "Octave Feuillet", in René Doumic, *Contemporary French Novelists*. Trans. Mary D. Frost. New York: Thomas Y. Crowell & Co., pp. 3–40.

Dubuisson, Lorraine Michelle, 2013. *The Epitome and Portrait of Modern Society: Ouida As Social Barometer of the Victorian Era*. Doctoral Thesis, University of Mississippi.

———, 2021. "The Intolerable Kodak: Ouida on Victorian Celebrity Culture", in Brian Cowlishaw (ed.), *The Rail, the Body and the Pen: Essays on Travel, Medicine and Technology in 19th Century British Literature*. Jefferson: McFarland & Co., pp. 188–204.

Du Camp, Maxine, 1905. "Preface", in *Monsieur de Camors*. Paris: Maison Mazarin, pp. v-vii.

Dumas fils, Alexandre, 1848 [2000]. *La Dame aux Camélias*. Trans. David Coward. Oxford: Oxford World's Classics.

Egerton, George, 1894 [2005]. "Virgin Soil", in Angelique Richardson (ed.), *Women Who Did: Stories by Men and Women 1890–1914*. London: Penguin Classics, pp. 103–14.

Elfenbein, Andrew, 1995. *Byron and the Victorians*. Cambridge: Cambridge University Press.

Ella, 1877. "Ouida", *Victoria Magazine*, 28, pp. 369–72.

Embry, Kristi, 2010. "Towards an 'Entente Cordiale': The Cultivation of Cosmopolitan Sympathies in Ouida's *Under Two Flags*", *Studies in the Novel*, 42.3, pp. 227–48.

Erickson, Jesse Ryan, 2020. "Confessions of a Black Ouidaite: Autoethnographic Neo-Victorianism", in Felipe Espinoza Garrido, Marlena Tronicke and Julian Wacker (eds.), *Black Neo-Victoriana*. Leiden: Brill, pp. 33–54.

Esser, Helena, 2022. 'Material Girls: *Moulin Rouge!*'s Neo-Victorian Spectacle and the Real Courtesans of Paris', *Victorian Popular Fictions Journal*, 4.1, pp. 111–25. DOI: https://doi.org/10.46911/IRPL4110.

——— forthcoming [2024]. "Tauchnitz and Ouida: An Anglo-German Friendship in Difficult Times", in Melanie Mienert, Stefan Welz and Dietmar Böhnke (eds.), *English Literature in Your Pocket: The Tauchnitz Edition and Other Paperback Series*. London: Palgrave.

Evangelista, Stefano, 2021. *Literary Cosmopolitanism in the English Fin de Siècle: Citizens of Nowhere*. Oxford: Oxford University Press.

Feuillet, Octave, 1867 [1905]. *Monsieur de Camors*. Paris: Maison Mazarin.

Ffrench, Yvonne, 1938. *Ouida: A Study in Ostentation*. London: Cobden-Sanderson.

Figes, Orlando, 2011. *Crimea: The Last Crusade*. London: Penguin.

———, 2019. *The Europeans: Three Lives and the Making of a Cosmopolitan Culture*. London: Penguin.

Fiske, A.K., 1880. "Profligacy in Fiction: Zola's *Nana*. Ouida's *Moths*", *North American Review*, 285, pp. 79–88.

Fitzsimons, Eleanor, 2015. *Wilde's Women: How Oscar Wilde Was Shaped by the Women He Knew*. London: Duckworth Overlook.

Foucault, Michel, 1978. *The History of Sexuality. Volume 1: An Introduction*. New York: Pantheon Books.

———, 1984. "Of Other Spaces", *Architecture/Mouvement/Continuité*, 5 (October), pp. 46–49.

Friedman, Dustin, 2019. *Before Queer Theory: Victorian Aestheticism and the Self*. Baltimore: Johns Hopkins University Press.

Furneaux, Holly, 2016. *Military Men of Feeling: Emotion, Touch, and Masculinity in the Crimean War*. Oxford: Oxford University Press.

Garval, Michael D., 2012. *Cléo de Mérode and the Rise of Modern Celebrity Culture*. London: Routledge.

Gedge, Rev. J. Denny, 1920. "Reader Letter", *Athenaeum* (17 September), p. 387.

Genz, Stéphanie, 2009. *Postfemininities in Popular Culture*. London: Palgrave Macmillan.

Geraghty, Lincoln, 2019. "Destination Antwerp! Fan Tourism and the Transcultural Heritage of *A Dog of Flanders*", *Humanities*, 8.2, pp. 1–11. DOI: https://doi.org/10.3390/h8020090.

Gere, Charlotte, 1998. "European Decorative Arts at the World's Fairs 1850–1900", *The Metropolitan Museum of Art Bulletin*, 56.3 (Winter 1998/99), pp. 3–55.

Gilbert, Pamela K., 1999. "Ouida and the Other New Woman", in Nicola Diane Thompson (ed.), *Victorian Women Writers and the Woman Question*. Cambridge: Cambridge University Press, pp. 170–88.

———, 2005. *Disease, Desire and the Body in Victorian Women's Popular Novels*. Cambridge: Cambridge University Press.

———, 2013. "Ouida and the Canon: Recovering, Reconsidering, and Revisioning the Popular", in Jane Jordan and Andrew King (eds.), *Ouida and Victorian Popular Culture*. Abingdon: Routledge, pp. 37–52.

Girouard, Mark, 1981. *The Return to Camelot: Chivalry and the English Gentleman*. New Haven: Yale University Press.

Gledhill, Christine, 1992. "Speculations on the Relationship between Soap Opera and Melodrama", *Quarterly Review of Film and Video*, 14.1–2, pp. 103–24.

Goellner, Sage, 2018. *French Orientalist Literature in Algeria, 1845–1882: Colonial Hauntings*. London: Lexington Books.

Gosse, Edmund, 1911. "Feuillet, Octave", in *Encyclopædia Britannica*, 10, pp. 304–5.

Greenslade, William, 2010. *Degeneration, Culture and the Novel: 1880–1940*. Cambridge: Cambridge University Press.

Grewe, Astrid, 1974. *Die Literatur der Krinoline: Eine historisch-soziologische Studie*

zum Werk von Octave Feuillet. Frankfurt Main: Peter Lang.
Guidi, Angelo Flavio, 1908. "Ouida"', *Nuova Antologia*, 217 (16 February), pp. 649–56.
Guigon, Catherine, 2012. *Les Cocottes: Reines du Paris 1900*. Paris: Parigramme.
Hager, Lisa, 2014. "Embodying Agency: Ouida's Sensational Shaping of the British New Woman", in Anne-Marie Beller and Tara MacDonald (eds.), *Rediscovering Victorian Women Sensation Writers*. London: Routledge, pp. 90–101.
Haggard, H. Rider, 1885 [1951]. *Three Adventure Novels of H. Rider Haggard: She, King's Solomon's Mines, Allan Quartermain*. New York: Dover Publications.
Hall, Donald E., 1994. *Muscular Christianity: Embodying the Victorian Age*. Cambridge: Cambridge University Press.
Hall, Stuart, 1981 [2019]. "Notes on Deconstructing 'The Popular'", in *Essential Essays, Vol. 1*. Durham: Duke University Press, pp. 347–61.
Hallum, Kirby-Jane, 2015. *Aestheticism and the Marriage Market in Victorian Popular Fiction: The Art of Female Beauty*. London: Routledge.
Harrison, Frederic, 1894. *The Meaning of History, and Other Historical Pieces*. New York: Macmillan.
Hatter, Janine and Helena Ifill, 2021. "Making Space: Key Popular Women Writers Then and Now", *Victorian Popular Fictions*, 3.1, pp. 4–32.
Hawthorne, Julian, 1890. "The Romance of the Impossible", *McBride's Magazine*, 46 (July-December), p. 413.
"Helianthus. By Ouida", 1908. *Saturday Review* (12 December), pp. 5–6.
Hemingway, Ernest, 1964 [2010]. *A Moveable Feast*. London: Arrow Books.
Houlbrook, Matt, 2003. "Soldier Heroes and Rent Boys: Homosex, Masculinities, and Britishness in the Brigade of Guards, circa 1900–1960", *Journal of British Studies*, 42.3, pp. 351–88.
Hughes, Thomas, 1857 [2008]. *Tom Brown's Schooldays*. Oxford: Oxford World's Classics.
Hume, Hamilton, 1867. "Literature", *Will-o-the-Wisp*, 1 (23 February), p. 7.
Jenkins, Henry, 1992 [2013]. *Textual Poachers: Television Fans and Participatory Culture*. London: Routledge.
Jenkins, Henry, Sangita Shresthova, Liana Gamber-Thompson, Neta Kligler-Vilenchik, and Arely Zimmerman, 2016. *By Any Media Necessary: The New Youth Activism*. New York: NYU Press.
Johnson, Myra T., 1977. "Asexual and Autoerotic Women: Two Invisible Groups", in Harvey L. Gochros and Jean S. Gochros (eds.), *The Sexually Oppressed*. New York: Association Press, pp. 96–109.
Jordan, Jane, 1995. "Ouida: The Enigma of a Literary Identity", *Princeton University Library Chronicle*, 57.1, pp. 75–105.
———, 2009a. "'Everything is true as solemnly as I can declare it': The Case of Ouida and her Biographers", in Meg Jensen and Jane Jordan (eds.), *Life Writing: The Spirit of the Age and the State of the Art*. Newcastle upon Tyne: Cambridge Scholars Publishing, pp. 183–94.

———, 2009b. "The English George Sand? Ouida, the French Novel and Late Victorian Literary Censorship", *Anglistica Pisana*, 6.1/2, pp. 107–16.

———, 2009c. "The Peasant and the Picturesque in Ouida's Italy", in Alessandro Vescovi, Luisa Villa, and Paul Vita (eds.), *The Victorians and Italy: Literature, Travel, Politics and Art*. Monza: Polimetrica Publisher, pp. 61–79.

———, 2011a. "Ouida: How Conceptions of the Popular Reader Contributed to the Making of a Popular Novelist", in Beth Palmer and Adelene Buckland (eds.), *A Return to the Common Reader: Print Culture and the Novel, 1850–1900*. Farnham: Ashgate, pp. 37–54.

———, 2011b. "Ouida", in Pamela K. Gilbert (ed.) *A Companion to Sensation Fiction*. Chichester: Wiley-Blackwell Publishing Ltd., pp. 220–31.

———, 2013. "'Between Men': Romantic Friendship in Ouida's Early Novels", in Jane Jordan and Andrew King (eds.), *Ouida and Victorian Popular Culture*. Abingdon: Routledge, pp. 53–71.

———, 2014a. "'Literature at nurse': George Moore, Ouida and *Fin-de-Siècle* Literary Censorship", in Ann Heilmann and Mark Llewellyn (eds.), *George Moore: Influence and Collaboration*. London: Rowman & Littlefield, pp. 69–82.

———, 2014b. "'Romans Français Écrits En Anglais': Ouida, the Sensation Novel and Fin-de-siècle Literary Censorship", in Anne-Marie Beller and Tara MacDonald (eds.), *Rediscovering Victorian Women Sensation Writers*. London: Routledge, pp. 102–18.

———, forthcoming [2024]. "Writing for the Masses: Ouida and Newspaper Syndication", in Carolyn Oulton and Adrienne Gavin (eds.), *Women's Writing from the 1840s to 1940s*. Vol. 3. London: Palgrave.

Jordan, Jane and Andrew King (eds.), 2013. *Ouida and Victorian Popular Culture*. Abingdon: Routledge.

Kestner, Joseph A., 2010. *Masculinities in British Adventure Fiction, 1880–1915*. London: Ashgate.

King, Andrew, 2009. "The Origins of Ouida's *Pascarèl* (1873): The Combination Novel, Myths of the Female Artist and the Commerce of Art", *Anglistica Pisana*, 6.1/2, pp. 77–86.

———, 2011a. "Introduction", in Ouida, *The Massarenes*, ed. Andrew King. London: Pickering & Chatto, pp. vii-xx.

———, 2011b. "The Sympathetic Individualist: Ouida's Late Work and Politics", *Victorian Literature and Culture*, 39.2, pp. 563–79.

———, 2013a. "Crafting the Woman Artist: Ouida and Ariadnê", in Kyriaki Hadjiafxendi and Patricia Zakreski (eds.), *Crafting the Woman Professional in the Long Nineteenth Century: Artistry and Industry in Britain*. Farnham: Ashgate, pp. 207–26.

———, 2013b. "Introduction", in Jane Jordan and Andrew King (eds), *Ouida and Victorian Popular Culture*. London: Routledge, pp. 1–9.

———, 2013c. "Ouida 1839–1901: 'Quantities, Aesthetics, Politics'", in Jane Jordan and Andrew King (eds). *Ouida and Victorian Popular Culture*. London:

Routledge, pp. 13–37.

——, 2015. "Ouida (Marie Louise Ramé)", in Dino Franco Felluga, Pamela K. Gilbert, and Linda K. Hughes (eds.), *The Encyclopedia of Victorian Literature*, New York: Wiley-Blackwell, pp. 1225–31.

Kukavica, Sebastian, 2023. "The Splendour of Decadence: The Moral Geography of the European South in Victorian Travelogues", *Victorian Popular Fictions*, 5.1, pp. 124–41. DOI: https://doi.org/10.46911/MXNR9140.

Law, Graham, 2013. "22 May 1891: Ouida's Attack on Fiction Syndication", Dino Franco Felluga (ed.), *BRANCH: Britain, Representation and Nineteenth-Century History. Extension of Romanticism and Victorianism on the Net*, https://branchcollective.org/?ps_articles=graham-law-22-may-1891-ouidas-attack-on-fiction-syndication. Accessed: 9 June 2023.

Lawrence, George Alfred, 1857 [1886]. *Guy Livingstone; or: "Thorough"*. New York: Harper & Brothers.

——, 1859. *Sword and Gown*. New York: Harper & Brothers.

"The Latest and Last of Ouida's", 1908. *Los Angeles Times* (13 December), p. 8.

Le Queux, William, 1911. *Revelations of the Secret Service*. London: F. V. White & Co.

Ledger, Sally, 1997. *The New Woman: Fiction and Feminism at the Fin de Siècle*. Manchester: Manchester University Press.

Lee, Elizabeth, 1914. *Ouida: A Memoir*. London: Fisher Unwin.

Linde, Zane, 2021. "Intended by Nature to be Left Intact: An Asexual Reading of *Jude the Obscure*", *Thomas Hardy Journal*, 27 (Autumn): pp. 81–8.

London, Jack, 1917 [1994]. "Eight Factors of Literary Success", in Earle Labor (ed.), *The Portable Jack London*. London: Viking Penguin.

Love, Heather, 2007. *Feeling Backward: Loss and the Politics of Queer History*. Cambridge: Harvard University Press.

Mallett, Phillip, 2015. "Masculinity, Imperialism, and the Novel", in Phillip Mallett (ed.), *The Victorian Novel and Masculinity*. London: Palgrave Macmillan, pp. 151–71.

Mallock, W. H., 1920. "Memories of Men and Places", *Harper's Monthly Magazine*, 141 (June-November), pp. 118–27.

Maltz, Diana, 2009. "Ouida, 'Impossible' Socialism, and the Appeal of Anachronism", *Anglistica Pisana*, 6.1/2, pp. 99–106.

Marcus, Steven, 1966 [2009]. *The Other Victorians: A Study of Sexuality and Pornography in Mid-Nineteenth-Century England*. New York: Routledge.

Markovits, Stefanie, 2009. *The Crimean War in the British Imagination*. Cambridge: Cambridge University Press.

Marrone, Claire, 1997. "Male and Female Bildung: The *Mémoires de Céleste Mogador*", *Nineteenth-Century French Studies*, 25.3–4, pp. 335–47.

Marucci, Franco, 2009. "Ouida: The Fascination of Moral Laxity", *Revue LISA*, 7.3, pp. 593–604. DOI: https://doi.org/10.4000/lisa.149.

——, 2020. *Authors in Dialogue: Comparative Essays in Nineteenth-and Early*

Twentieth-Century English Literature. Oxford: Peter Lang.

Matsui, Midori, 1993. "Little Girls Were Little Boys: Displaced Femininity in the Representation of Homosexuality in Japanese Girls' Comics", in Sneja Gunew and Anna Yeatman (eds.), *Feminism and the Politics of Difference.* St Leonards: Allen, pp. 177–96.

Matthews, J. Brander, 1881. *French Dramatists of the 19th Century.* New York: Charles Scribner's Sons.

Maugham, F. Somerset, 1930 [2000]. *Cakes and Ale.* New York: Vintage International.

Mauris, Maurice, 1880. *French Men of Letters.* New York: D. Appleton & Co.

McLelland, Mark J., 2000. "The Love between 'Beautiful Boys' in Japanese Women's Comics", *Journal of Gender Studies,* 9.1, pp. 13–25.

McRobbie, Angela, 2009. *The Aftermath of Feminism: Gender, Culture, and Social Change.* London: SAGE Publications.

[Meynell, Alice], 1895. "'Praises of Ouida", *Pall Mall Gazette* (16 August), p. 4.

Middleton, Alex, 2015. "French Algeria in British Imperial Thought, 1830–70", *Journal of Colonialism and Colonial History,* 16.1. DOI: https://doi.org/10.1353/cch.2015.0012

Milne-Smith, Amy, 2011. *London Clubland: A Cultural History of Gender and Class in Late Victorian Britain.* London: Palgrave Macmillan.

Mitchell, Sally, 1981. *The Fallen Angel: Chastity, Class and Women's Reading 1835–1880.* Bowling Green, Ohio: Bowling Green University Popular Press.

Mogador, Céleste, 1854 [2001]. *Céleste Mogador: Memoirs of a Courtesan in Nineteenth-Century Paris.* Trans. Monique Fleury Nagem. Lincoln: University of Nebraska Press.

Molloy, Carla, 2008. *The Art of Popular Fiction: Gender, Authorship and Aesthetics in the Writing of Ouida.* Doctoral Thesis, University of Canterbury.

Montesquiou, Robert de, 1913. *La Divine Comtesse: Étude d'après Madame de Castiglione.* Paris: Goupil & Co.

Moody, Nickianne, 2013. "Defending Female Genius: The Unlikely Cultural Alignment of Marie Corelli and Ouida", in Jane Jordan and Andrew King (eds), *Ouida and Victorian Popular Culture.* London: Routledge, pp. 109–30.

Moore, Rory, 2011. "'The Penalties of a Well-Known Name': Ouida, Celebrity, and a Sensational Friendship", *Nineteenth-Century Contexts,* 33.5, pp. 483–97.

Moulin Rouge!, 2001. Directed by Baz Luhrman. [DVD Disc 2]. USA: Twentieth Century Fox Home Entertainment Inc.

Munro, Ealasaid, 2013. "Feminism: A Fourth Wave?", *Political Insight* (September), pp. 22–5.

Murray, Vincent E. H., 1873. "Ouida's Novels", *Contemporary Review,* 22, pp. 921–35.

Nagem, Monique Fleury, 2001. "Translator's Introduction", in Céleste Mogador, *Memoirs of a Courtesan in Nineteenth-Century.* Trans. Monique Fleury Nagem. Lincoln: University of Nebraska Press, pp. ix-xxii.

Nead, Lynda, 1988. *Myths of Sexuality: Representations of Women in Victorian Britain.*

Oxford: Basil Blackwell.

Nelson, Camilla, 2024. "'A public orgy of misogyny': Gender, Power, Media, and Legal Spectacle in Depp v Heard", *Feminist Media Studies* (25 January), pp. 1–17. DOI: https://doi.org/10.1080/14680777.2024.2304225

Neville, Lucy, 2018. *Girls Who Like Boys Who Like Boys: Women and Gay Male Pornography and Erotica*. London: Palgrave.

"New Novels", 1878. *Standard* (15 August), p. 2.

"Novels", 1880. *Examiner* (10 July), p. 841.

"Novels of the Week", 1885. *Athenaeum* (19 December), pp. 803–05.

"Novels of the Week", 1889. *Athenaeum* (1 June): pp. 693–4.

Ouida, 1863 [1891]. *Granville de Vigne, or: Held in Bondage*. London: Chatto & Windus.

———, 1866 [1879]. *Chandos*. London: Chatto & Windus.

———, 1867 [1902]. *Idalia*. London: Chatto & Windus.

———, 1867 [1995]. *Under Two Flags: A Story of the Household and the Desert*, ed. John Sutherland. Oxford: Oxford University Press.

———, 1869. *Tricotrin*. London: Chapman & Hall.

———, 1870. *Puck: His Vicissitudes, Adventures, Observations, Conclusions, Friendships, and Philosophies*. 2 Vols. Leipzig: Tauchnitz.

———, 1871 [1872]. *Folle-Farine*. 2 Vols. Leipzig: Tauchnitz.

———, 1872. "A Leaf in the Storm"; "A Dog of Flanders"; *and Other Stories*. Leipzig: Tauchnitz.

———, 1876 [1892]. *In A Winter City*. London: Chatto & Windus.

———, 1877 [1891]. *Ariadnê: The Story of a Dream*. Philadelphia: Lippincott.

———, 1878. *Friendship. A Story*. 2 Vols. Leipzig: Tauchnitz.

———, 1880 [2005]. *Moths*, ed. Natalie Schroeder. Plymouth: Broadview.

———, 1881. *A Village Commune*. London: Chatto & Windus.

———, 1882 [1895]. "Romance and Realism", letter to *The Times* (12 October), pp. 3–4, reprinted in *Frescoes: Dramatic Sketches*. London: Chatto & Windus, pp. 299–310.

———, 1883 [1895]. *Frescoes: Dramatic Sketches*. London: Chatto & Windus.

———, 1884 [1886]. *Princess Napraxine*. London: Chatto & Windus.

———, 1885 [1893]. *Othmar*. London: Chatto & Windus.

———, 1885. "The Tendencies of English Fiction", *North American Review*, 141 (September), pp. 213–25.

———, 1887 [1895]. "Vulgarity", *North American Review*, 144 (February), pp. 148–60, reprinted in *Views and Opinions*. London: Methuen & Co., pp. 327–46.

———, 1889. *Guilderoy*. 2 Vols. Leipzig: Tauchnitz.

———, 1891. "New Literary Factors", *The Times* (22 May), p. 3.

———, 1891 [1895]a. "Has Christianity Failed?", *North American Review*, 152 (February), pp. 221–33, reprinted as "The Failure of Christianity" in *Views and Opinions*. London: Methuen & Co., pp. 111–30.

———, 1891 [1895]b. "The State as Immoral Teacher", *North American Review,* 153 (August), pp. 193–204, reprinted in *Views and Opinions.* London: Methuen & Co., pp. 347–67.

———, 1894 [1895]a. "The Legislation of Fear", *Fortnightly Review,* 56 (October), pp. 552–61, reprinted in *Views and Opinions.* London: Methuen & Co., pp. 382–99.

———, 1894 [1895]b. "The New Woman", *North American Review,* 158.450, pp. 610–9, reprinted in *Views and Opinions.* London: Methuen & Co, pp. 205–22.

———, 1894 [1895]c. "L'Uomo Fatale", *Fortnightly Review,* 61 (March), pp. 355–64, reprinted in *Views and Opinions.* London: Methuen & Co., pp. 187–203.

———, 1895a. "The Italy of To-day", in *Views and Opinions.* London: Methuen & Co., pp. 145–59.

———, 1895b. *Views and Opinions.* 2nd edn. London: Methuen & Co.

———, 1896 [1900]. "The Ugliness of Modern Life", *Nineteenth Century,* 39 (January), pp. 28–43, reprinted in *Critical Studies: A Set of Essays by Ouida.* London: Fisher Unwin, pp. 210–38.

———, 1897 [1900]. "Georges Darien", *Fortnightly Review,* 62 (September), pp. 341–57, reprinted in *Critical Studies: A Set of Essays by Ouida.* London: Fisher Unwin, pp. 50–84.

———, 1897 [1904]. *The Massarenes.* London: Chatto & Windus.

———, 1898. "An Impeachment of Modern Italy", *Review of Reviews,* 18 (September), pp. 245–54.

———, 1899 [1900]. "Joseph Chamberlain", *Nuova Antologia,* 168 (1 December), pp. 576–85, reprinted in *Critical Studies: A Set of Essays by Ouida.* London: Fisher Unwin, pp. 165–80.

———, 1900a. "Imperialismo Inglese", *Nuova Antologia,* 170 (16 April), pp. 729–30.

———, 1900b. "The Decadence of Latin Races", in *Critical Studies: A Set of Essays by Ouida.* London: Fisher Unwin, pp. 264–79.

———, 1900c. "Wilfred Scawen Blunt", in *Critical Studies: A Set of Essays by Ouida.* London: Fisher Unwin, pp. 143–64.

———, 1900d. *Critical Studies: A Set of Essays by Ouida.* London: Fisher Unwin.

———, 1900 [1902]. *The Waters of Edera.* London: Chatto & Windus.

———, 1908. *Helianthus.* London: Macmillan and Co.

———, 1909. "The Woman Problem. I. Shall Women Vote? A Study of Feminine Unrest – Its Causes and Remedies", *Lippincott's Monthly Magazine,* 83.497 (May), pp. 556–92.

Oulton, Carolyn W. de la L., 2007. *Romantic Friendship in Victorian Literature.* Aldershot: Ashgate.

Parkins, Wendy, 2009. *Mobility and Modernity in Women's Novels, 1850s-1930s: Women Moving Dangerously.* London: Palgrave Macmillan.

Pater, Walter, 1893 [2020]. *The Renaissance: Studies in Art and Poetry.* Berkeley: University of California Press, 2020.

Peck, John, 1998. *War, the Army, and Victorian Literature*. London: Palgrave.
Pélissier, Georges, 1893. *Essais de littérature contemporaine*. Paris. Lecène, Ouidin, & Co.
Phillips, Celia G., 1978. "Ouida and her Publishers: 1874–1880", *Bulletin of Research in the Humanities*, 81, pp. 210–5.
Pilcher, Jane, and Imelda Whelehan, 2017. "Mainstreaming or New Activism? Gender Studies and Gender Politics", in Jane Pilcher and Imelda Whelehan (eds.), *Key Concepts in Gender Studies*. 2nd Edition. London: SAGE Publications, pp. xiii-x.
Pireddu, Nicoletta, 2014. "Between Darwin and San Francesco: Zoographic Ambivalences in Mantegazza, Ouida, and Vernon Lee", *Gothic Studies*, 16.1 (May), pp. 111–27. DOI: http://dx.doi.org/10.7227/GS.16.1.9
Pollock, Mary Sanders, 2005. "Ouida's Rhetoric of Empathy: A Case Study in Victorian Anti-Vivisection Narrative", in Mary Sanders Pollock and Catherine Rainwater (eds.), *Figuring Animals: Essays on Animal Images in Art, Literature, Philosophy, and Popular Culture*. London: Palgrave, pp. 135–60.
Poster, Carol, 1996. "Oxidization Is a Feminist Issue: Acidity, Canonicity, and Popular Victorian Female Authors", *College English*, 58.3 (March), pp. 287–306.
Preston, Harriet Waters, 1886. "Ouida", *The Atlantic Monthly*, 58, pp. 47–58.
Primorac, Antonija, 2018. *Neo-Victorianism on Screen: Postfeminism and Contemporary Adaptations of Victorian Women*. London: Palgrave Macmillan.
Przybylo, Ela, 2006 [2016]. "Introducing Asexuality, Unthinking Sex", in Nancy L. Fisher and Steven Seidman (eds.), *Introducing the New Sexuality Studies*. 3rd Edition. London: Routledge, pp. 181–91.
Puccini, Giacomo, 1896 [2001]. *La Bohème*. Coral Gable: Opera Journeys Publishing.
Pykett, Lyn, 1992. *The 'Improper' Feminine: The Women's Sensation Novel and the New Woman Writing*. London: Routledge.
———, 2002. "Foreword", in Angelique Richardson and Chris Willis (eds.), *The New Woman in Fiction and in Fact: Fin-de-Siècle Feminisms*. London: Palgrave Macmillan, pp. xi-xii.
———, 2013. "Opinionated Ouida", in Jane Jordan and Andrew King (eds.), *Ouida and Victorian Popular Culture*. Abingdon: Routledge, pp. 147–64.
———, 2016. "*Fin-de-Siècle* Ouida: A New Woman Writing Against the New Woman?", in Holly A. Laird (ed.), *The History of British Women's Writing, 1880–1920*. London: Palgrave Macmillan, pp. 35–46.
Rainwater, Crescent, 2021. "'I want bad things – strong bad things': Ouida, Walter Pater, and Aestheticism in Dorothy Richardson's *Backwater* (1916)", *Feminist Modernist Studies*, 5, pp. 89–105. DOI: https://doi.org/10.1080/24692921.2021.1932178.
Reidy, Kerry, Abbott, Keeley, and Samuel Parker, 2023. "'So they hit each other': Gendered Constructions of Domestic Abuse in the YouTube Commentary of

the Depp v Heard trial", *Critical Discourse Studies* (12 December), pp. 1–18. DOI https://doi.org/10.1080/17405904.2023.2291130.

"Review of *La Vivandière*, by W. S. Gilbert", 1868. *The Times* (24 January), n. p., reprinted at The Gilbert and Sullivan Archive, https://www.gsarchive.net/gilbert/plays/vivandiere/times1868.html. Accessed: 10 April 2023.

Richardson, Angelique, 2002. "Introduction", in Angelique Richardson (ed.), *Women Who Did: Stories by Men and Woman 1890–1914*. London: Penguin Classics, pp. xxxi–lxxxi.

Richardson, Dorothy M., 1917. *Pilgrimage*, Vol. 1. London: The Cresset Press.

Richardson, Joanna, 1967. *The Courtesans: The Demi-Monde in 19th-Century France*. London: Phoenix.

Rivers, Nicola, 2017. *Postfeminism(s) and the Arrival of the Fourth Wave: Turning Tides*. London: Palgrave.

Robinson, Charles, 1894. "Ouida at Home", *Tuapeka Times*, 26.4127 (15 August), p. 5.

Robinson, Sandra, and Emily Hiltz, 2024. "Platformed Misogyny in Depp v Heard: #justiceforjohnny and Networked Defamation", *Feminist Media Studies*, 24.1, pp. 162–5. DOI: https://doi.org/10.1080/14680777.2023.2284107

Rounding, Virginia, 2003. *Grandes Horizontales: The Lives and Legends of Four Nineteenth-Century Courtesans*. London: Bloomsbury.

Saintsbury, George, 1878 [1891]. *Essays on French Novelists*. 2nd edn. London, Percival & Co.

Schaffer, Talia, 2000. *The Forgotten Female Aesthetes: Literary Culture in Late-Victorian England*. Charlottesville: University Press of Virginia.

———, 2001. "Nothing but Foolscap and Ink: Inventing the New Woman", in Angelique Richardson and Chris Willis (eds.), *The New Woman in Fiction and Fact: Fin-de-Siècle Feminisms*. London: Palgrave Macmillan, pp. 39–52.

———, 2002. "The Origins of the Aesthetic Novel: Ouida, Wilde, and the Popular Romance", in Joseph Bristow (ed.), *Wilde Writings*. Toronto: University of Toronto Press, pp. 212–29.

———, 2011. "Aestheticism and Sensation", in Pamela Gilbert (ed.), *A Companion to Sensation Fiction*. Chichester: Wiley-Blackwell Publishing Ltd., pp. 614–26.

Schmidt, Michael, 2014. *The Novel: A Biography*. Cambridge, MA: Harvard University Press.

Schroeder, Natalie, 1988. "Feminine Sensationalism, Eroticism, and Self-Assertion: M. E. Braddon and Ouida", *Tulsa Studies in Women's Literature*, 7.1, pp. 87–103.

———, and Shari Hodges Holt, 2008. *Ouida the Phenomenon: Evolving Social, Political, and Gender Concerns in Her Fiction*. Newark: University of Delaware Press.

———, and Ronald A. Schroeder, 2011. "*Under Two Flags*", in Pamela K. Gilbert (ed.), *A Companion to Sensation Fiction*. Chichester: Wiley-Blackwell Publishing Ltd., pp. 232–43.

Sedgwick, Eve Kosofsky, 1985. *Between Men: English Literature and Male Homosocial*

Desire. New York: Columbia University Press.
Severi, Rita, 2009. "Ouida: Wilde's *Lionne and The Woman's World*", *Anglistica Pisana*, VI, 6.1/2, pp. 99–106.
Seward, Desmond, 2013. *Eugénie: The Empress and Her Empire.* London: Thistle Publishing.
Shaw, George Bernard, 1886 [1991]. "Ouida's Latest Novel", *Pall Mall Gazette* (25 January), reprinted in Bran Tyson (ed.), *George Bernard Shaw's Book Reviews.* University Park: Pennsylvania State University Press, pp. 105–9.
Showalter, Elaine, 1977. *A Literature of Their Own: British Women Novelists from Brontë to Lessing.* Princeton: Princeton University Press.
"*Signa*", 1875. *Saturday Review,* 39 (June 26), pp. 830–1.
Smith, Alison, David Bayney Brown, and Carol Jacobi (eds.), 2016. *Artist and Empire: Facing Britain's Imperial Past.* London: Tate Publishing.
Solomon-Godeau, Abigail, 1986. "The Legs of the Countess", *October,* 39 (Winter), pp. 65–108.
Spencer, Herbert, 1884. *The Man Versus the State.* London: Williams & Norgate.
Stafford, David A. T., 1981. "Spies and Gentlemen: The Birth of the British Spy Novel, 1893–1914", *Victorian Studies,* 24.4 (Summer), pp. 489–509.
Stanfill, Mel, 2021. "Straight (White) Women Writing about Men Bonking? Complicating our Understanding of Gender and Sexuality in Fandom", in Marnel Niles Goins, Joan Faber McAlister, and Bryant Keith Alexander (eds.), *The Routledge Handbook of Gender and Communication.* London: Routledge, pp. 446–57.
Stearn, Roger T., 2004. "Burnaby, Frederick Gustavus (1842–1885)", *Oxford Dictionary of National Biography.* DOI: https://doi.org/10.1093/ref:odnb/4047.
Steel, Tom, 1990. *The Langham: A History.* London: Langham.
Stevenson, Robert Louis, 1882 [1887]. "A Gossip on Romance," *Longman's Magazine,* 1.1 (November), pp. 69–79, reprinted in *Memories and Portraits,* Edinburgh: T. Nelson & Sons, Ltd., pp. 234–58.
———, 1883 [1905]. "A Note on Realism", in *Essays in the Art of Writing.* London: Chatto & Windus, pp. 93–110.
———, and friends, 1892 [1900]. *An Object of Pity, or: The Man Haggard.* New York: Dodd, Mead, & Co.
Stirling, Monica, 1950. *The Fine and Wicked: The Life and Times of Ouida.* London: Gollancz.
St. John, John. 1990. *William Heinemann: A Century of Publishing 1890–1990.* London: Heinemann, pp. 23–4.
Stokes, Roy B., 1983. "Ouida", in Ira B. Nadel and William E. Fredeman (eds.), *Dictionary of Literary Biography, Vol. 18: Victorian Novelists after 1885.* Detroit: Gale Group, pp. 239–46.
Street, G.S., 1895. "An Appreciation of Ouida", *Yellow Book,* 6, pp. 167–76.
"A Study in Puppydom", 1890 [1908]. *St James's Gazette* (24 June). Reprinted in Stuart Mason, *Oscar Wilde: Art & Morality A Defence of The Picture of Dorian*

Gray. London: J. Jacobs, p. 9–11.

Sullivan, Courtney, 2016. *The Evolution of the French Courtesan Novel From de Chabrillan to Colette*. London: Palgrave Macmillan.

Sutherland, John, 1995. "Introduction", in Ouida, *Under Two Flags: A Story of the Household and the Desert*. Oxford: Oxford Popular Fiction, pp. ix-xxi.

Symons, Arthur, 1892 [2012]. "Nini Patte-en-l'Air", in Jane Desmarais and Chris Baldick (eds.), *Decadence: An Annotated Anthology*. Manchester: Manchester University Press, p. 139.

———, 1893 [2012]. "The Decadent Movement in Literature", in Jane Desmarais and Chris Baldick (eds.), *Decadence: An Annotated Anthology*. Manchester: Manchester University Press, pp. 251–62.

———, 1922. "The Nietzschean Follies, IV: Feminine Fiction", *The Smart Set*, 67.4, pp.123–7.

Tennyson, Alfred, 1855. "The Charge of the Light Brigade", in Alfred Tennyson, *Maud, and Other Poems*. Boston: Ticknor and Fields, p. 157.

Tintner, Adeline R., 1991. *The Cosmopolitan World of Henry James: An Intertextual Study*. Baton Rouge: Louisiana State University Press.

"Translator's Preface", 1891. In Octave Feuillet, *A Man of Honor: M. de Camors*. Chicago: Laird & Lee, pp. 11–4.

Turgenev, Ivan, 1867 [1906]. *Smoke*. Trans. Constance Garnett. New York: Macmillan.

Vamplew, Wray, and Joyce Kay, 2006. "Captains Courageous: Gentlemen Riders in British Horseracing 1866–1914", *Sport in History*, 26.3, pp. 370–85.

Van Vechten, Carl, 1926. *Excavations*. New York: Alfred A. Knopf.

Verdi, Giuseppe, 1853 [2001]. *La Traviata*. Coral Gable: Opera Journeys Publishing.

Villa, Luisa, 2019. "With Gordon, Kitchener and Others in the Sudan: Mapping Fictional Engagement with the Imperial Frontier", *Victorian Popular Fictions*, 1.2, pp. 61–74.

Vrachnas, Barbara, 2013. "Ouida's Publishing History: Prolific Then, Peripheral Now", *Gramma: Journal of Theory and Criticism*, 21, pp. 115–29.

———, 2017. "Ouida's Female and Male Players from 1860 to 1880", *CEA Critic*, 79.1, pp. 58–77.

Waugh, Evelyn, 1948. *The Loved One*. London: Chapman & Hall.

Wharton, Edith, 1920 [1996]. *The Age of Innocence*. London: Penguin Classics.

Whelehan, Imelda, 1995. *Modern Feminist Thought: From the Second Wave to 'Post-Feminism'*. New York: New York University Press.

"The 'Whitehall' Portraits. XCVIII. – Ouida", 1878. *The Whitehall Review* (5 October), p. 484.

Wilde, Oscar, 1889. "Ouida's New Novel", *The Pall Mall Gazette*, 5 (17 May), p. 3.

———, 1890 [2008]. *The Picture of Dorian Gray*, in *The Complete Works of Oscar Wilde: Stories, Plays, Poems, & Essays*. New York: HarperCollins, pp. 17–167.

———, 1891a [2008]. "The Decay of Lying", in *The Complete Works of Oscar Wilde: Stories, Plays, Poems, & Essays*. New York: HarperCollins, pp. 970–93.

———, 1891b [2008]. "The Soul of Man under Socialism", in *The Complete Works of Oscar Wilde: Stories, Plays, Poems, & Essays*. New York: HarperCollins, 1079–105.

Willy [Henry Gauthier-Villars], 1904. *Danseuses*. Paris: A. Méricant.

Yates, Edmund Hodgson, 1879. "Ouidà at Villa Farinola", in Edmund Hodgson Yates, *Celebrities At Home*, First Series. London: Office of "The World", pp. 239–47.

Zimmerman, Tegan, 2017. "#Intersectionality: The Fourth Wave Feminist Twitter Community", *Atlantis*, 38.1, pp. 54–70.

Zola, Émile, 1880 [2009]. *Nana*. Trans. Douglas Parmée. Oxford: Oxford World's Classics.

Zweig, Stefan, 1943 [1947]. *The World of Yesterday*. 4th Edition. London: Cassell and Company.

Index

#MeToo, 19, 116, 119

Adultery, 3, 79, 81, 98, 100, 102, 107, 109
Adventure fiction, 2, 5, 18–21, 28, 39–46, 47–51, 56–9, 76–8, 179, 183–4, 186; Heroes, 23–4, 39, 187
Adventuress, 9, 21, 26, 34–5, 50, 4, 0, 95, 99, 112
Aestheticism, 5, 10, 15, 102, 111, 123–7, 130, 142–4, 149–54, 161, 182, 186; Female Aestheticism, 21, 120–1, 132–6; and Walter Pater, 102, 121, 146, 149; and Oscar Wilde, 2, 5, 124–5, 130, 142, 183
Ambrosini, Richard, 148, 169, 172, 176
Arendt, Hannah, 172
Ariadnê (Ouida), 7, 10, 122, 146–7, 149–50, 155, 177; Hilarion, 150–4; Giojà, 150–4
Aromantic, aromanticism, 128–30, 141
Artist (female), 4–7, 18, 21–2, 145–58, 173–6, 182–9
Asexual, asexuality, 120, 127–33, 141, 153, 183
Aurora Floyd (*see*: Braddon, Mary Elizabeth)
Autonomy, 13, 61, 93, 110–1, 133, 136, 138, 158

Baden Baden, 36, 38, 84–6
Balzac, Honoré de, 98, 185
Barney, Natalie Clifford, 92, 187
Baudelaire, Charles, 83, 151–2
Beau Geste (P. C. Wren), 44
Beau Sabreur, 9, 17, 20, 23, 28, 30, 41, 44, 47–9
Bedouin, 25, 41–6, 170
Beerbohm, Max, 2, 3, 5, 6, 180, 182
Bell, Gertrude, 44
Bentzon, Thérèse, 95–6
Bernhardt, Sarah, 10, 97
Bigland, Eileen, 11
Blunt, William Scawen, 107, 148
Boer War, 39, 148, 159–60, 166, 176
Braddon, Mary Elizabeth, 2, 10, 24, 32, 34, 97–8, 107; *Lady Audley's Secret*, 24, 32, 34; *Aurora Floyd*, 107
Bristow, Joe, 121, 124
Broughton, Rhoda, 2
Bulwer-Lytton, Edward, 24
Burnaby, Frederick, 25, 38–9
Bury St. Edmunds, 8, 11

Caird, Mona, 110–1, 114–5, 127, 134
Carroll, Alicia, 163
Castiglione, Countess, (see: Oldoïni, Virginia)
Cather, Willa, 5

Cecil, Bertie (*see: Under Two Flags*)
Chamberlain, Joseph, 148, 166, 176
Chandos (Ouida), 9, 25, 33, 57, 99
Chapman & Hall, 6, 9–10, 185
Chatto & Windus, 6, 10, 105, 185
Cigarette (*see: Under Two Flags*)
Clubland, 20, 25, 29, 37–8, 49
Colette, 187
Collins, Wilkie, 2, 84, 97, 118
Commodity culture, 11, 20, 66, 80, 83, 89, 91, 95, 108–9, 137, 190
Conrad, Joseph, 46, 56
Corelli, Marie, 3–4, 6, 11, 80, 184
Corrèze, Raphael (*see: Moths*)
Cosmopolitanism, 6–8, 16, 56–7, 81–9, 95–6, 102, 104, 106–8, 119, 122, 135, 148–9, 176, 180, 186–8
Courtesan (*also*: Celebrity courtesans, *see also*: *lionne*), 21, 81–9, 91–5, 107–8, 187; Courtesan novels and memoirs, 86–8, 91–3, 187
Crimean War, 20, 24, 27, 29, 32, 45, 47, 63
Crispi, Francesco, 149, 166

D'Alençon, Emilienne, 156
D'Annunzio, Gabriele, 176
Dame aux Camélias, La (Alexandre Dumas *fils*), 82
Dandy, dandyism, 20, 24–6, 29–30, 34, 38, 50–1, 99, 105, 120–1, 126, 143, 188; Female dandy, 120–1, 135
Dare, Avice, (*see*: Pearl, Laura, *Puck*)
Darien, Georges, 47, 167–8
Daudet, Alphonse, 80, 98
De Mérode, Cleo, 84, 89
De Pougy, Liane, 84, 92, 156, 187
Decadence, 3, 15, 31, 94, 105, 125, 149–52, 154–5, 160, 175, 182, 184, 186
Della Stufa, Marchese, 10, 108, 146, 155

Demi-monde, 37, 81, 86, 89, 92–3, 96, 98, 107–8, 187
Desert adventure, 18, 40, 46, 76, 186
Disraeli, Benjamin, 24
Dorian Gray, The Picture of (Oscar Wilde), 124, 132
Douglas, Norman, 176, 180, 184
Doumic, René, 77, 102, 181
Doyle, Arthur Conan, 25, 40, 46
Du Camp, Maxine, 97
Dumas, Alexandre *fils*, 21, 82, 86–8, 92, 94, 96, 98, 106
Dumas, Alexandre *père*, 58–9, 76, 97–8, 190
Duplessis, Marie, 21, 82, 85–7

Egerton, George, 115, 127, 141
Eliot, George, 84, 185
Ellis, Havelock, 31, 127
Environmentalism, also: eco-criticism, 11, 16, 18, 124, 161, 163, 176
Erceldoune (*see: Idalia*)
Erickson, Jesse Ryan, 188
Espionage (also: spy fiction), 54–5, 58, 62, 73
Eugénie, Empress, 10, 62, 82–3, 97

Fallen Woman, 21, 35, 67, 75, 92, 101, 110, 153
Faubourg St Germain, 97, 107
Female body, 55–6, 66, 74–5, 78, 82
Female dandy (*see*: Dandy)
Feminism, 12, 15–6, 56, 78, 109–10, 127, 158, 161, 176, 188, 191; Second Wave, 1, 12–5, 110, 188; Fourth Wave, 18–9
Femme fatale, 24, 54, 58, 63, 143
Femme Galante, 21, 60, 80–3, 96–109, 111, 118, 120–2, 126–8, 135–6, 148, 155–7
Feuillet, Octave, 21, 77, 82, 97–108; *Julia de Trecoeur*, 98; *Monsieur de Camors*, 99–100; *Marriage in High*

INDEX

Life, 99; *Parisian Romance, A*, 99; *Romance of a Poor Young Man, The*, 98
Ffrench, Yvonne, 11
Fin de siècle, 3, 15, 18, 84, 144, 149, 156
Firbank, Ronald, 183
First World War, 11, 24, 44, 47, 149, 176
Flaubert, Gustave, 41, 84, 102
Folle-Farine (Ouida), 10, 55, 73–7, 82, 116, 150, 162
Foucault, Michel, 54, 127
Franco-Prussian War, 8, 97
French Algeria, 25, 41–6, 63, 65, 71, 73
French novels, 3–4, 79, 82, 97–8, 105–8
Friedmann, Dustin, 123, 133
Friendship (Ouida) 10, 146, 190
Friendship (romantic or homosocial), 17, 24–6, 33–5, 46, 49, 54
Furneaux, Holly, 29, 45

Garibaldi, Guiseppe, 57, 61, 165–6
Gautier, Théophile, 41, 83
Genius, 3–5, 22, 70, 80, 122, 146–55, 158–9, 172–5, 189
Germany, 2, 9, 44, 84, 97, 148, 167–8, 172, 176
Gilbert, Pamela, 4, 14–7, 30, 73, 75, 79, 110, 184
Giojà (*see: Ariadnê*)
Gordon, General (of Khartoum), 25, 39
Gothic, 21, 59, 111, 116–9, 134, 143
Granville de Vigne (Ouida), see *Held in Bondage*
Guilderoy (Ouida), 10, 111, 136–40, 141
Guy Livingstone (see: Lawrence, George Alfred)

Hager, Lisa, 15
Haggard, Rider H., 20, 25, 39, 46
Hardy, Thomas, 140–1
Heineman & Balestier, 147, 185
Held in Bondage (also *Granville de Vigne*, Ouida), 9, 24–6, 34, 99, 110
Helianthus (Ouida), 11, 148–9, 163–77
Hemingway, Ernest, 187
Henty, George Alfred, 20, 25, 40
Heterotopia, 21, 54–6, 62, 65–6, 71–4, 76, 164
High society, 5, 10, 29, 58, 62, 76, 80–4, 89, 97–108, 112, 118–9, 124, 139, 155, 179
Hilarion (*see: Ariadnê*)
Holt, Shari Hodges, 34, 61, 72, 90, 149
Homosocial, homosociality (desire, friendships), 17, 20, 25, 33–7, 50–1, 54, 72, 131
Hope, Anthony, 164
Horses, horsemanship, 26–7, 32, 37, 86, 91–2, 107, 134, 143, 157, 176–7
Household Cavalry (also: Horse Guards), 26, 31, 33, 39
Hugo, Victor, 58, 76, 83–4, 98

Idalia (Ouida), 9, 20, 54–66, 70, 76–8, 82, 160; Erceldoune, 59–61, 160, 181
In a Winter City (Ouida), 81, 83, 93, 95–6, 111, 120–2, 141, 143; Lady Hilda, 106, 120–4, 126, 133, 142–3; Madame Mila, 97, 100–2, 106, 118, 122
Individualism, 1, 16, 153, 158–9, 188, 190
Invasion fiction, 56, 187
Italy, 2–3, 8, 10, 18, 56–62, 97, 143–9, 160–4, 166–8, 175–7, 180, 184, 187

211

James, Henry, 3, 102, 180, 185
Jingoism, 166, 169
Jordan, Jane, 4, 6, 9, 17–8, 24, 79

Kaiser Wilhelm II, 148, 166
King, Andrew, 6–7, 12, 17, 122, 145, 147, 150, 153, 173, 190
Kitchener, Herbert, 40

Lachman, Esther (*also*: La Païva), 82–4
Lady Audley's Secret (*see*: Braddon, Mary Elizabeth)
Lady Dolly (*see*: *Moths*)
Lady Hilda (*see*: *In A Winter City*)
Langham Hotel, 2, 9, 11, 25, 143
Lawrence, George Alfred, 2, 9, 17, 20, 23–8, 36; *Guy Livingstone*, 23–8; *Sword and Gown*, 25, 26
Lawrence, T. E., 44
Le Queux, William, 56, 187
Léblanc, Leonide, 93
Lee, Elizabeth, 11
Lee, Vernon, 3, 11
Lionnes (*see also*: courtesans), 31, 83–5, 88–99, 101, 104, 107–8, 113, 118, 150–1
Lippincott, 9, 189
Literary marketplace, 4, 6–7, 20
Loti, Pierre, 41, 80
Luhrman, Baz, 87

Madame Mila (*see*: *In a Winter City*)
Male gaze, the, 55, 66–7, 74–5, 90, 119, 127
Mallett, Phillip, 49, 76
Mallock, W. H., 2, 143, 148, 158
Marriage, 13, 15, 21, 26, 35, 37, 88–9, 95, 98, 107–20, 128–9, 134–43, 156–7; Marriage market, 10, 15, 21, 49, 67, 72, 110, 142; Marriage plot, 110, 124, 133, 160
Marx, Karl, 171

Masculinity, 5, 15, 19–20, 24–8, 31–50, 54–62, 70–1, 76, 145, 150, 189
Massarene, Katherine (*see*: *Massarenes, The*) 157–20
Massarenes, The (Ouida), 11–2, 15, 105, 149, 155–60, 164, 171, 177
Maugham, Somerset W., 105, 187
May, Karl, 44
Meynell, Alice, 132
Militarism, 11, 47, 164–8, 172–3, 177
Mogador, Celeste, 82, 92–3
Molloy, Carla, 185
Montez, Lola, 93
Moths (Ouida), 5, 10, 12, 15, 79, 83, 96, 102, 100–1, 115, 134; Corrèze, Raphael, 102, 117, 120, 181; Lady Dolly, 80, 96, 100, 102–6, 111–2, 118–9, 131, 156–7; Vere, 104, 112–20, 126, 129, 142–3, 157, 181; Zouroff, Serguis, 80, 112–20, 137
Mouse (*see*: *Massarenes, the*) 100, 155–7
Muscular heroism (*also*: muscular adventure, muscular Christianity), 2, 20, 24–6, 28, 31, 38–9

Nana (Émile Zola), 10, 79, 82, 92–4, 150
Napraxine, Nadine (*see*: *Princess Napraxine*)
New Imperialism, 20, 25, 28, 39, 48, 169
New Woman, 1, 3, 12–6, 18, 21, 33, 54–6, 109–11, 115, 127, 140–4, 188–9

Offenbach, Jacques, 84, 90, 101
Oldoïni, Virginia (*also*: Countess Castiglione), 61–2, 76, 81
Oliphant, Margaret, 184

Orientalism, 73, 117, 125, 179
Otero, Carmen, 84
Othmar (Ouida), 10, 133
Othmar, Otho (*see*: *Princess Napraxine, Othmar*)
Ottoman Empire, 44, 56
Oulton, Carolyn, 12

Païva, la (*see*: Lachman, Esther)
Paris, 3, 8, 36–7, 49, 57–8, 62–3, 81–99, 104–8, 112–8, 122, 125, 150, 153–6, 181, 187
Pascarèl (Ouida), 10, 57, 146, 148
Pater, Walter (*also*: Paterian aesthetics), 102, 121–2, 125, 143, 146, 149–50, 154
Patriarchy, patriarchal, 8, 14, 19, 21, 34–7, 49–51, 61–3, 74–5, 82, 86, 89–92, 111, 115, 120, 128–30, 140–2, 157, 183
Pearl, Cora, 21, 82–3, 85–6, 90–3, 107
Pearl, Laura, (see: Dare, Avice *Puck*)
Popular fiction, 7, 16–7, 20, 22, 56, 144, 149,177, 183–4, 191
Pre-Raphaelite, 116, 118, 120, 143
Princess Metternich, 62
Princess Napraxine (Ouida), 10, 15, 100, 111, 118–20, 124–5, 133–4, 137; Napraxine, Nadine, 119–20, 124–37, 140–3, 153, 156; Othmar, Otho, 119–20, 129, 131–5; Yseulte, 118–20, 131, 143
Prisoner of Zenda, the (Anthony Hope, *see*: Ruritania)
Puck (Ouida), 10, 82, 88–91, 107; Dare, Avice, (*also*: Laura Pearl) 82, 88–91, 94, 103, 108, 135
Pykett, Lyn, 15, 17, 146, 169, 177

Queen Victoria, 165, 176
Queer, 19, 21, 51, 92, 111, 123, 127, 133, 183

Ramé, Louis, 8, 49–50
Realism, 1, 5, 80, 102, 179, 182–6
Richardson, Dorothy, 3, 7, 182
Risorgimento, 54, 56, 59, 62, 76, 146, 148, 165
Romance (style or genre), 2–3, 16, 23, 49–51, 56–9, 76–8, 80, 102, 106–8, 121, 124, 150, 163, 175, 179–81, 188, 190
Romantic friendships (*see*: homosocial friendship)
Ross, Janet, 10, 108, 146
Ruritania (*The Prisoner of Zenda*), 149, 164, 181
Ruskin, John, 2–3, 13, 64, 143, 187

Sabatier, Appolonie, 82–3, 151
Salon, 2, 9, 25, 38, 49, 51, 83, 92, 151, 154, 187
Sand, George, 58, 76, 79
Schaffer, Talia, 13–5, 17, 116, 118–9, 142
Schroeder, Natalie, 12, 17, 34, 61, 72, 90, 149
Scott, Walter, 58, 77, 190
Second Empire, 21, 80, 82–3, 94–5, 98–9, 101–2, 106, 108
Sedgwick, Eve Kosofsky, 33–4
Self-commodification, 61, 89, 91, 94, 104, 108
Self-fashioning, 91, 95–6, 103, 126, 130, 136, 142–4, 145
Sensation fiction, 2, 4–5, 9, 17, 24, 32, 34, 47, 50, 98, 107, 110, 116, 118, 143, 184–5
Seraph, the (*see*: *Under Two Flags*)
Sexuality, female, 49–50, 54–5, 58, 62, 66, 73–4, 94, 110–1; Queer, 19, 123, 128, 141; Homosexuality, 31, 156; Asexuality (*see*: Asexual)
Shaw, George Bernhard, 180
Showalter, Elaine, 13
Skittles (see: Walters, Catherine)

213

Soldiers, 27–9, 64, 66, 162, 181; Soldier hero 20, 25, 28, 32, 42–3, 45–7, 51; Soldier heroine, (*see also*: Cigarette, *Under Two Flags*) 54, 63, 68, 70–3, 76
Soudan, 39–40, 44
Spy fiction (*see*: Espionage)
Steeplechase, 32
Stevenson, Robert Louis, 179, 181–3
Strathmore (Ouida), 9, 25, 29, 33–5, 99, 179; Vavasour, Marion, 26, 34–5
Suffrage, 13, 15, 188
Sutherland, John, 12, 44
Swinburne, Charles Algernon, 2, 11
Sword and Gown (*see*: Lawrence, George Alfred)
Symons, Arthur, 122, 157, 160

Tauchnitz, Bernhardt, 9, 145, 147, 167, 185–6
Tennyson, Alfred, 2, 27
Tinsley Brothers, 24, 185
Tom Brown's Schooldays (Thomas Hughes), 26, 28
Tricotrin (Ouida), 10, 88–9
Turgenev, Ivan, 84–5

Under Two Flags (1936 film), 44, 105, 182, 187
Under Two Flags (Ouida), 5, 9, 12, 15, 17, 20, 24, 29, 32, 36, 40, 43–4, 48–9, 54, 63, 76, 82, 84, 99, 105, 124, 170; Cecil, Bertie, 20, 24–9, 33–47, 53–5, 64–73, 99, 105, 135, 160, 181; Cigarette, 42, 46, 49–56, 63–77, 82, 162, 181, 186; Seraph, the, 31–3, 37, 46; Venetia, 45–6, 49, 6, 71–2; Zu-Zu, the, 36, 38, 82, 86–9, 108

Van Vechten, Carl, 50, 182–4, 186
Vavasour, Marion (*see*: *Strathmore*)
Venetia (*see*: *Under Two Flags*)
Vere (see: *Moths*)
Villa Farinola, 9, 143, 177
Villa, Luisa, 40

Wagner, Richard, 84
Walters, Catherine (Skittles), 93, 107
Waters of Edera, The (Ouida), 11, 149, 160, 177, 180
Waugh, Evelyn, 187
Wharton, Edith, 187
Wilde, Oscar (see also: *Dorian Gray*), 1, 5, 10–1, 31–3, 103, 109, 122, 124–5, 130, 132, 136, 142–3, 158, 182–3, 191
Worth, Charles Frederick, 83, 101, 142
Wren, P. C., 44, 46

Yates, Edmund, 10, 143
Yseulte (see: *Princess Napraxine*)

Zola, Émile, 2–3, 5, 10, 21, 79–84, 86, 92–3, 98, 111, 150
Zouroff, Sergius (see: *Moths*)
Zu-Zu, the (*see*: *Under Two Flags*)
Zweig, Stefan, 174–5

Also in the series......

Forthcoming.......

www.ingramcontent.com/pod-product-compliance
Lightning Source LLC
Chambersburg PA
CBHW052038300426
44117CB00012B/1883